BENJAMIN FRANKLIN TRACY
Father of the Modern American Fighting Navy

BENJAMIN FRANKLIN TRACY
Secretary of the Navy, 1889-1893
[Official Navy Department portrait by Ayer Whipple, 1896;
official U.S. Navy photo]

BENJAMIN FRANKLIN TRACY

Father of the Modern American Fighting Navy

by
Benjamin Franklin Cooling

ARCHON BOOKS
1973

Library of Congress Cataloging in Publication Data

Cooling, B   Franklin.
    Benjamin Franklin Tracy: father of the modern American fighting Navy.

    Bibliography: p.
    1. Tracy, Benjamin Franklin, 1830-1915. 2. United
States. Navy—History. I. Title.
E664.T72066   353.7 [B]   73-6645
ISBN 0-208-01336-9

*To my mother for her patience and confidence
through the arduous doctoral program*

Contents

Tables

Illustrations

Preface

Benjamin Franklin Tracy explained his contribution to the re-naissance of American naval power to a *New York Herald* reporter shortly before his death. The old gentleman told the newsman on June 27, 1915:

> The defence of the United States required the creation of a fighting force. I felt that we must be able to divert an enemy's force from our own coast by threatening his own, for a war, though defensive in principle, may be conducted most effective-ly by being offensive in its operation. So I advocated right from the start a fighting plan that meant taking the offensive. That's why, I guess, I've been called now and then the "Father of the Fighting Navy."

The term "fighting navy" means different things to different peo-ple as anyone may attest who has witnessed the various applications of American seapower in the twentieth century. Tracy's contribu-tion from 1889 to 1893 lay in the best tradition of John Paul Jones, Stephen Decatur, Isaac Hull, and others, although it also implied a dramatic departure from the traditional naval policy of commerce destruction and coastal protection under which those heroes labored for God and country.

Tracy obviously could not work alone. He was but one of six very able secretaries who, in unparalleled succession, contributed to the rise of the "New Steel Navy"—William H. Hunt (1881-1882), William E. Chandler (1882-1885), William C. Whitney (1885-1889), Tracy, Hilary A. Herbert (1893-1897), and John D. Long (1897-1902). Moreover, other supporters of a strong navy in Congress, in the service itself, and among the general public, sought to revitalize America's first line of defense during this era.

It was Tracy, however, who, by shrewd maneuver and by co-operation with other enthusiasts, introduced at a key moment several elements demanded by the new technology and by the nation's development—the concept of a balanced battle-fleet deterrent; nickel steel armor and armament superior to that of foreign navies; and a full appreciation of professionalism. Tracy translated the latter into abandonment of the spoils system in the navy yards, federal support for the state naval militia, merit promotion within the officer corps, and better education and training for all ranks. His term was too short to see successful completion of all these endeavors, but he worked actively for their enactment.

Research in naval history of the period indicates that it is not enough to speak merely of strategic policies and types of ships. Examination must be made of the personalities and ideas of the secretaries, their ability to manage daily tasks, to negotiate contracts for materiel, and to project the overall ability of the department to construct a fleet and to direct the men and vessels constituting that tool of national power. Tracy's career, from small-town lawyer, Civil War veteran, and municipal figure, presaged his services at national cabinet rank. He matured in his career, participating in the expansionist diplomacy of the administration of Benjamin Harrison. The aggressive diplomacy of the Harrison period was a prelude to the expansionism and imperialism at the turn of the century and can be understood more fully by examining the role of Secretary of the Navy Tracy. His intense nationalism and drive to establish American power in the eyes of the world reinforced the bold if bumbling posture in foreign affairs assumed by the Chief Executive himself.

One of the last human links with the Tracy era snapped in 1971 with the death of Admiral Richard Harrison Jackson, a hero of the Samoan hurricane of 1889, who retired as commander of the U.S. Battle Fleet in 1930. Still another link remains, not just in the form of the modern nuclear navy as an awesome strike force, but also in continued preservation of the last of the steel fighting ships of the "New Navy" of the late nineteenth century. U.S.S. *Olympia*— Admiral George Dewey's flagship at Manila Bay, the opening battle of a conflict which symbolized America's naval renaissance—lies berthed as a national historic shrine at Philadelphia. It forms the best monument to Tracy and his contemporaries who sought to project the national power and prestige of the United States before the eyes of an expansionist-minded world.

Acknowledgements

I am indebted to a number of people who provided advice and encouragement in my work. Professors Thomas C. Cochran, Warren Hassler, Walter R. Herrick Jr., Kenneth Hagen, and James I. Robertson all contributed to its early stages. My thanks go also to Lawrence G. Williams, M.C., and W. Pat Jennings, Clerk of the U.S. House of Representatives for permission to see key Congressional records. The staffs of the Manuscript Division, Library of Congress; Old Military Records Division, National Archives and Records Service; Navy Department Library; Indiana State Library; Miss Juliet Wolohan, New York State Library; and Mr. William Lay, Jr., Tioga County Historical Society, Owego, were all helpful.

Abbreviations

BHLC   - Benjamin Harrison Papers
SLLC   - Stephen B. Luce Papers
WRLC   - Whitelaw Reid Papers
DPLC   - David D. Porter Papers
ACLC   - Andrew Carnegie Papers

BENJAMIN FRANKLIN TRACY
Father of the Modern American Fighting Navy

CHAPTER 1

Formative Years on the Southern Tier

Flowing gently westward from its headwaters in the Catskill Mountains the Susquehanna River crosses the so-called "Southern Tier" counties of lower New York State before dipping sharply southward across Pennsylvania toward Maryland and the Chesapeake Bay. Today, large cities, broad highways, and railroads line the stream. Once sparkling waters are now polluted, but on a warm summer day young boys can still be found in places with fishing poles slung across youthful shoulders, or following the tracks of wildlife through overgrown thickets. A century ago, however, these things were the rule and not the exception.

In the early decades of the nineteenth century a stranger might gaze upon a broad river valley cutting across worndown ridges of the Allegheny Mountains which rose 250 to 400 feet above the valley floor. White pine covered the hillsides while the rich loamy bottom land enabled settlers to plant an ample crop of wheat. The Susquehanna Valley in lower New York state epitomized rustic America and it was here in Tioga County that Benjamin Franklin Tracy was born on April 26, 1830. Tracy's active life would carry him far from such rural beginnings, but he never would lose his affection for nature and the quiet, ordered pace which it seemed to demand of all beings.

The Tracy family traced its lineage to the sylvan countryside of France and Great Britain. A Norman family assumed the name Tracy from Traci-Boccage near Caen. Sir William de Tracy, companion to William, the Duke of Normandy, transplanted the name to English soil soon after the Norman conquest and their other relatives became the lords of Barnstaple in Devonshire. Having embraced reformist religious beliefs, it was William's great-grandson, Stephen, who cast his lot with the Pilgrims and sailed first for Holland and then to Plymouth colony in North America, landing there in 1623.[1]

The Tracys remained New Englanders through two generations before Thomas Tracy, a veteran of the Revolution, decided to move westward with his family during the great postwar migration. They drifted down the Susquehanna by raft, acquired land near the tiny frontier hamlet of Apalachin in New York state, and began to grow wheat for sale downriver. Thomas's son, Benjamin, continued to cultivate the land and he also erected a small sawmill near the river from which lumber could be rafted to market at Harrisburg in Pennsylvania. Income from the white pine lumber and cultivation of cereal crops induced Benjamin Tracy to think of marriage and family. In 1820 or 1821, he took as his wife Bathsheba Woodin Jewett, a local widow with four children. She bore four sons to Tracy over the subsequent thirteen years; of these, Benjamin Franklin was the third.

Young Tracy's boyhood experiences revolved generally about his father's farm and sawmill. Benjamin Tracy, Sr., though by no means wealthy, managed to supply his large household with the necessities of life and some of its comforts. He reared his eight children according to the Congregational faith and young Benjamin Franklin developed early the sense of moral integrity and personal discipline implied in his puritan heritage. Then, too, farm chores and life among the shadowy hills cultivated a lasting interest in horses and Tracy's lifelong affinity for them would provide many hours of pleasure.[2]

Tracy's father wanted his children to receive whatever rudimentary education could be secured even in those rustic surroundings. Young Tracy began to attend the district school when he was five and there for the next eight years, winter and summer, he grappled with Lindley Murray's "English Reader" and elementary arithmetic.

Tracy was eight when his father became the local Justice of the Peace and it may have been then that the youth first thought of a legal career.[3]

These childhood years contained more than just work and study for Tracy since they were times of excitement in Tioga County. In addition to the usual play in the fields and outbuildings near home—play which on one occasion reputedly cost Benjamin Franklin the sight of an eye—the Tracy children could always look forward to the lure of Owego, the bustling little county seat nearby. A thriving commercial center of about 3,000 people, this growing hamlet enjoyed river and turnpike connections with the outside world. Indeed, the Tioga County Court House was the setting of a convention in December 1831 which has been credited as the birthplace of the New York and Erie Railroad. Some eight or nine years were to pass before the rails were finally laid at Owego. But as the construction neared the village, young Benjamin and his family must have been fascinated by the sounds and sights of axe and hammer as workmen forged the road close to their farm. When the first passenger train finally pulled into Owego at ten o'clock on the morning of June 1, 1849, the Tracys probably gathered with the rest of the large crowd to witness the linking of Tioga County with ocean and lake by rail.[4]

Tracy's year-round schooling ended in 1843 when farm chores demanded his presence during the peak summer months. He recalled years later that he helped at light work on the farm during the summer and went to school during the winter until his sixteenth year, later spending a short period at the school run by C. R. Coburn in Owego.[5] This brief sojourn ended Tracy's life at home but it added to his basic education. Among his new schoolmates was Thomas Collier Platt, son of an Owego lawyer.[6] Platt was three years Tracy's junior and he went on to study at Yale, an opportunity beyond the reach of Tracy, but the two forged a lifelong friendship during their attendance at Coburn's academy.

Tracy assumed the task of teaching a large and unruly group of students in the district school at Canawana, a suburb of Owego, during the winter of 1846-47. The young teacher proved his mettle despite the belief of his old principal at the academy that the Canawana school needed an older and more experienced teacher. The job carried a stipend of $16.00 a month, but more importantly it gave Tracy an opportunity to lead, to judge others fairly, and to forge within himself a strong sense of duty as well as an awareness of the importance of regularity and order—attributes that were to prove invaluable to him in his later career.

Tracy cultivated his incipient interest in law while teaching at Canawana. He had joined a debating society in Owego a year earlier where his "clearness of statement of proportion and the force of his logic greatly impressed those who listened to him."[7] On one occasion when the discussion centered upon the annexation of Texas he opposed the move declaring that annexation would lead to dissolution of the Union. When he left teaching, first to return to the Owego Academy and then to the farm, he further nourished his interest in law by reading his father's legal compendium whenever he could find time from other chores.

Formal legal training was now necessary for the nineteen-year-old Tracy. He entered the law office of Colonel Nathaniel W. Davis in Owego in order to prepare for admission to the New York State Bar. Two years of intensive preparation exposed Tracy to the intricacies of Blackstone, Coke on Littleton, Fearne, Sugden, Preston, Chitty, Archbold, and Graham and he became particularly attracted to Chancellor Kent as a never-failing source of intellectual stimulation. He was convinced that a lawyer needed to be familiar with the sources of legal knowledge as well as with the appropriate places to find the most dissimilar principles and to know how such principles might be applied to the written law. At the same time Tracy was gaining practical experience by conducting trials in the local so-called "Justices' Court." Here a fledgling lawyer faced a crosscut of legal opponents ranging from rural hacks known for bluster, conceit, and ignorance to many of the ablest members of the bar. Tracy learned to study hard, to reason closely, and to act with energy or with caution as the situation and opponent demanded. He was ready for admission to the New York State Bar in 1851. That same year he made another important move; he took Delinda E. Catlin of neighboring Nichols as his wife.

Tracy's demonstration of professional brilliance and personal integrity brought him great success within the next two years. He was compelled to measure himself against some of the best lawyers on the Southern Tier, including Daniel S. Dickinson, Alexander S. Divin, John A. Collier, George Sidney Camp, and John M. Parker. Also, as was usual for young lawyers of the period, Tracy met politicians and officials at the county seat. He soon developed a warm interest in local politics.

Renewal of Tracy's friendship with Tom Platt undoubtedly stimulated such an interest. Platt left Yale because of ill health, returning to Owego to manage a drugstore. Like Tracy, he began to take an interest in politics. Platt probably imparted much of his own enthusiasm to his older friend. When the leaders of the Whig county organization became interested in the successful young lawyer and courtroom orator and named him as their candidate for District Attorney of Tioga County in 1853, Platt assisted Tracy as leader of the campaign glee club. They stumped the county together. Tracy proved such an effective candidate that he emerged the sole Whig victor in Tioga County that year, to become the youngest district attorney ever elected in the state up to that time.[8]

Tracy, twenty-four years old when he became district attorney at Owego, combined a sharp mind and an engaging personality with a handsome physical appearance. He stood nearly six feet tall and carried about 170 pounds on a frame further developed by rowing, swimming, and baseball. Straight-forward blue eyes, a sharp nose, and a firm chin gave his face an attractive look. His well-kept dark brown hair and carefully chosen clothing announced meticulous habits and conservative tastes. The young attorney moved in the best social circles of small-town Owego. He was noted for cutting a fine figure on the dance floor, often appearing in blue swallow-tail coat with brass buttons, silk hose, patent leather pumps, and a large ruffle on his shirt front. As one admirer recalled:

> He was an authority on matters of costume, and successfully banished straps from the trousers of Owego dancing men. He was a supreme waltzer, dancing from his hips, avoiding his partner's toes, and always keeping time to the music. Such difficult old-time round dances as the "Deux Temps," the "schottische," "the Esmeralda," the "Varosovienne" and the "Danish Dance" were his habit and delight. And, on the old-fashioned five-step waltz he was simply peerless.[9]

These were happy days for Tracy. His family soon numbered three children: Emma Louise, Mary Farrington, and Frank Broadhead, born in 1852, 1854, and 1856 respectively. Furthermore, lawyer Tracy emerged successfully from all jury trials in which he was counsel in any court of record between 1851 and 1857. After 1853 his civil practice became the busiest and most lucrative in the county. Finally, Tracy became involved in the formation of a new political party in New York state.

By 1854-55 many "Conscience Whigs" in the state began to shift their allegiance to the infant Republican party. Tioga County became a scene of much activity in this respect and Tracy and Platt were both among the county's early converts to the Republican ranks. Tracy himself admitted to being an old-line Whig and follower of William Henry Seward, but his opposition to further extension of slavery led him to embrace the cause of Northern Whigs and those Democrats who opposed the policies of the national administration of President Franklin Pierce. Thus the young district attorney found himself in the forefront of the local movement to raise a phoenix from the ashes of the dying Whig organization.[10]

Tracy attended many local conventions held by Free Soilers throughout the state in an effort to convince this group of the affinity of its ideas with those of the Republicans. He persuaded and cajoled individual citizens at home in Tioga County, and he helped organize mass rallies, once driving thirty miles over rough country roads from Owego to Towanda, Pennsylvania, in order to secure the aid of David Wilmot, the famous author of the Wilmot Proviso. He also participated as a delegate in the joint Whig-Republican convention at Auburn, New York, in September 1855.[11]

Local Democrats naturally sought to silence the popular young district attorney. They named Gilbert Carlton Walker to oppose Tracy's reelection to office in 1856. Walker, a partner of Colonel Davis in Owego, later became governor of Virginia as well as a United States Representative from that state during Reconstruction. In the 1850s, he moved from Binghamton to pursue a career in Tioga County soon after Tracy entered independent practice—the two young men became fast friends despite differences in political persuasion. Walker ran far ahead of his party in New York state in 1856, but Tracy's record proved too agreeable to Tioga County and the voters returned him to office for a second time. Tracy, recognizing a good man when he saw one, asked Walker to join him in law partnership. The firm of Warner, Tracy and Walker appeared unusually prosperous at the outset, but it was dissolved abruptly in 1859 when Walker moved to Chicago.[12]

Tracy did not seek reelection upon the expiration of his second term as district attorney. Tired and overworked, he wished to devote himself exclusively to private practice. He fell ill soon after Walker's departure from Owego and abandoned his own legal activity temporarily, convalescing with Delinda and the children on his father's farm at Apalachin for over a year. Yet events prevented the young lawyer from remaining absent from the political and professional arena for long. Just before Tracy became sick, the Tioga Republicans elected him chairman of their executive committee. Due to his poor health, perhaps, Tracy relinquished this position to his friend Tom Platt in 1860, thus paving the way for the personal political empire that Platt built in Tioga County during the subsequent decade. But events on the national stage by this time eclipsed provincial happenings in the small towns and rural counties along the Southern Tier.

Tioga County voted for Abraham Lincoln in 1860 by a margin of 1,000 votes over the Democratic opposition.[13] Subsequent dissolution of the Union followed by the outbreak of war caught many Tioga citizens off guard. Never any hotbed of abolitionist sentiment, the locale was strongly Unionist nonetheless and the fall of Fort Sumter and Lincoln's call for troops in April 1861 had a deep effect. A cyclone of patriotic fury swept the community and resulted in an irresistable impulse to enlist. As Tracy's brother-in-law, Isaac Catlin, recalled:

> Business was practically suspended throughout the entire community. Farms and shops and schools all over the County were substantially deserted. The people were beside themselves with excitement.[14]

Tracy, as a loyal Unionist and Republican, was swept up in the excitement, but did not rush to join the army for he was too involved in politics. His law practice and family considerations naturally shaped many of his actions.

In the autumn of 1861, as echoes of Federal disasters at Bull Run and Balls Bluff, Virginia, resounded throughout the North, Republicans and War Democrats from Tracy's district sent him to the New York legislature, dedicated to the Unionist cause of vigorous prosecution of the war. The freshman member of the Assembly took his seat at Albany on January 7, 1862, and he quickly proved to be an astute judge of men, a shrewd political operator, and a capable orator.

The New York legislature, especially the General Assembly, contained a distinguished group of Unionist supporters, including Lemuel Stetson, former Congressman Benjamin Pringle, Calvin T.

Hulburd, Darium Ogden, and Thomas G. Alvord, all members of previous legislatures, and Henry T. Raymond, a former speaker of the Assembly and later lieutenant-governor. Benjamin Tracy might well have felt overawed by such experienced colleagues. Like sixty-six other members of the one hundred seven member body, Tracy was elected on a Unionist ticket and the vast majority of the Assembly enjoyed affiliation with the Republican Party.[15] An assemblyman could expect a flood of letters from constituents, petitions, and committee meetings, in addition to normal sessions of the Assembly. All told, Tracy found little time to worry about inexperience.

The 1862 legislature was remarkably free of party manifestations and strife, yet opportunities developed for interesting alliances and political maneuvers at Albany. Tracy became embroiled from the outset as he participated actively in the calling of a caucus to select a candidate for speaker. The prominent names included Raymond, Hulburd, and Alvord; a Weed Republican, a Republican of Democratic origin, and a Union Democrat respectively. Tracy knew Raymond, a New York City editor, from the Auburn convention. Although the Tioga assemblyman previously favored the Seward faction in the party to that of Weed, he supported Raymond against the wishes of the State Senator from Tracy's district who backed Hulburd. Tracy joined numerous assemblymen who, while strongly favoring emancipation, nonetheless preferred the moderate Raymond.[16]

Assemblyman Tracy worked behind the scenes organizing a caucus and soliciting votes for Raymond. The newspaperman won and when the full assembly met on January 7, Raymond was chosen Speaker over his Democratic rival, Horatio Seymour of Erie County. All the members of Republican affiliations, whether elected on the straight or on the Unionist ticket, and nearly all the Union Democrats voted for Raymond. Thus the 1862 session began with relative harmony between Republicans and the Union men.

Raymond thereafter attributed his good fortune largely to Tracy's activity. He rewarded the young legislator with the chairmanship of the Railroad Committee, a gesture to Owego and the birthplace of the Erie, as well as with the second place on the Judiciary Committee. Later in the session Tracy was named Chairman of the subcommittee of the whole, or "Grinding Committee" which collected bills from the general calendar entitled to early consideration and reported them to the whole Assembly for immediate consideration. Tracy emerged as the acknowledged floor leader of the Republicans and Unionists, an unprecedented feat for a freshman legislator.[17]

The 1862 legislature focused primarily upon mundane matters of local interest. Canals, roads, and other internal improvements, private relief bills, and various acts to incorporate, amend, or alter public and private institutions in the state, kept Tracy and his colleagues busy. The *New York Herald* correspondent noted toward the end of the session that: "Everything that has approximated a party movement has been simply a struggle between the two great wings of the Republican party."[18]

Nevertheless, several national issues tended to shatter the apparent calm at Albany. These included instruction of the New York senators in Washington to favor expulsion of their colleague, John Bright of Indiana, who indiscreetly addressed a letter to "His Excellency, Jefferson Davis, President of the Confederate States," as well as additional issues such as adoption of a resolution favoring abolition of slavery in the District of Columbia, national taxation for funding the war effort, a harbor defense bill, and soldier relief measures.[19] Tracy's warm support of a vigorous prosecution of the war prompted him to follow Speaker Raymond's lead on these matters.

Tracy showed strong feelings on two other major issues. He voted with the opposition to prevent enactment of a prohibition amendment to the state constitution. He also voted with Speaker Raymond on a proposed health bill for metropolitan New York City. The latter measure involved more than purely medical considerations since a large patronage package was at stake. Mayor George Opdyke bore a grudge against the Speaker for packing the Assembly's committee on cities with up-state legislators and the health measure also discriminated against Opdyke's following at City Hall when it came to filling the various new offices mentioned in the legislation. Tracy, animated by loyalty to Raymond as well as by his own aversion to municipal corruption—a theme which appeared later in his career—voted with the Speaker and the bill passed 60-44. But the Senate later emasculated the bill, giving partial victory to Opdyke's people.[20]

Notwithstanding a rather poor voting record—he participated in only slightly over half of the 800 roll call votes—Tracy worked

hard in his first year as a legislator. He served his rural constituency by pushing measures concerning education, county administration, and local improvements for roads and canals. He served
ably as a committee member and apparently provided a steady
hand whenever a small political squall threatened the calm of the
session. Usually reserved, Tracy impressed even casual acquaint-
ances with his quiet good humor, tact, and sympathy. His role was
that of a capable, determined manager whose high principles and
courtesy could bend the will of the most hard-bitten colleague.

Many of Tracy's personality traits emerged when he occupied
Seat 60 in the Assembly that spring. His point of view mirrored
an essentially rural, conservative upbringing. He espoused no
radical causes. Yet he evidenced a sharp, analytical mind which
enabled him to grasp both fine points of the law as well as intricate political moves. At times the Southern Tier legislator appeared
to be shackled by an almost unswerving loyalty to friend, political affiliation, and patriotism. But, when put to the test, he unobtrusively blended idealism with pragmatism as demanded by
the political realities of Albany.

Political opponents, caught napping by Tracy's cordiality, soon
learned that he could be a man of iron determination. His high
principles of political morality prevented blind allegiance to any
organization. Tracy dutifully followed Speaker Raymond's lead
on 264 occasions, or with roughly two-thirds of his votes. But he
showed an independent streak on 138 other occasions, thereby dis-
playing an ability to play the political game with integrity as well
as skill.

The 1862 session of the legislature adjourned at 11:00 A.M. on
April 22, and Tracy returned to the quiet of Owego, his neglected
law practice, as well as to a reunion with his wife and family. Meanwhile, several hundred miles to the south a Federal army moved
slowly up the long Virginia peninsula toward the Confederate
capital at Richmond. Events there in the Tidewater, independent
of Tracy's knowledge or involvement, were soon to have a pro-
found effect upon the future life and career of the Tioga lawyer.

CHAPTER 2

Forged on the Anvil of War

Benjamin Tracy returned to Owego in the spring of 1862 to find his friends and neighbors waiting impatiently for news of Union victories and a quick conclusion to the Southern rebellion. Meanwhile, Tracy immersed himself once more in his law practice, and together with Delinda and the children he felt refreshed by the warm days and chilly nights which accompanied spring along the Southern Tier. Both Albany and the war must have seemed far away indeed.

The early summer of 1862 brought another series of Union defeats in the eastern theater. Major General George B. McClellan and his Army of the Potomac suffered defeat at the very doorstep of the Confederate capital. But McClellan's campaign meant more than just tactical setbacks. Long casualty lists resulted from the battles and on July 1st, in response to a message of confidence from loyal Northern governors, President Lincoln called for 300,000 additional volunteers.[1] Governor Edwin D. Morgan of New York reacted quickly by dividing the state into thirty-two regimental districts corresponding to the state's senatorial districts, appointing a committee of citizens in each district to raise one or more regiments. Morgan named his friend and loyal party member, Benjamin F. Tracy, to head the committee in the Twenty-Fourth District, which included Tioga, Broome, and Tompkins counties.

The district committee soon needed someone to take charge of the troops which they hoped to raise but no one volunteered for the task. At last Tracy, although disavowing military ambition before the committee, agreed to shoulder the burden. Elected commandant of the regimental district by his fellow committeemen at a meeting in the Owego Hotel on July 21, he received a commission as colonel of state troops from Governor Morgan on the following day. As Tracy reflected later on:

> When I was appointed Commandant of the Rendezvous in the 24th Senatorial District I had never looked inside the Army Regulations and was utterly ignorant of military forms and procedures. I was told that the pressing need of the time was *men* and that I was to spare no effort to obtain them as fast as possible.[2]

Tracy soon discovered that everything was disorganized throughout the district. He quickly pushed for appointment of a Quartermaster, Adjutant, and Surgeon, as well as of numerous recruiting officers. Officials selected a rendezvous of twenty acres on the south side of the Susquehanna River at Binghamton and recruits quickly began to pour into "Camp Susquehanna."[3] Tracy and his assistants rushed to secure blanks and posters since neither Albany nor the War Department at Washington saw fit to provide the supplies necessary for the business of recruiting men. Bounties from the state and Federal authorities speeded recruitment further so that by the middle of August Tracy had completely filled the ranks of one regiment (the 109th New York Volunteer Infantry).

Immediately the question arose about the disposition of the additional recruits in camp. Talk of filling veteran regiments in Virginia caused an abrupt decline in volunteers and Tracy hurried to Albany to obtain permission to recruit a second new regiment. His recruiting appeals proved so successful that this second unit, the 137th New York, quickly exceeded its authorized strength and the Tioga lawyer again petitioned the governor to raise still another regiment. This time Governor Morgan decided that Tracy and his district had done enough. Within thirty days Tracy had reached the district's quota of approximately 2,400 men. Now lay ahead the greater task of training and mustering these raw troops.[4]

Command of the troops also posed a problem and Tracy finally agreed to lead the 109th New York. The new colonel drilled and trained his men during the hot August days. Bending New York farm boys to army discipline, squad and company drills, and camp police proved arduous work although the daily schedule was not especially strenuous for the recruits. Rising at 5:00 they bathed in the river and then read or wrote letters until breakfast, a meal lasting from 6:00 to 8:00 A.M. because of the large number of men and inadequate messing facilities. Drill occupied the mornings and afternoons, dress parade took place daily before sundown, and "lights out" capped the day's activities. There were also the lighter incidents of camp life including harassment of sutlers, the usual boyish pranks played upon one another, and more formal events such as the presentation of regimental flags and officers' swords.[5] Then, the apparent fun of war abruptly ended when on August 30, at 11:00 A.M., Tracy led his regiment to the railroad depot for departure south.

Tracy and the 109th New York left Binghamton on the Erie Railroad to the cheers and shouts of assembled citizens and the patriotic music of the Ithaca brass band. The route of the troop train first led westward to Elmira. As the nineteen cars pulled slowly through Owego, Tracy probably felt some twinges of emotion at leaving the sedate life of law and family for the unknown rigors of war. But as the miles sped by after leaving Owego, a contagious tone of hilarity and mirth spread among the troops and at least subtly to their regimental commander.[6] Turning southward the train which carried the main elements of Tracy's unit reached Baltimore about noon on Sunday, August 31.

Gloom enshrouded that Maryland city as news came over the telegraph telling of yet another Union defeat at Bull Run near Washington. The 109th waited in the mud and soot of the Baltimore depot while Tracy went to VIII Corps headquarters to learn about transportation to the nation's capital. There he found something of a panic. Rumors placed General Robert E. Lee and his Confederates across the Potomac in Maryland and Union authorities fully expected Baltimore and Washington to be under siege at any moment. Thus, when Tracy's men detrained at Baltimore they had stepped into a fluid situation in the war zone, a condition which changed Tracy's ultimate destination.

Major General John Wool, VIII Corps commander, needed troops to guard against major Confederate raids on isolated posts, bridges, and transportation arteries under his jurisdiction. He quickly ordered Tracy and his inexperienced regiment southward to Annapolis Junction astride the railroad midway between Baltimore and Washington.[7] They reached the junction during the afternoon of September 1. Having selected their campsite and pitched their tents, the New Yorkers scoured the neighborhood for straw to make themselves more comfortable in the face of an approaching storm. Tracy was greeted within the week by local citizens complaining that his incorrigible men were "plunderers and common thieves."[8]

The New Yorkers spent the next year and one-half engaged in the unsung but vital task of guarding railroads in the vicinity of Baltimore and Washington. Tracy took command of a so-called "Railway Brigade" and, when not occupied with preparing his positions against possible Confederate cavalry and guerrilla raids during the Antietam and Gettysburg campaigns, he sought to perfect the training and discipline of the two regiments in his charge— the 109th and 141st New York.

The monotony of the duty eventually took its toll of officers and men. Regimental records attest to Tracy's determination to retain the effectiveness of his command despite the ravages of sickness, uncleanliness, gambling, and intemperance.[9] He constantly sought to instill his men with a sense of responsibility for protection of the invaluable supply and communication link between Washington, the Northern states, and the fighting front. In time Tracy himself succumbed to the inaction. He sought to brigade his own regiment with its sister unit, the 137th New York, declaring to his old friend ex-governor Morgan: "such an order . . . would be hailed with delight by the friends and soldiers of both regiments." He petitioned the new state administration of Horatio Seymour to re-outfit the unit as cavalry, thinking that this course might carry with it a call for more active service. At one point the restless colonel sought his own reassignment as acting assistant provost-marshal general in Albany. Tracy probably longed for the more familiar scenes of the state capital and the chance to mend political fences.[10]

All of Tracy's schemes came to nothing. By the winter of 1863-64, his command found itself divided between Falls Church, Virginia, Mason's Island, D.C., and Laurel, Maryland. The colonel could not exercise proper control and supervision and he continued to bring pressure on friends and higher authority for some other duty.

COLONEL BENJAMIN F. TRACY, U.S.V.
109th New York Volunteers
[From the collections of the Library of Congress]

Writing that the New York Unionist members of Congress desired
Tracy's return to his native state, his friend Morgan suggested command of the draft rendezvous at Elmira. But Assistant Secretary
of War Charles A. Dana rebuffed the request by stating simply:
"recruiting request cannot be complied with consistently with the
exigencies of the service."[11]

Tracy's problems did not entirely escape notice at headquarters.
During the summer of 1863 the rigidly proper colonel incurred the
indignation of an influential member of the staff of the United
States Senate. Tracy claimed to have found a stolen government
horse in the possession of a local horsetrader. He seized the animal
only to learn that it allegedly belonged to G. E. Brown, Sergeant-
at-Arms of the Senate. Tracy categorically refused to yield the
animal without written proof of Brown's ownership and Brown in
turn accused Tracy of horse-stealing and conduct unbecoming an
officer and gentleman.

The New Yorker's sharp legal mind suspected something amiss
when Brown tried to duck the request for proof of ownership.
Tracy protested his innocence and dedication to duty to Secretary
of War Edward Stanton before declaring somewhat sardonically:
"The said Tracy [quoting Brown] may be a very 'contemptible and
cowardly' fellow but he is not so jolly as to suppose for an instant
that a Congressional official would use his office to cover stolen
property . . . ."[12] The matter soon closed but Tracy continued to
interpret rather rigidly his responsibility as a military representative of the Federal government.

Suddenly, in March and early April of 1864, Lieutenant General
Ulysses S. Grant, the new General in Chief of Union armies,
stripped the Washington garrisons of all but a skeleton force in
order to strengthen eastern forces for the seasonal campaigning.
The 109th New York was ordered to Annapolis to be brigaded in
Major General Ambrose Burnside's IX Corps. Tracy and his men
soon joined Brigadier General John F. Hartranft's First Brigade
of the Third Division, commanded by Brigadier General Orlando
B. Willcox. The well-drilled New Yorkers must have cut a sharp
appearance as they passed through Washington enroute to the
Army of the Potomac's staging area near Culpeper Court House,
Virginia. A cheering throng watched as Burnside's whole corps
swung down 14th Street with bands playing and colors flying.
President Lincoln, who reputedly had met Tracy during one of his

tours of inspection around the defenses of Washington, and the corps commander reviewed 'the parade from a second story balcony of the renowned Willard's Hotel.[13] But the glitter and glamour faded rapidly for the blueclad soldiers as only the long road stretched southward.

Burnside's corps initially assumed the task of protecting the Orange and Alexandria Railroad, lifeline for the army. Tracy's men must have found it ironic to return to their old job of guarding a rail line, this time near Warrenton, Virginia. The 109th New York soon left this duty, however, for on May 4 Grant started his drive against Lee's forces south of the Rappahannock and Rapidan rivers. Several days later Tracy's New Yorkers followed the rest of the army across the Rapidan and entered that dreary wasteland known to history as the "Wilderness of Virginia."

Tracy's men almost immediately felt the eerie spell cast by the Wilderness. Once a primeval forest of stately pine and oak, ironmongers in an earlier day had denuded the land and a second growth of scrub trees, dense underbrush, and thorny vines now covered the area. Gloomy shadows over stagnant pools and marshy creek bottoms mingled with a crackling rifle fire in the distance to create a distinctly unpleasant night for the Union soldiers.

Tracy's unit formed part of a force of IX and VI corps forces covering the Germanna Plank Road and the Germanna Ford crossing over the Rapidan. The rest of the army lay to the south in several separate masses—all part of Grant's plan to outflank Lee's Confederates moving eastward from Culpeper and Orange court houses. Action quickly developed along two major east-west roads, and Burnside's units found themselves committed to battle.

Lee pushed his army eastward along the Orange Turnpike and Orange Plank Road, forcing Grant to turn and give battle. Firefights developed in two separate sectors along these roads. Grant, reinforced by Burnside's corps during the night of May 5, determined to overwhelm Lee before the latter could secure additional men and artillery. Therefore, he ordered a general advance of all his forces for 5:00 A.M. on the following day. Tracy's regiment left its bivouac at that hour and swung southeastward along the Germanna Plank Road with the rest of Hartranft's brigade. Their orders were to close the gap between the two sectors of fighting, but Burnside's corps moved slowly and Tracy and his men did not enter the dense woods near the Confederate line until nearly noon.

Fighting was already in progress and Burnside's delay only compounded the impatience of his fellow corps commanders. As one historian has concluded: "Burnside's tardy appearance opposite the gap between [R.S.] Ewell and [A.P.] Hill is generally regarded as the dissipation of an opportunity that seldom comes in war to a general of tarnished reputation to rehabilitate his past ,fame and, by the simple expedient of rapid movement and tough fighting, to clinch a decisive victory for the army he had once commanded."[14] Yet, Burnside was neither quick nor tough, and Tracy's regiment had to share the ignominy of the lost opportunity.

The Confederates held a strong position and by early afternoon were ready to thwart any Union thrust in this sector. Lieutenant Colonel Isaac Catlin, Tracy's brother-in-law and his second in command, recalled that "after a suffocating march through the intricate and tangled meshes of burning woods, while marching by the left flank in columns of four, we suddenly came upon the enemy in force, whose infantry from behind works poured volley after volley of musketry into our surprised ranks."[15] Experiencing their baptism of fire, Tracy's New Yorkers and other IX corps units moved resolutely into the volleys of veteran Alabama and Florida troops. At this time Tracy acted with the gallantry which years later would gain him the Medal of Honor.

When some of his men wavered under the Confederate fire, Tracy seized the regimental colors and rushed toward the enemy lines. The Federals quickly followed him and swept over the light entrenchments of the opposition, capturing men and equipment. But the veteran Confederates mounted a savage counterattack and in turn swept Hartranft's inexperienced troops back in panic. Burnside prudently withdrew his units and entrenched without further harassment from the Confederates. It was a bitter lesson in warfare for the young New Yorkers as they mourned the loss of seventy-eight of their comrades. Moreover, Tracy himself suffered from heat prostration and was on the verge of a breakdown. Carried temporarily to an aid station in the rear, the colonel refused to yield his command.[16]

Tracy rejoined his regiment two days later when it passed the old battlefield of Chancellorsville on the line of march toward Spotsylvania Court House. He rode up just as the 109th was brewing coffee during a break in the march. Raising three cheers and closing ranks behind their commander, the New Yorkers once more followed Tracy toward the sound of the guns. From May 9 through May 12 the regiment participated in heavy skirmishing along the Ny River near the courthouse hamlet as Burnside's corps attempted to outflank the Confederates. Meanwhile both armies gathered in large numbers north of the town. A major battle unfolded rapidly west of Burnside's position around a U-shaped angle in the Confederate line.

Burnside received orders to support the attack of Major General Winfield S. Hancock's II corps against this salient on May 12. That morning Tracy's regiment deployed as supporting infantry for a section of field guns; then, in the early afternoon, the 109th moved forward in a general attack against the Confederate entrenchments held by Ewell's corps. But Tracy's men enjoyed no repetition of their success in the Wilderness. The attackers made only local gains and suffered nearly twice the casualties of their first battle. Tracy instructed his men to fall back and throw up entrenchments. The New Yorkers huddled in their rifle pits with spirits dampened further by heavy spring rains and the complete incapacitation of their commander—for the strain of battle had finally caught up with Tracy. He was carried to the regimental hospital where Surgeon William Johnson found that ". . . his previous physical condition had been such to render him entirely unfit for active field service, he having suffered and [is] suffering from dilation of the left ventrical of the heart and has suffered from its effect for the past year."[17] Johnson believed that Tracy could never resume field duties and he recommended a change of climate and removal from camp in order to avoid permanent disability.

The surgeon's judgment came as a blow to the energetic and patriotic Tracy. The colonel sent his resignation of command to IX corps headquarters on May 14, stating tersely: "Satisfied from actual experiment that I have not the physical strength requisite to the command of the Regiment in active service I deem it both honorable and just that I give place to one who has."[18] Thus Tracy left his brother-in-law to carry on and returned to the Southern Tier of New York for rest and recuperation.

Here, during the summer of 1864, he nursed his health, enjoying the reunion with home and family, and perhaps testing the political climate in Owego. But, like most restless convalescents, Tracy soon yearned for a return to active service. He hoped at first to rejoin his old command. When that proved impossible, on September

7 he accepted appointment as commander of the 127th United States Colored Troops. Tracy never saw this command, for in the meantime events intervened decisively.[19]

Tracy's old political colleague, former Speaker of the Assembly Henry J. Raymond, suggested to Secretary of War Stanton that Tracy was the perfect man for a special assignment in New York state. Stanton needed a commandant for the vital draft rendezvous and prisoner of war depot at Elmira, thirty-seven miles from Tracy's home. Tracy arrived in Elmira pursuant to Stanton's orders on September 20, 1864, ready to undertake a totally new assignment.[20]

Elmira, the "Queen City of the Southern Tier," had become a local military center in 1861. Its 15,000 inhabitants first witnessed the mustering of a number of local regiments in May and then in July Governor Morgan named Elmira along with Albany and New York City as state military depots. Three large barracks were built at Elmira and in 1863 they became the draft rendezvous for that part of the state. In May of 1864 Lieutenant Colonel Seth Eastman, the local commander, received instructions to "set apart the barracks on the Chemung River as a depot for upwards of 10,000 prisoners" who would be transferred there from other Northern prison compounds.[21]

Eastman wired Washington by the end of June that the prison depot was ready for occupancy. A board fence surrounded a camp of nearly forty acres. The first prisoners arrived early in July to discover what they thought to be a "garden spot"—the sparkling Chemung River; quaint reed-lined Foster's pond within prison boundaries; thirty-five two-story, white-washed barracks; and warm, comfortable weather. But the Confederates were to find later, as one Virginian commented wryly, that the compound "was a pleasant summer prison for Southern soldiers, but an excellent place for them to find their graves in the winter."[22]

Colonel Tracy knew nothing of the difficulties which lay ahead when he took over from Eastman at Elmira. The assignment probably seemed like a welcome change from the blood and grime of war, and one well-adapted to his training in the law. In any event, he was not well-prepared for the dual role called for. First, as Commandant of the Prisoner of War Depot, he inherited Eastman's problems with camp administration, care and treatment of prisoners, and stockade hygiene. In addition, he was simply one link in a chain of command which began with the local prison commander located physically at Barracks No. 3, passed through Tracy's hands at local headquarters, and ended with Colonel William Hoffman (and later Colonel H. W. Wessels) as Commissary General of Prisoners in Washington.

Furthermore, Tracy bore responsibility as commanding officer of the draft rendezvous, a separate operation from the prison camp.[23] Here he was accountable to Brigadier General A. S. Diven, a prominent local citizen and Erie Railroad official who commanded the Military Division of Western New York. Diven shared headquarters facilities with Tracy in the same building in downtown Elmira. In turn, the administrative chain of command beyond Diven led to the Commanding General, Department of the East, and then to either the Adjutant General or the Provost Marshal General in Washington. In either case, Tracy was merely a middleman. He observed:

> Lt. Col. Eastman was so dangerously ill as to be unable to do more than simply turn over the command by a written order. I was compelled therefore to grope my way in the dark, learning the details and needs of a most intricate and difficult command as rapidly as I could.[24]

Tracy immersed himself quickly in the functions of the draft rendezvous. He cut through some of the administrative confusion left in the wake of a change of command. He re-posted troops to proper assignments either at the prison camp or the draft rendezvous as necessity dictated. Clerks took charge of huge account ledgers at headquarters, set up by Tracy to better control the hundreds of men passing from home draft districts through the rendezvous on their way to distribution points with the armies in Virginia.

He established strict inspection procedures to insure that the 2,500 drafted recruits at Barracks Number 1 remained healthy, learned the rudiments of army life, and did not desert or tear up the city before leaving for the front. Tracy, backed by Diven, issued regulations pertaining to sutlers, the conduct of soldiers off-duty, liquor sales, and prostitution—all carefully coordinated with Elmira officials. He also secured permission to repair mess and barrack facilities at the draft rendezvous and to insure sufficient guards from units of the Veteran Reserve Corps, Regular Army, and New York militia. Civil War draftees seldom acted like willing soldiers and Tracy undoubtedly felt that he was managing not one, but two "prison camps."[25]

As the duties of the draft rendezvous became increasingly routine over the passing weeks, Tracy found that he could not solve all problems so expeditiously. Imbroglios developed over office space at headquarters, management of the post fund based upon contributions of the garrison, and bounty payments to recruits, as well as over the complexity of shipping hundreds of draftees and substitutes south. These difficulties often revealed Tracy's rigid approach to duty as he conceived it.

Tracy's headquarters consisted of a twenty-two foot square room subdivided by a partition and housing two adjutants and sixteen clerks in addition to himself. Visitors added to the turmoil. The post commander's solution lay in centralizing post headquarters and the quartermaster office in larger quarters. He hastily ordered requisition of some rooms nearby—whose owner sought to extort a high rent from the government. But Tracy had forgotten to consult General Diven, going directly to the Adjutant General in Washington for the needed authority. Diven reacted predictably over his subordinate's disregard for the chain of command. He vetoed the scheme with a testy comment to Washington authorities: "There is no necessity certainly in this city that can for a moment justify the running a business man out of his store, and any officer doing it would [be] himself in trouble and bring disgrace upon the service."[26] Washington officials apparently agreed with Diven. Tracy was doubtless pleased when Diven resigned from the service in April 1865.

Tracy also expressed displeasure with the state of finances at Elmira and the propriety of having the prison guards share the benefits of the post fund accumulated at the draft rendezvous. He queried the Adjutant General about administration of bounties to recruits, believing the bounty money which accompanied the recruit from his home to the draft rendezvous only heightened the man's temptation to desert.[27] Later he protested against the practice of discharging or rejecting men for disabilities which had existed prior to enlistment and returning their local bounty to these men. As Tracy wrote Secretary of War Stanton:

> It seems to me clear that, if localities are credited with these
> rejected men the government should retain the local bounty.
> I utterly fail to comprehend why a man who has cheated him-

self or the government to the credit of some locality, should be
rewarded for his rascality by pocketing from $300 to $1000
local bounty. Either the Government should retain the bounty
or the locality be deprived of the credit.[28]

Records fail to show that Tracy received any satisfaction on his
complaint.

A more serious and a continuing problem involved both the
transportation of draftees southward and their proper distribution
to assigned regiments. Tracy reported on November 23, 1864, that
the Elmira rendezvous had forwarded over 13,000 men to the
armies at a rate of 300 to 800 per day. It was inevitable, perhaps,
that many were incorrectly designated on muster rolls or turned
over to the wrong receiving officers at Baltimore and Washington
instead of to regiments at the front. Corruption among escort
troops contributed to desertion and, indeed, the insufficiency of
escorts for the draftees many times delayed their transit to the forward staging areas. Orders from Washington often seemed unclear
and the harried colonel worked long hours to insure that the steady
stream of replacements continued to flow toward Grant's forces in
Virginia.

Tracy fought hard against the corruption and desertion which
accompanied the forwarding of recruits. He stripped escort officers of command when they lost over five percent of their draftees
enroute to the front. Most of the difficulties ended with the discharge of 100-day New York militiamen in late autumn, although
desertions were never eliminated completely. Higher authorities
often seemed oblivious to Tracy's problems despite his efforts. They
censured him for the lateness of monthly returns and the slow dispatch of recruits and the Adjutant General's office reprimanded
him severely when he inadvertently dispatched one group of recruits to an incorrect rendezvous point at Philadelphia.[29]

An especially thorny problem involving both the speed of shipping recruits and their comfort brought Tracy into conflict with
the Northern Central Railroad and graphically illustrated the problems of Union manpower management during the war. Both sides
had a good case in this instance and, in deference to the railroad,
if Southern lines suffered from the ravages of war, Northern rolling
stock seldom escaped unscathed even from the convoy of loyal
troops. I. N. DuBarry, General Superintendent of the Northern
Central, told a Washington official in October 1864:

. . . this Railway Co. has assigned for the movement of troops, over 100 new cars, that two months since the cars were new, had never been used in any service, that during the very heavy movement of troops commencing August 10, the side of the cars have been entirely knocked off by the troops, seats taken up and thrown away, and not a single window or stove remains in the cars. . . . Every regiment or squad of men consider it their duty to do every possible amount of damage to the equipment of our Rail Roads.[30]

Tracy, and others responsible for getting men to the front, saw the matter somewhat differently. They considered that the railroad provided poorly lighted box cars which invited desertion and he complained about service that took up to forty-eight hours to make the trip of 234 miles from Elmira to Baltimore. Tracy thought that troop trains should follow passenger schedules, be well-lighted, and that the cars should be open at both ends.[31] The service became so poor by early January 1865 that Tracy secured War Department approval to withhold further payment to the Northern Central until service improved. The issue found eventual solution when Tracy received orders on February 25 to forward men via the Erie and New York Central railroads despite added expense and greater danger of desertion by shipment through urban areas such as New York City.[32]

Soldier riots in Elmira, draft protests in Auburn, and the national elections in 1864 occasionally upset the routine of the rendezvous. The election especially called for stringent measures to prevent the soldiers from interfering with voters at the polls. Also there were numerous attempts to raid Tracy's headquarters contingent of clerks for more fighting men. Even the regimental headquarters of Tracy's regular command, the 127th U.S. Colored Infantry, demanded his transfer to that unit. But such requests always received the answer: "Colonel Tracy cannot be at present relieved from duty at Elmira without detriment to the service."[33]

If Tracy remained submerged beneath paper-work from the draft rendezvous that fall and winter, his other responsibility as commandant of the prison depot caused even more strain. Tracy's performance of that duty in fact shadowed him for much of his postwar career. Command of a draft rendezvous lacked glamor,

ELMIRA PRISON CAMP, 1864-1865
[Courtesy National Archives]

but responsibility for a prison depot was an even more thankless task. Both duties, as witnessed at Elmira, symbolized the absence of planning as well as the confused and often contradictory policies of administrative management during the Civil War.

When Tracy assumed his dual assignment, he soon discovered that affairs were just as entangled at the prison depot as at the draft rendezvous. The number of prisoners had reached 9,508 by the time of Tracy's arrival at the post. These pitiful captives brought ill-clothed, dirty, emaciated, and diseased bodies from other prisons such as Point Lookout, Maryland, and Old Capitol Prison in Washington, as well as directly from the battlefields. They literally swamped the limited facilities beside the Chemung River. Insufficient housing, coupled with a summer drought, turned the compound into a miniature dust bowl and made Foster's Pond ". . . a festering mass of corruption, impregnating the entire atmosphere of the camp with its pestilential odors, night and day."[34] Eastman, to his credit, had alerted Washington to the problem, but officials there could provide little positive guidance, divorced as they were from the local conditions.

Tracy spent the first month studying the difficulties besetting the depot as well as means of shipping numerous prisoners southward for exchange. The *Elmira Avertiser* observed optimistically: "Colonel Tracy is inaugurating many changes and improvements. Barracks are to be created at once to take the place of tents now in use."[35] Indeed, by early October, the new commandant began to act upon many of the issues and plans which Eastman had formulated but had been obliged to leave unresolved.

The industrious Tracy prodded Washington authorities with frequency on such matters as drainage of Foster's Pond, wooden barracks for prisoners and guards, proper clothing for prisoners, and the perennial quarrels over transportation with the Northern Central Railroad. At best he achieved moderate success. Over all hung the stench of disease, death, and infamy which Tracy never succeeded in eradicating from the name "Elmira."

Grim statistics tell the tale of suffering at the so-called "Andersonville of the North." On the surface they seem to be a monument to Tracy's failure as an administrator. But if the conditions reflected by these statistics dogged Tracy's footsteps long after the war ended, they also tended to hide the humanitarian efforts he took to ameliorate the situation at the camp.

TABLE 1 — ELMIRA PRISON CAMP 1864-1865[36]

Month	Prisoners	Sick	Dead
August 1864	9606	394	115
September 1864	9480	563	398
October 1864	9441	640	296
November 1864	8258	666	207
December 1864	8401	758	269
January 1865	8602	1015	285
February 1865	8996	1398	426
March 1865	7102	823	491
April 1865	5055	647	267
May 1865	4885	509	131
June 1865	3610	218	54

Tracy spent most of the fall securing official permission to initiate various projects to improve conditions and work was begun on them. Frugal by nature and conservative by official mandate, the commandant built up a secure prison fund. Commissary General regulations dictated that the fund be based upon withholding certain parts of the prisoners' ration allowance. Tracy saved $120, 459.18 and expended $30,547.60 between September and December.[37] Although this method seemed to stimulate undernourishment among the prisoners, Tracy reinvested the money in improved health facilities. The prison fund, for instance, paid for construction of a wooden drainage pipe to alleviate the critical situation at Foster's Pond.

Many of Tracy's difficulties lay beyond his control. A lack of lumber in the area at the time, the onset of a harsh New York winter which blanketed Elmira with cold and snow by mid-October, the lengthy delays in communication with the bureaucracy in Washington, and confusion surrounding shipment of cotton to pay for prisoner clothing emerge from the record. It took, for example, two months for Tracy to receive a requisition submitted in December for 4,000 bootees, 10,000 pairs of socks, 3,000 blankets, and 1,500 caps, which the prisoners needed desperately to face the winter.[38] Strict Army regulations concerning the type and color of prisoner clothing, provision of fresh vegetables and sutlers' supplies, even civilian visitation to the camp also constricted many of Tracy's humanitarian inclinations.

Nearly every letter of inspection endorsement from Elmira to the Office of Commissary General of Prisoners bore Tracy's terse comment: "Many men are in tents without floors or blankets"; "Bar-

racks should be erected instead of tents"; "hospital accommoda-
tions insufficient at present"; and "it seems to me that a due regard
for the lives of prisoners confined here requires that some method
of introducing a running stream of water through this camp should
be adopted. . . ."[39] But, while Tracy wrote of prisoner care,
Washington officials talked in terms of cost. Instructions from the
Office of Commissary General of Prisoners contained phrases such
as ". . . it is desirable that no more clothing shall be provided by
the Government than is absolutely demanded by the ordinary dictates of humanity."[40]

The official position was understandable. War weariness in an
election year dictated a rapid end to the conflict and hence any
financial expedient must help the forces at the front, not prisoners
in the rear. In addition, northern propogandists began to portray
the prison pens of the Confederacy as filled with atrocities, soaring death rates, starvation, and unnecessarily harsh security regulations. Thus Secretary Stanton and his advisers ordered northern
prison authorities to reduce food, fuel, shelter, and clothing partly
in retribution, partly in order to concentrate resources for an ultimate battlefield solution to the rebellion.

Red tape tied Tracy's hands and he could do little. Perhaps he
felt he could satisfy no one. He turned away solicitous citizens and
relatives with baskets of food and clothing for the prisoners because of a regulation which stipulated that all such requests had
first to be cleared with Washington officials. Tracy even received
a reprimand from those officials for permitting an agent of the
Sanitary Commission access to the prison, since "formal inspection of a military prison station by private individuals is highly
improper, and the publication of a report cannot be permitted
unless under direction of the Department of War."[41]

Differences with General Diven extended to the prison camp.
Needing at least 2,000 men for guards, Tracy watched as the actual
numbers by late fall fell below 1,100. Diven also failed to help by
requesting use of prison guards for dress parades. Notwithstanding
Elmira's low escape record—the lowest of any Federal prison
camp—Tracy feared a massive breakout. He complained to the
Commissary General of Prisoners:

> Now who is to say how many troops can be taken from their
> position to join in the reviews! If while these troops are absent

under Genl. Diven's orders a rush should be made by the
Prisoners and an escape follow, will his orders protect me?[42]

Washington authorities provided few answers, even to Tracy's
repeated requests that his old command be sent to Elmira. He
promised to recruit the now-decimated 109th New York to full
strength, but the War Department needed men in the field, not
promises. Tracy was forced to content himself with invalids of the
Veteran Reserve Corps and a sprinkling of regular contingents.

The Army and Navy Journal expressed concern in December
that desertion among Union prison guards could be attributed to
their quartering in tents while the prisoners enjoyed wooden barracks. One of Tracy's spokesmen quickly set the record straight,
noting that while many of the guards did live in tents they had
ample rations, bedding, and firewood, "for the Government has
been most munificent and watchful towards them. . . ."[43] Other
misunderstandings also developed especially with medical authorities. Major E. F. Sanger, surgeon in charge at the prison camp,
accused Tracy of hampering coordination between hospital staff
and administrative personnel causing a breakdown in measures
taken to prevent disease, a deterioration in camp hygiene, and an
onset of malnutrition. Far from content with local medical treatment anyway, and fearful of criticism from superiors, Tracy requested a formal inspection of the camp by the Surgeon General's
office. The first inspection tended to confirm Sanger's contentions
but a later visit by Dorthea Dix gave Tracy's administration a
better report. Finally, a medical inspector from the Office of Commissary General of Prisoners simply overlooked the Tracy-Sanger
feud and pressured his own superior to order erection of oil stoves
in barracks and the lining of hospital wards against the cold. Sanger, disliked both by prisoners and administrators, soon found
himself transferred from Elmira.

Medical problems also plagued Tracy's efforts in the late winter
to ship prisoners south for exchange. Unwittingly he forwarded a
number of sick men who could not tolerate the long trip. Medical
examiners in Baltimore complained that prisoners were dying enroute. The Office of Commissary General of Prisoners refused to
listen to Tracy's counter-charges about poor service on the Northern
Central Railroad: "It requires a pretty strong man . . . to endure
a railroad journey of forty-one hours during such weather as pre-

vailed at the time this party of prisoners was forwarded." Rather, the Commissary General of Prisoners reprimanded: "You are responsible that this service is properly performed, you can relieve yourself from censure only by holding the parties who neglect your orders to a strict accountability."[44]

The long winter of suffering, frustration, and disheartening duty ended with the first spring breezes in 1865. The winter months witnessed Confederate defeats before Petersburg in Virginia and Nashville in Tennessee. In April, guns boomed the news of Lee's surrender as well as that of Lincoln's assassination. Tracy's duties then turned to shipping increased numbers of prisoners south and to receiving homeward-bound Federals for final muster. Yet he could never escape so quickly the onus of Elmira. Eleven years after he left the service the prison camp emerged to haunt him once more. On January 11, 1876, Congressman Benjamin H. Hill of Georgia attacked the administration of the Elmira depot from the floor of the House of Representatives. Hill declared, in a debate with James G. Blaine, that conditions at Andersonville had been no worse than those at Elmira and he introduced a letter by the camp doctor, possibly the resentful Sanger, as an authority for the charges.

Tracy learned of the debate from his morning newspaper. He quickly telegraphed his old friend, Tom Platt, one of Hill's colleagues at the capitol in 1876, denying emphatically the existence of "cruelty, inhumanity or neglect" in the treatment of prisoners at Elmira. "There was no suffering there which is not inseparable from a military prison," he declared.[45] Platt read Tracy's message to the House—a message in which the former post commander pointed to the absence of any dead line, prisoner shootings, or burial of prisoners in unmarked graves. These phenomena were reputedly commonplace at Andersonville. Tracy exaggerated when he praised the quality and quantity of the food, comfort of prisoner barracks, and conditions of the camp hospital. But his message proved, as Hill admitted afterward, that the abominable death rate of 24 percent—the highest of any Federal prison camp—and even the illness rate at Elmira were not the product of calculated neglect or callousness on the part of local prison officials. Besides, it undoubtedly helped Tracy's cause that he had served on the winning side and professed a loyal Republican persuasion.

Subsequent years of study have failed to quiet the controversy as historians have either rationalized or condemned the "scourge

of Elmira."[46] But by concentrating upon the local conditions themselves they have implicitly castigated the camp administrators of
whom Tracy stands preeminent. He had been caught in the middle,
forced to trust subordinates who actually administered the camp—
from all reports they formed a mixture of responsible and irre-
sponsible individuals. Some like Lieutenant Colonel Stephen
Moore and Major Henry Colt received the respect of friend and foe
alike. Others like Sanger and personnel of lower rank, who may
have enjoyed even closer contact with the prisoners than Tracy,
Colt, or Moore, were not liked and perhaps engaged in suspicious
practices. Tracy had tried to ferret out corruption with the use of
detectives but, in the final analysis, with little effect upon the
prisoners' plight.

The record shows Tracy to have been a conscientious, well-
intentioned official who, during the trying winter and spring of
1865, spent liberally from prison funds to provide such little extras
as cooking utensils and table furniture, as well as wash houses and
enlarged quarters and hospital facilities for the prisoners. Compared with his frugality in the fall of 1864, Tracy had spent roughly
double what he collected from the prison fund during the first six
months of 1865. A large sum went toward rehabilitating the camp
from the ravages of a March flood. Tracy also ordered confiscation
of an offensive spectator platform erected by a local entrepreneur
so that Elmira citizens might gaze upon the "Rebels." All in all,
Tracy showed more than normal concern for the prisoners while
still carrying out the orders of Washington officials—correctly
but without imagination.

The infamy of Elmira can be attributed rather to deficiencies in
planning by absent officials in the nation's capital, the physical
breakdown of Southern prisoners ill-prepared for a frigid winter,
and delays in communications and supplies of clothing and building materials. However, Tracy's desire to follow orders and func-
tion within the bounds of military bureaucracy tacitly contributed
to many of these delays. A rule-book administrator, he may have
been too prone to await Washington's final approval at a time
when greater imagination combined with his evident capacity for
hard work and a strong personality might have saved many lives
at Elmira. A later commentator wrote:

> For all its brilliance . . . Tracy's mind functioned within the
> bounds set by a conservative frame of reference. This limitation

impaired his legal talent not at all, but it engendered in him a
dedication to the established order of things which tended to
narrow his outlook.[47]

Still, Tracy mirrored many military and civilian authorities of the
period who possessed little conception of, let alone experience with,
the management demanded by modern warfare. Like most military officials of any age, he courted the approval of superiors and
tended to take the safe course, anxious to avoid court martial for
dereliction. As post commander at Elmira, Tracy appreciated the
government's desire to end the war quickly; indeed, such a purpose
had contributed to his original entry into his country's service in
1862. He felt that the Federal authorities wanted a job done at Elmira with maximum efficiency. Incarceration of "rebels" prevented
their return to Confederate fighting ranks, and, in Tracy's mind,
meant a speedier end to the war.

Overburdened with two assignments at Elmira, Tracy simply
could not do justice to both. Perhaps he may have divided his
efforts too greatly between the draft rendezvous and prison camp.
He had entered the Army in 1862 completely untutored in military
affairs. He emerged from experiences at Binghamton, near Washington, in the Wilderness, and at Elmira as a more enlightened and
sobered individual in ways of administering institutions and bodies
of men.

Tracy's thoughts increasingly turned toward the future as the
war reached a conclusion in the spring of 1865. He submitted his
resignation from the army on June 5, 1865, stating simply: "I have
made arrangements to resume the practice of law in New York
City and have formed a connection there which I regard as very
advantageous.[48] The veteran officer wanted to be in the metropolis
by mid-June but it was not until June 13 that special orders discharged him. Four days later Tracy passed the command at Elmira
to Colonel I. R. Lewis and turned toward a new life.

CHAPTER 3

The Road to National Recognition

New manufacturing, the extension of transportation facilities, and the acceleration of immigration, all stimulated by the Civil War, combined to increase the country's urbanization as the nation sought to forget the conflict. Many returning veterans headed westward, but countless others were drawn to the cities by the lure of wealth and excitement. Colonel Benjamin F. Tracy, late of the United States Volunteers, provided a case in point as he briefly rejoined his family at Apalachin in the summer of 1865 enroute to a new life in New York City. He realized that his political fortunes had collapsed on the Southern Tier. Prolonged absence from the political battlefront allowed Thomas Platt, his boyhood friend, to capture the organization and votes in Tioga County.[1] The colonel now sought the new challenges and wider opportunities provided by metropolitan New York.

Tracy decided to manage his father's farm from Manhattan and he arranged for the construction of a quaint vacation house on land adjacent to the family homestead. Then with Delinda and the children, he took the train for New York to resume his law career with the firm of Benedict, Burr and Benedict at 76 Wall Street. The inevitably fatiguing search for a permanent residence led the Tracys to the attractive and mushrooming suburb of Brooklyn. This city,

with its population of nearly 300,000, in 1865 offered pleasant resi-
dences, numerous churches, a burgeoning economy, and proximity
to Manhattan. That fall Tracy bought a comfortable brownstone
house at 148 Montague Street in the heart of Brooklyn's "Heights"
section. Overlooking most of the city, the area boasted trees and
grass until after the turn of the century. It was populated "by gentle-
men of solid respectability and well lined simplicity,' who left their
offices shortly after three; returned from Manhattan on the Wall
Street Ferry; dined at four; and then during the long spring twilights
went on a sedate drive to the outskirts of the city."2 Such an atmosphere well suited an aspiring individual like Tracy. The family
could watch activity in upper New York Bay at Bedloe's Island
from an upstairs window. In the distance to the left lay Fort Wads-
worth and the quarantine station on Staten Island; while in the
opposite direction busy harbor traffic of ferries and lighters created
a flurry on the southeastern side of New York's Battery Park. The
Tracy children were enchanted with the urban bustle and even the
colonel and his wife must have enjoyed the difference from bucolic
Apalachin.

Tracy soon established his reputation in New York's legal circles
and he returned to active partisan politics while Republican chief-
tans kept an attentive eye upon his personal and professional development. But his opposition to radical reconstruction measures led
him to eschew the policies of the state machine preceding the mid-
term elections of 1866. He particularly disliked Roscoe Conkling's
support of the Fourteenth Amendment and, placing loyalty to personal beliefs above political career, Tracy attended the National
Union Convention in Philadelphia backing the non-enfranchise-
ment of Negroes in the South. Urging rapid and painless restoration
of the rebel states, Tracy was recorded as siding with President
Andrew Johnson and his administration.3

The President rewarded Tracy's loyalty by naming him to succeed
Benjamin Silliman as United States District Attorney for the
Eastern District of New York in October 1866. That Tracy openly
sought the position can be discerned from his unabashed solicitation of help from the well-known politician Thurlow Weed: "I
desire this place *very much*—not that I expect any pecuniary compensation from it (for I learn the office is not worth a dollar after
giving a reasonable compensation to an assistant) but being a
stranger here it will serve to distinguish me a little from the great
mass of mankind by which I am surrounded."4

The district encompassed one of the richer and more populous areas in the nation and one of its foremost residents, "Boss" William Marcy Tweed, provided countless legal challenges for the District Attorney's office. Tracy thus undertook the job in a period requiring courage, legal acumen, and energy on the part of a Federal prosecutor. In addition to Tweed's activities the district was a major center for whiskey production on the Eastern seaboard. More than five hundred distilleries could be counted within its limits, many of them illicit.[5] For two years Tracy threw his skill into the fight against this so-called "whiskey ring." The struggle proved to be severe, for the distilleries used their immense profits to bribe revenue officers and to subsidize the best legal talent; but Tracy persisted and succeeded in cleaning up to the point where the local collector of internal revenue was indicted, convicted, and sent to prison for fraud.

At this time it was not a crime for two or more persons to conspire to defraud the Federal government and as Tracy observed later: "One man leased the distillery, one man bought the grain, and another sold the whiskey, but all acting together, I found the law would not cover the cases. . . ." Therefore, the District Attorney set out to draft corrective legislation and when Washington authorities learned of Tracy's work they wholeheartedly backed his efforts. Congress passed an act in March 1867, drafted chiefly by Tracy, which made it a crime for two or more men to conspire to defraud or to commit a crime against the United States where any overt act had been committed by one or more of the conspirators in furtherance of the conspiracy.[6]

Tracy refused to relax his crusade despite numerous threats of bodily harm and proffered temptations, as well as lack of police protection when collection of Federal revenue threatened to erupt into riots. He contended that the existing law for the collection of taxes on distilled spirits was defective and proceeded to draft a new one, submitting it to the House Committee on Ways and Means. In turn a subcommittee of Robert G. Schenck, William B. Allison, and Samuel Hooper, assisted by Tracy, perfected the details of corrective legislation which passed Congress early in the summer of 1868. According to the District Attorney:

> In one year after the passage of this law, $50,000,000 was secured for the United States instead of $13,000,000 collected the previous year. The law provided that every man asking for a

license should present to the collector . . . a draft of his distillery, giving the size and showing every pipe and quantity of
whiskey that could be produced in 24 hours. The result was
that ninety percent of the whiskey distilled paid a tax.[7]

Three years later, Tracy reported that 366 Internal Revenue cases
in 1871 alone had netted the Federal coffers some $66,509.27, al-
though the aggregate amount of judgments in favor of the United
States was more than double that amount. The District Attorney
told Justice Department officials that similar progress had been
made in Customs and Post Office cases which also fell within his
jurisdiction.[8]

Tracy apparently stood "almost omnipotent before a jury" at the
time and his record as a public prosecutor caught the eye not only of
Andrew Johnson but also of political opponents to the president.
When Ulysses S. Grant succeeded Johnson, he reappointed Tracy
to a second term in 1871. At various times Tracy's name was suggested for the Southern as well as the Eastern District. But his
"desire to be freed from this office" rather than further serve the
corrupt Grant regime marked the New Yorker as expendable in the
eyes of administration spokesmen. Grant's friends used the public
press to seek Tracy's resignation and finally caused the frustrated
District Attorney to tell Grant: "Conscious that it is wholly un-
deserved, that I have been faithful in all things to my trust and that
my action as a member of the Republican party which is well known
and approved furnishes no cause of complaint, I feel that I have a
right to complain of the action taken without notice to me." Nevertheless, the Attorney General invited Tracy's resignation in December 1872 and, despite minor outcries from concerned citizens and
friends in Brooklyn, Tracy complied in February of the following
year.[9]

The six and one-half years in office proved to be a profitable experience, for in addition to invaluable lessons in legal prosecution,
governmental responsibility, and guardianship of the public trust,
Tracy won another honor. President Johnson appointed him a
Brevet Brigadier General of Volunteers on July 16, 1867, "for
gallant and meritorious services during the War" to date from
March 13, 1865.[10] General Tracy, as he became known after that,
resumed private practice in partnership with his brother-in-law
Isaac Catlin, with offices at 26 Court Street in Brooklyn. He soon
provided amply for his family on an income of nearly $19,000 a

year after 1873. Shrewd business sense and capable planning enabled him to add comfortable stock dividends to his earnings and he was able to maintain not only the Brooklyn city house but also sizable country holdings on the Southern Tier. He purchased a 550 acre farm known as "Marshland" where he indulged his love of horses by raising and breeding trotters. At one point this farm stabled over 100 trotters including the famous "Mambrino Dudley" and "Marshland Stud" both known in racing circles for their beauty and stamina.[11]

Tracy's primary attention centered on his law practice. Soon after he departed the District Attorney's job, he became ensnarled in the famous litigation known as the Beecher-Tilton trial. The scandal first broke into public view in October 1872 when the *Woodhull and Claffin Weekly,* published by suffragettes, Victoria Woodhull and Tennessee Claffin, carried an account of an alleged affair between the Reverend Henry Ward Beecher of Plymouth Church, Brooklyn, and the wife of a parishioner, Theodore Tilton. Beecher immediately sought legal counsel from Tracy, a long-time friend and a member of the church vestry. In one of his last acts as District Attorney, the general jailed the publishers of the *Weekly* for sending an "obscene utterance" through the mails. At least one student of the case has contended that Tracy's move formed the initial blunder in a series of events which must have all the earmarks of *opera bouffe* to modern Americans.[12] In any case, while the indictment against Miss Woodhull and Miss Claffin was soon dropped, Tilton filed a complaint against Beecher, charging him with adultery and demanding $10,000 in damages. Beecher asked Tracy to join the defense counsel.

The case of *Tilton versus Beecher* came to trial in Brooklyn City Court before Chief Justice Joseph Neilson on January 11, 1875. Attracting a wide variety of reporters, scandal mongers, and curiosity seekers, it dragged on for six months until a hung jury of nine for Beecher and three opposed concluded the spectacle on July 2. Tracy failed to play the preeminent role for the defense expected by many people. The trial record shows that on several occasions he participated in the examination of witnesses as well as making the opening address for the defense. But illness and rebuke from the bench for obvious hostility to plaintiff witnesses marred his performance. Personal loyalty to a friend, in this case, reduced Tracy's usual grace and effectiveness before a jury.

Indeed, when the trial ended there was a movement to indict the general for perjury. Criticism of "professional treachery and personal dishonor" was also showered upon Tracy. But, in the context of the courtroom practices of the time, Tracy's performance displayed little that was unethical or dishonorable. More suspect was his pre-trial badgering of certain principals involved, and Beecher himself may have placed greater reliance upon other members of the defense team when the case went to court. Later observers have suggested various political implications whereby an unfriendly press attempted to stress Tracy's association with Boss Tom Platt in the hope of reducing his usefulness to Beecher.[13] As one commentator explained it:

> General Tracy was one of the leading Republican machine politicians of New York. There was no danger of his being indicted for anything short of murder.[14]

Yet if any cloud hung over Tracy's name as a result of the Beecher trial it did little to disturb his political position in Brooklyn. His control of Federal patronage while District Attorney earned for him a place among the "Three Graces" who controlled Brooklyn Republicanism early in the decade. Along with General James Jourdan, Assessor of Internal Revenue, and Silas B. Dutcher, Supervisor of Internal Revenue, they formed one faction based upon strong conventional partisanship for the minority Republicans in Brooklyn. Tracy, an honest politician, was also a loyal party-man, as evidenced on one occasion when he opposed all attempts by Brooklyn reformers to shape a bipartisan charter for that city.

Brooklyn, like Manhattan, was run by the Democrats for much of the period. However, the state legislature in Albany (dominated by rural Republicans) maintained control of the police department and a vast number of special commissions instituted for local improvements such as sewers and roads.[15] Thus Tracy and his colleagues who supported the regular Republican organization locally in the seventies stood in a superb position for broader recognition of their talents by party leaders at the state and national level.

Tracy's involvement in Republican politics paid off when he went to the National Convention as a delegate in 1880. Roscoe Conkling and Tom Platt tightly controlled the New York delegation at this gathering and they wanted Grant to stand for a third term. Tracy nearly departed from the organization on several occasions during the convention until he was finally whipped into line in support of

Grant. In some ways the general's actions proved somewhat contradictory. Tracy sided with delegates of a fourteen-state minority,
Robert T. Lincoln among them, in a fight to abolish the traditional
practice of unit rule. It was broken and one political observer stated
later: "It was the greatest defeat the Grant group could possibly
have suffered."[16] Inasmuch as James A. Garfield led the reform
drive as chairman of the rules committee, it might appear that
Tracy supported the Ohio politician for the party's nomination.
But, in the end, either from personal loyalty to fellow New Yorkers,
or because of severe party discipline, General Tracy cast his vote for
Grant. Along with Platt and Conkling, he suffered the ignominy of
watching Garfield emerge as the standard bearer of the party.

The Brooklyn attorney enjoyed especially close affiliation with
Platt in this period. Platt conducted an unofficial headquarters in
the Fifth Avenue Hotel, located north of Manhattan's Washington
Square. Tracy visited him frequently in the first floor rendezvous
known as the "Amen Corner," and here the New York boss persuaded his boyhood friend to run for the mayoralty of Brooklyn.[17]
But if 1881 proved to be a successful year for Platt, who engineered
his own election to the United States Senate through political
manipulation in Albany, it was not similarly auspicious for Tracy.
The Brooklyn lawyer ran on the regular Republican ticket and he
received powerful support from the party organization. However,
realizing that he could not unite all the reformist elements of both
parties, he withdrew and threw his support to a nonpartisan candidate, Seth Low. Thus strengthened, Low triumphed and became
Brooklyn's first reform mayor.[18]

Any disappointment which Tracy might have felt as a result of
the election was dispelled in December of that year when Governor
Alonzo Cornell named him an associate justice of the Court of Appeals. At first Tracy appeared reluctant to assume such an esteemed
position but other members of the bench prevailed upon him. Tracy
proved himself capable of taking the position of trust beside Justices Rapallo, Miller, Earl, Danforth, and Finch. His opinions in
cases involving the legality of marriages contracted in other states,
and in the relatively new field of urban railroad and transit litigation
established long-standing precedents. His written judgments ex-
emplified Tracy's ability by "their clearness of expression, research,
logical compactness, pointed illustration, and absence of all preten-
sion and show."[19]

The heavy chores and schedule of the Court of Appeals took

their toll of Tracy's health. In one year he handed down more controlling opinions than any single judge in the history of that court. He declined renomination to the bench in 1882, only to be named by the Republican state convention for the Supreme Court of the Second District. The Brooklyn judge ran far ahead of the ticket but the Republicans suffered overall defeat as the Democrats elected Grover Cleveland governor. Actually the release from heavy work came none too soon. Tracy's health broke in the winter of 1882-1883, and he was forced to relinquish his law practice as well as politics for awhile. A long rest at Marshland, and a tour of Europe with his family restored Tracy's health and provided a long-neglected opportunity to enjoy the company of his wife and children. But, Tracy's natural energy and his doctor's instructions soon conflicted, and he resumed his law practice in 1885, forming the firm of Tracy, MacFarland, Boardman and Platt with offices at 35 Wall Street in Manhattan.

The new firm enjoyed certain favors in Albany chiefly because the junior partner, Frank H. Platt, was Tom Platt's son. Since "four-fifths of the legislators at Albany would have no wish 'except to record his wants,'" Tracy as a member of the firm became privy to a number of schemes and questionable deals involving the political fortunes of the elder Platt.[20] Thus the general occupied a rather favored position in the Platt organization when the New York boss went to the national convention at Chicago in June 1888 as head of the state's "Stalwart" (or conservative) delegation. At first Platt disciplined his people to back favorite son candidate Chauncey Depew, even though he personally favored Russell A. Alger. Subsequent conversations between Platt and Stephen B. Elkins of West Virginia, a member of the party's national committee and former "Half Breed" (or liberal) supporter of James G. Blaine, changed the picture abruptly. The New York boss interpreted a chance remark from Elkins as a promise that Benjamin Harrison, the Half Breed candidate, would name Platt as Secretary of the Treasury in return for support at the convention. Platt immediately swung his fifty-eight delegates behind Harrison who became the Republican nominee and eventually President.[21]

Thus the fourth in a succession of former Civil War officers became Chief Executive in November 1888 when Harrison narrowly defeated Cleveland. The new administration became identified with high tariffs, overseas expansion, and a modernized navy. President-elect Harrison set the tone by indicating to his advisers that he wished cabinet nominees to be men who represented Republican policy and ideas rather than merely factions or cliques. His avowed desire to make the cabinet posts a personal decision and thus to exclude state bosses from a share in the spoils put many senators, congressmen, and local party leaders on the defensive. But Harrison remained adamant.[22]

Harrison wanted to keep his choices secret until they could be announced simultaneously. He was handicapped, in part at least, by the very internal party policies which he sought to avoid, namely the placating of state bosses. The pivotal state of New York provided the focal point of controversy. Harrison no doubt owed a large debt of gratitude to the Empire State both for support at Chicago and at the polls. Platt naturally expected recompense for his "king making" chores at the convention. He strongly advanced his claim, totally unfounded, that he had a letter from Harrison which promised him the Treasury post.[23] But Platt's claims conflicted with other aspirations like those of former Senator Warner Miller who lost his bid for the New York governorship in 1888. Westerners were also clamoring for recognition, so that the selection of a New Yorker for a cabinet post vexed the President-elect from the day of his election until two days before his Inauguration.

Casting about for a solution, Harrison wrote to Stephen Elkins that perhaps it was best to give the Treasury spot to a Westerner. "Now if the Treasury should go to the West," said the new President, "and the friends of the New York men who have been named for that place should accept this decision as disposing of the whole question . . . the way would be opened to select some suitable person for say the Navy Department—though I do not want to limit suggestions to that place."[24] Harrison went on to say that New York ought to be especially interested in warships and harbor defenses, adding that he still wanted a Navy secretary of high character and good administrative ability, for ". . . there is a chance for fame in that office and that implies a chance for shame as well."

The factional fight between Platt and Miller grew more bitter by the time Harrison arrived in Washington. Compromise seemed out of the question. Finally, and against the advice of some advisers, Harrison talked with Senator Frank Hiscock, a New York middleman, and they reached agreement. The name of Benjamin Franklin Tracy of Brooklyn—acceptable to both factions and also to Harrison—emerged for the post of Secretary of the Navy. As was Harrison's wont, the candidate was immediately summoned to Washington for consultation.[25]

Tracy's reaction to the summons may have been a mixed one. Assumption of a cabinet post meant dislocation of family and career, as well as facing the high cost of living in Washington. Yet he was no stranger to public life; his reputation alone called attention to service, principle and loyalty. When the nation and party beckoned, Tracy felt obliged to accept the call. As Harrison's private secretary tersely recorded in his diary for March 1, 1889: "General Tracy reached here and had an interview with the General [Harrison] at night. Offered Navy and accepted it."[26]

Tracy was probably taken by surprise with the offer of the Navy Department. As a lawyer of great repute he had been mentioned, and perhaps led to expect, appointment as Attorney-General. When one Brooklyn reporter met Tracy on the street three days before the Inauguration and queried whether the General was going to Washington for that event, Tracy replied in jest: "I do not think I shall go unless General Harrison invites me to participate as a member of his Cabinet." Thinking he was serious, the newsman pressed the question: "Well, General, you would make a first class Attorney-General." "It seems that you are not the only Brooklynite who thinks so," quipped Tracy.[27] Nevertheless, he readily accepted the navy portfolio with mixed pleasure and humility.

Harrison soon realized that his appointment, while personally satisfying, did not settle the party feud at home. Neither the Platt nor Miller factions felt encouraged and one Brooklyn ward boss, Ernest Nathan, observed: "General Tracy represents Platt. I know of my own knowledge that he did all he could to have Platt placed in the Cabinet, and I suppose that is the main reason why he finds himself there now." Platt also claimed later that Harrison "finally permitted me to name General Benjamin F. Tracy, from my own county," as naval secretary.[28]

On the other hand, letters poured into the office of the new President in a chorus of praise for the Brooklyn attorney. The Union League of New York listed Tracy's name among its preferred candidates for a cabinet post and one New York attorney wrote ecstatically to Harrison:

> Alexander the Great cut the 'Gordian Knot,' you have done better—you have untied it . . . the choice of General Tracy as

one of your advisers . . . will be received with a deeper and a more general satisfaction throughout the State than any other you could have made. He is a broad man—natural not personal in his politics—he leads no faction—he is simply and thoroughly Republican.[29]

Republican and Democratic editors alike joined the bipartisan applause. One Brooklyn editor declared: "In General Tracy he selected a strong man, one who has trained with the Stalwarts, but who is [not] a Stalwart himself, and who will be Secretary of the Navy on his own account, for the good of the Administration, the party, and the country, and not in behalf of any blizzard obliviated [sic] faction of the party."[30]

Perhaps Americans felt cheered more by the comments of the outgoing Secretary of the Navy, William C. Whitney:

I am personally acquainted with Judge Tracy, and consequently can truthfully congratulate you upon his selection. He is a man of probity and ability, and will make an excellent Secretary of the Navy. It is a good appointment.[31]

After all, Whitney was in a superb position to know the demands of office.

CHAPTER 4

National Service Leads to a Policy Revolution

Rainy weather marred inaugural activities in Washington on March 4, 1889, but it failed to dampen President Benjamin Harrison's ardor in declaring that "the construction of a sufficient number of modern warships . . . should progress as rapidly as is consistent with care and perfection in plans and workmanship."[1] He also called for acquisition of overseas naval bases. Two days later the new Chief Executive signed the commissions of all cabinet members and they were inducted formally into office. Secretary of the Navy Benjamin F. Tracy qualified first; it was to be a prophetic omen for the next four years.

The Harrison administration found itself the object of great public expectation as the nation prepared to celebrate its Centennial. Economic and psychological changes following the turbulence of civil war and reconstruction once more permitted Americans the luxury of asserting manifest destiny and a place in the sun. The nation possessed enormous confidence that it would offer something truly unique to the rest of the world, that its institutions were superior, its progress greater, and its civilization higher than other peoples. Americans looked to Washington and their national officials to reflect such glory.

The stirrings of manifest destiny developed slowly in the seventies and eighties. An earlier, mid-century expression of that spirit disappeared with much of antebellum society. Men like Tracy and Harrison might recall personally that new interests took hold of them after Appomattox. Neglected families and occupations, financial strain, and disrupted careers all bothered veterans of the conflict. Americans in general became preoccupied with other things. It was the era of the emergence of modern America, of change from farm to factory, from rural to urban living. Looking inward, most Americans allowed issues of foreign affairs to drift beyond their gaze. The navy of Reconstruction days certainly mirrored this development and numerous historians have subsequently recounted its vicissitudes.[2]

Briefly, the naval service drifted backward into its pre-war condition. Tracy told a Brooklyn audience in 1889:

> At the close of the Civil War the United States had the largest and most powerful navy in the world, but at the conclusion of peace we disbanded our armies, neglected our navy, and devoted the energies of our people to building inland transportation routes and developing internal trade and commerce. But while we built railroads other nations built navies. Now at the end of twenty-five years we find we have dropped from the top to the very bottom of the list of naval powers.[3]

Pre-war restoration seemed so complete, indeed, that some later analysts contended: "A visitor returning in 1870 after ten years absence might never have guessed that the Navy had passed through any war . . . much less a war that hastened a revolution in naval architecture and thoroughly demonstrated the inadequacy of the strategic theories in vogue on the eve of the conflict."[4]

The American sea service enjoyed few moments of grandeur during the early years of Reconstruction. The Navy list, showing 700 vessels aggregating half a million tons and mounting almost 5,000 guns in 1864, had shrunk considerably by 1870. In that year the navy numbered but 200 ships of 200,000 tons aggregating about 1,300 guns. Even this array included store and hospital vessels and the 52 actual warships mounted only 500 obsolete cannon. Naval appropriations from 1865 to 1881 showed a similar decline. From a figure of $122,613,000 spent in the final year of the Civil War, the sum fell to $13,537,000 in the election year of 1880. Active duty personnel, numbering 58,296 officers and men in 1865, slipped to a peacetime level of 9,361, and naval tonnage dropped finally to 146,725 tons when James Garfield entered the White House.[5]

Not that the Navy Department always advanced its best interests before Congress and the people. Misconception if not utter neglect of the lessons of the Civil War concerning ironclads, rifled ordnance, and ship design; internal squabbles between line and staff officers; reactionary senior officers such as Admiral David Porter; rife corruption at naval installations; and the strife between prerogative-conscious bureau chiefs and ineffectual political hack secretaries like George M. Robison, Adolph Borie, and Richard W. Thompson—all projected the very opposite of a taut combat-ready, peacetime navy. The celebrated *Omaha* case of 1880 provided a classic example of the state of the service.

Someone in the department decided to rebuild the *Omaha,* an old wooden vessel. Half a million dollars (more than the cost of a new vessel of comparable size) went into the project; yet four years later the *Omaha* put to sea only to have her captain discover a coal supply sufficient for merely four-days steaming. Except for the issue of culpable neglect, probably few observers either on Capitol Hill or in the Navy Department felt disturbed over the incident. After all, why should the peacetime service do anything more than show the flag and shepherd America's commercial interests abroad? Wooden ships like the *Omaha* could effectively handle such responsibilities naval secretaries claimed in their annual reports. Congress might review naval policy and make annual decisions about naval expenditures but, except for a few extreme navalists, that body could see little cause for redirection of naval policy or strategy.[6]

Actually, Congress may have judged rather accurately the American temper about foreign affairs. Random incidents such as the acquisition of Alaska and its inherent strategic problems of defense, the *Virginius* affair in 1871 which exposed the worthlessness of American wooden warships when faced with first-class Spanish vessels, the rise of Chilean seapower, the prospect of a French-owned canal in Central America, or the perennial bogey-man of Britannia ruling the waves—all failed to arouse the American people to the policy of neglect of its first line of defense. Atrophy lingered on until the eighties. Meanwhile, other harbingers of American expansion rapidly outdistanced strategic policy.

The early postwar years may not in fact have been so bereft of activity as hitherto believed. Recent scholarship has uncovered cer-

PRIDE OF THE OLD NAVY
U.S.S. *Hartford*, Veteran Steam Frigate of the Civil War, still in
Commission in 1905
[Courtesy National Archives]

tain "subterranean forces of change" which accompanied the idle chatter and unproductive foreign policy of the postwar decades. The concern for internal matters, political battles in Washington, and sterile diplomacy may have only hidden a sequence of phenomena viewed by a new group of historians as illustrating America's turn towards the imperialist era. Indeed, the sequel from industrial expansion to the search for markets to a larger navy for protection, and thence to acquisition of bases for making naval strength viable, has been advanced to explain the "spread-eagle nationalism" which surfaced so vividly near the end of the century.[7]

The rumblings, however muted, certainly were present all along. Such men as Secretaries of State Seward and Fish, President Grant, Ohio capitalist S. J. Ritchie, navalists like Commodore Robert Shufeldt and Senator Eugene Hale, and American men of letters like Samuel Clemens, served as advance agents of American expansion. Revival of the foreign service, as pushed by civil service reformers; and participation in international conferences on matters like the Red Cross (1864 and 1882), formation of an international postal union 1874, 1878), marine affairs (1882, 1889), as well as monetary issues (1881), obviate the usual image of a completely isolationist America following the Civil War. Noteworthy too was American representation at trade expositions such as the Paris Exposition in 1867, Vienna in 1873, and even fairs held in Sydney and Melbourne in 1879 and 1880. Such were the manifestations of a quickening concern for world affairs.

The attitude of American business toward expansion may have been even more important. While historians continue to differ as to the real significance of economic considerations to overseas expansion of the period, none completely avoids discussion of economic imperialism during the Gilded Age.[8] The United States was never isolated commercially from the rest of the world. But domestic markets gradually approached a point of saturation. Businessmen began to look elsewhere for markets—to Europe, Canada, Latin America, even to the Pacific world.

It was perhaps illogical for American businessmen to think that Europe would sit back complacently while the United States stole her commercial supremacy. England reacted predictably as Americans chipped away at her control of world finances and leadership in the international marketplace. In turn, tariff matters rapidly supplanted the Southern question as a topic of conversation in Washington. It may be that the economic factor was but one element of a confusing melange of philosophical idealism, domestic frustration, political expediency, and quest for national prestige that led to expansionism. One thing remains abundantly clear, however. By 1889, when Harrison became president, any notion of commercial isolation lay buried beneath industry's search for new markets. America's exports began to exceed her imports in value from 1874 onward. Whether commerce followed the flag or vice versa, the inherently adventurous and speculative American businessman pushed his government to reevaluate its foreign policies. Indeed, lights burned longer into the night in foreign ministeries on both sides of the Atlantic by late in the decade as commercial issues became inextricably interwoven with larger questions of national power and strategic policy.

This international revival of colonial expansion after 1880—the "acquisitive imperialism" of loans, leases, spheres of influence, protectorates, colonies—remains intrinsic to any understanding of America's subsequent naval revival. Certainly the tempo of expansion had been increasing since the conclusion of the Napoleonic struggles in 1815. Growth of European technology and industry enlarged trade with all parts of the world. Superior European military techniques overwhelmed Islamic and Asiatic states, yet colonial annexation remained essentially unplanned by European statesmen. It emerged mainly because some local European interest in Africa, Asia, or the Pacific rendered annexation or protectorship inevitable. Land-hungry settlers expanded their domains in Canada, South Africa, and Australasia. Local officials in India, Java, and Algeria sought frontier buffer zones, and the activities of Christian missionaries and explorers in heretofore "dark continents" led to added European involvement.

New elements were injected into this situation in the eighties and thereafter. Continuation of trends evident from 1815-1880 received added impetus from the theory that tropical colonies were necessary to provide markets for manufactures, fields for investment of surplus capital, and an assured source for raw materials. Intensified international rivalries followed the unification of Germany and Italy and the defeat of France in 1870-71, and colonies became sources of national power and symbols of prestige.

In 1884-85 came the introduction of still another element. Chancellor Otto von Bismarck advanced Germany's claim to colonies and, at that time, imposed the new power politics of the continent on the maritime nations which had formerly regarded colonies as their special preserve. Overseas possessions became diplomatic pawns and bargaining chips at the international conference table. The tranquility of European diplomacy was shattered since it was now less a question of value of a particular section of the globe, and more a fact that any European power which failed to advance its own claims was apt to find itself shut out from further expansion. Peace and harmony in Europe became linked inextricably to events in Tunisia, or Fiji or Nicaragua. Strategy joined economic motive in the imperialist rhetoric of the late nineteenth century.

As the race for trade and empire embroiled the great powers of Europe in a relentless campaign to carve up the weaker nations of the world, repercussions were soon felt in several ways by an expansion-minded United States. Questions arose not only about protection for American commerce or development of United States hegemony in the Americas but also about the underlying cause of American navalism—the issue of national defense expressed through the historic role of seapower. The theme of national security and power governed the plans and policies of European nations in the eighties and the United States reacted in no small measure to their lead.[9]

American officials began to realize that the antiquity of their post-Civil War navy combined with the obvious technological superiority of such foreign fleets as those of Great Britain and France posed serious threats to the shores of the United States. British warships operating from Halifax or Jamaica could threaten the Atlantic seaboard and might even enter the Great Lakes through the improved Welland Canal. If British seapower could take Suez as it did in 1882, then why not Panama, an object of American interest? Also, there was the possibility of French intervention in Central America. Moreover, by the eighties, domestic conditions in the United States permitted increased consideration of expensive programs such as naval rearmament in the interest of defending American freedom.

By the time President Garfield took office in March 1881, national economic problems of the previous decade were over. Treasury figures showed a surplus and American industry, especially manufacturing, appeared to be expanding significantly. A favorable balance of trade pointed to a greatly revived merchant marine and thus to inevitable friction internationally. In general, then, the time seemed good for naval rebuilding.[10] It began under the leadership of William H. Hunt, Garfield's naval secretary. Cut short by the president's assassination, Hunt's action nonetheless set a precedent. Surrounding himself with capable advisors such as Admiral John Rogers' board of professionals, Hunt promulgated plans for rebuilding the navy. Board members called for the immediate construction of eighteen unarmored steel cruisers, twenty wooden cruisers, ten torpedo boats, and five rams. But Congress vacillated. Finally, Secretary Hunt brought together leading members of Congress and his department and this new departure helped to overcome hostility between the legislative branch and the navy.[11]

President Arthur, succeeding Garfield, endorsed Hunt's program and introduced into his cabinet a New Hampshire politician who ably implemented the latter's rebuilding schemes. William E. Chandler, a combination of energy and organizational talent, instituted the actual work of new construction despite intense criticism of his policies and practices. Congress, of course, continued to express its own collective will when it came to naval policy. It pared Hunt's requests to only two steel cruisers, then failed to fund them. But, pressed by many newspapers, business groups, lobbyists, and even some of its own vocal membership, Congress set up a second statutory advisory board under the guidance of Commodore Shufeldt, lately returned from opening Korean ports to American trade.

Then, in 1882, Congress proceeded to enact a law whereby no wooden warship should receive repairs amounting to more than 30 percent (later reduced to 20 percent), of the cost of a new vessel of the same size and rate. But merely retiring the remaining ships of the "Old Navy" was not enough; the policy had to be complemented with a modern expansion program. Thus Congress appropriated $1.3 million on March 3, 1883, towards construction of four new vessels from which emerged the "New Steel Navy." These ships, the protected cruisers *Atlanta, Boston, Chicago,* and the dispatch boat *Dolphin* provoked much controversy because of construction costs and performance. They carried four-inch armor and mounted a mixture of 8-inch, 6-inch, and 5-inch guns. Light in tonnage, yet speedy in performance, the "ABCDs"—as they were called—pleased no one from their builder, John Roach, to the Navy Department. Still, when grouped together in the "White Squadron"

with the blue-green waters of the Atlantic lapping gently against
their gleaming white sides—a departure in navy paint schemes
ostensibly reflecting their peaceful intent—they surely swelled the
pride of all Americans everywhere. Here was the keystone of a
"New Navy"—the first tangible proof that a renaissance had begun
in American naval affairs.[12]

A number of obstacles to naval progress remained for Chandler
and his successor, William C. Whitney. For instance, American
steel mills had never rolled hull plates before, nor had a vessel ever
been built completely of domestic steel. Shipbuilders lacked skill
in application of materials and their foundries remained ill-prepared
for forging steel for heavy ordnance. Additionally, bureaucratic
red tape riddled the Navy Department and party strife in Congress
interrupted passage of important naval legislation. Many people,
Democrat and Republican, naval officer and steelmaker, could
foresee benefits accruing from naval reconstruction. But they simply lacked experience in determining costs, lead-time, policies, and
priorities. Thus, the ugliness of party politics, patronage, the spoils
system, contract favoritism, as well as a tradition of political and
geographical isolation, all posed roadblocks for the supporters of
the steel navy.[13]

Secretary Tracy, reviewing progress in the spring of 1889, devoted most of his attention to the administration of Whitney, his
immediate predecessor. When the Democrats returned to the
White House in 1885, for the first time since the war, they arrived
in Washington with definite ideas about the management of national affairs. President Cleveland summoned Whitney, a prominent New York corporation lawyer, to lend direction to the Navy
Department.[14] Much of Whitney's attention subsequently went to
departmental administration, but his connection with New York
commercial interests stimulated his concern with building the navy
to protect foreign trade. His own accomplishments in office continued in the wake of Chandler's "ABCDs" but, in turn, European
developments also affected Whitney's actions and gave additional
direction to subsequent naval progress by the GOP.

The New York Democrat contributed significantly to many
areas of the navy's rebuilding in addition to 100,000 tons of shipping authorized by Congress during his tenure. Changes in administrative techniques resulted from politically motivated disclo-
sures of huge expenditures wasted on repairs of old wooden

PROTOTYPE BATTLE FLEET
Squadron of Evolution, 1889
[Courtesy National Archives]

warships by previous administrations. Moving to reduce the number of departmental bureaus charged with such matters as construction, supply, and personnel, Whitney also investigated the production of gun forgings and established a government ordnance factory at the Washington Navy Yard. He encouraged domestic steel production, soliciting bids on armor contracts with a thirty-month deadline for delivery before finally awarding the lucrative contract to the Bethlehem Steel Company. Whitney proved less responsive to the needs of the forward-looking Naval War College, established by his predecessor at Newport in 1884. His motives for the opposition to Commodore Stephen B. Luce's brainchild remain unclear, reflecting once more perhaps the internal struggle in naval circles between safe conservatism and uncertain innovation.

The policy ramifications of Whitney's shipbuilding programs have proved more controversial. Seeming contradictions existed, at least in retrospect, for the program blended modern armament with inadequate armor protection and sailing impedimenta, coast-defense monitors with several fairly large sea-going armored vessels. Congressional authorizations included provisions for constructing vessels from naval tugs to heavier cruisers (later termed second-class battleships). These latter vessels, *Texas* and *Maine,* were authorized in 1886 and included 7,000 tons displacement, a speed of 18.5 knots, heavy armor, and modern 10- and 12-inch rifled guns in their main batteries. Subsequently, the cruisers *New York* (8,000 tons), and *Olympia* (5,540 tons), were designed for speeds of 21 and 22 knots respectively and mounted 8-inch guns. These vessels could hardly be termed "commerce destroyers" in the traditional sense of American naval policy. Rather, their heavier tonnage and armament promised to better serve emerging American commercial enterprise of the era—the need to be able to give battle to enemy squadrons bent upon their own task of commerce destruction—something which the White Squadron and other weaker units of the steel navy could not do.

One modern historian contends that while appearing to represent a shift to offensive doctrine, these ships actually indicated nothing more than technological progress which had outrun policy. "The thirty ships added by Whitney reflected the haphazard planning of officers who grasped the tactical significance of mobility and fire-power, but failed to appreciate the strategic advantage inherent in

a unified battle force of significant strength and endurance to destroy an enemy fleet a thousand miles offshore."[15] Such an analysis appears too simple for explaining the myriad forces at work
during the Whitney period. Whitney himself saw European navies
expanding their inventories of armored vessels as a result of advances in firepower and intricacies of continental politics. But he
realized the American navy was entirely dependent upon European
manufactured armor and gun forgings, an untenable posture for
the United States in the event of war. Therefore Whitney subjected
construction programs to a three-year delay in order to prepare a
domestic facility for producing armor and armament (as it turned
out, the Bethlehem plant and the gun factory at Washington). A
drift in policy unfortunately accompanied delays in construction,
for neither the Navy Department nor Congress chose to define
specific types of armored fighting craft until after the nation possessed a capacity to build them.

Thus the contemporary reader of Whitney's final annual report
might find some interesting passages. On the one hand, the secretary sensed the future direction of warfare by citing the need for
torpedo boats (in a sense the prototype for both the modern submarine and destroyer classes of warship), and ready reserves of
organized seamen. Yet he still clung to archaic strategic concepts
by declaring: "We can not at present protect our coast, but we can
return blow for blow, for we shall soon be in condition to launch a
fleet of large and fast cruisers against the commerce of an enemy,
able to inflict the most serious and lasting injury thereon."[16] Whitney claimed that in terms of ships with 19 knot speeds and 3,000
tons or more displacement, the United States Navy ranked second
only to Great Britain's ten ships displacing 59,600 tons. America's
eight ships (32,010 tons) were more than France's five (24,630 tons),
Spain's three (14,400 tons), Japan's two (7,500 tons), and Russia's
one (5,030 tons). Thus, Whitney's ships represented an offensive
spirit, but one which continued to be couched within the traditional
framework of naval policy, and reflective of political and technological realities of the time.[17]

If anything, the Whitney programs pinpointed the confusion and
transitional nature of this phase of America's naval rebuilding.
More Americans agreed with naval modernization than a decade
before, but in the eighties a majority remained uncertain of the

direction to be taken by such programs. They would have applauded the sentiments of Tennessee Congressman, John D. C. Atkins, when he told a colleague in 1882:

> Now I do not see any very great necessity for being in a hurry about building up a navy. Let us wait, sir, until naval invention and construction shall have reached that perfection which will present a model that we may safely adopt.[18]

Slowly, as the decade advanced, perceptible signs of a shift in the political climate appeared on Capitol Hill. Many more legislators began to see a defenseless coastline of the United States and the possible implications from expanding overseas trade. Senator John F. Miller of California prophesied a new era for American trade in which European envy might lead to conflict; Senator Joseph Dolph of Oregon felt concern for possible consequences of European bombardment of American cities; and Senator John T. Morgan of Alabama wanted four fleets for the Atlantic, Pacific, Gulf of Mexico, and surprisingly, even for the Great Lakes.[19] Such perceptions were helped by growing international tensions which might embroil the United States.

Chilean hostility to American policies in the Southern Hemisphere mounted as the United States sought to offset possible European intervention and usurpation of markets in that area. Prospects of a Central American canal controlled by a European power continued to frighten Americans as witnessed by Whitney's action in 1885 when he dispatched an expeditionary force to Columbia to smother a revolution which threatened to disrupt the tranquility of that region and possibly lead to European intervention. Then, too, there were controversies with Canada and Great Britain over fishing rights, possible Far Eastern reverberations from restriction of Chinese immigration, and the conflicting interests of England, Germany, and the United States in Samoa. All these threatened to embroil the United States, not just with banana republics, but with first-class European powers who likewise felt a vested interest in those sections of the world.[20]

Few men in Congress, however, had a clear view of the correct policy on such matters, much less on the proper size and type of naval vessel to underwrite the nation's foreign policy. So they hedged. Designs of the *Maine* and *Texas* made sense to practical, economy-minded Congressmen and surely, thought the legislators, these vessels were more than adequate for the moment.

TABLE 2—RELATIVE STRENGTH OF SHIPS BUILT OR BUILDING 1888-1889

Class	Great Britain	France	Russia	United States
Battle-ships	37 (323,920 tons) (iron hulls)	33 (235,879 tons) (2 iron hulls)	7 (83,829 tons)	
Coast Defense Vessels	8 (33,110 tons)	14 (41,496 tons)	7 (24,441 tons)	
Harbor Defense Vessels	10 (30,940 tons)		15 (27,216 tons)	19 (50,820 tons) 2 rams (1,843 tons)
Armoured Cruisers	18 (137,050 tons) (all iron hulls)	7 (43,100 tons) (iron and wood hulls)	7 (40,312 tons) (all iron hulls)	2 (12,948 tons) (all iron hulls)
Unarmoured Cruisers	65 (171,880 tons)	34 (82,333 tons)	14 (25,999 tons)	14 (39,800 tons) (steel hulls) (incl. 4 classed as gun-boats, 1 dispatch boat, 1 dynamite cruiser) 24 (54,102 tons (wooden hulls)
				38 (93,902 tons) total
Grand Total	138 (696,900 tons)	88 (402,808 tons)	50 (201,797 tons)	61 (159,513 tons)

Source: Brassey's Naval Annual, 1888-89.

International naval progress to some degree forced the hands of the navy professionals. Great Britain and France at this time offered the greatest maritime threat to American interests whether commercial or strategic. The love-hate relationship of the United States with her mother country and traditional enemy, England, received added dimensions from the preeminence of British naval strength. Here was the model for all competitors, since Great Britain enjoyed a numerical and supposedly qualitative lead over her continental rivals in both battleships and cruisers. By 1889 the White Ensign was to fly above sixteen battleships of the first class and seventeen of the second class embracing main batteries varying in caliber from 12- to 16-inch guns. French vessels varied in armor plate and armament according to the fancy of their naval contractors and admittedly fewer battleships flew the tricolour than the British flag, there being twelve of the first class and eighteen of the second class in the French fleet. Similar numerical differences existed in other classes of warships, but in that era of experimentation and rapid technical advances in engineering, gun design, and naval architecture relatively few people outside of naval designers and key officials really knew who possessed the superior navy. One thing seemed obvious to everyone. The United States Navy in the eighties had nothing with which to counter the eighteen inch armor and 13.5-inch breechloading rifles of HMS *Anson, Camperdown, Howe,* and *Rodney,* or the twenty-two inch armor and 13.4-inch guns of *Admiral Duperré.* Together or separately, British and French navies were more than a match for American seapower.

British navalists of the time were naturally more concerned with the rapid progress of France, Russia, and even the new German empire in building up their fleets than with the United States Navy. A combination of France and Russia could strongly challenge the Royal Navy in first-class vessels. The Admiralty reacted predictably to fears of possible invasion of the home islands and *guerre de course* against the overseas trade lifeline by launching more heavy warships in the eighties.[21] As the international situation became threatening and the naval race escalated on the eastern side of the Atlantic, the contagion spread across the water to Washington.

American naval officers knew that they needed ships mounting bigger guns and more armor. Professionals like Rear Admirals Stephen B. Luce and Edward Simpson, Commodore John G. Walker, Commanders William T. Sampson, Caspar F. Goodrich,

Bainbridge Hoff, and Lieutenant Commanders French B. Chadwick and F. M. Barber, studied the activities of their counterparts abroad. Indeed, the Office of Naval Intelligence was set up for that purpose in 1882. Annual publications of that office as well as the *Proceedings* of the United States Naval Institute carried their findings to fellow professionals throughout the service. Foreign experience highlighted prominent issues of design and construction, ordnance, armor, steam engineering, even electrification and small arms training.[22] Together the amount of professional knowledge available to American naval officers, especially those stationed in Washington, convinced such men as Luce and Walker of the need for changes in their own service. Whether or not European intelligence information prompted any "revolution" in American naval attitudes, it certainly must be weighed when considering the basis of decision-making by top naval leaders and how the civilian secretary presented his programs to Congress and to the public. A carefully cultivated image of a major foreign threat to the United States might mean more money from Congress for naval defense. Naval defense required ships and new ships meant new openings for command, or so thought many naval officers.

A large percentage of these ideas came together during the eighties in the ". . . unmistakable indications of growing unrest and dissatisfaction with . . . traditional doctrines."[23] Spokesmen included the prize essayist in 1880 of the Naval Institute who stressed the inseparability of commercial and naval supremacy. The minority report of the naval members of the Endicott coastal defense board in 1886 assumed that thereafter the United States should build large numbers of armored sea-going ships which "would act offensively and not be confined to the defense of ports." While hesitating to jettison completely the accepted notions of strategic policy, naval officers such as Luce, and politicians like Senator Matthew C. Butler heralded the shift in focus. Both men spoke out late in the decade against the nebulous strategy of commerce raiding and passive coast and harbor defense. Heavy gunned, "line-of-battle" ships figured prominently in both their arguments.[24]

Translation of theory into programs proved to be another matter. Neither President Cleveland nor Secretary Whitney became proponents of extravagant naval expansion. Nevertheless, their programs —larger cruisers and weaponry, administrative reform, and stimulation of heavy industry—represented a departure from the "small navy" policies usually associated with the party of Jefferson and Jackson.[25] If the navy stood at a crossroads when the Cleveland administration left office in 1889, it was largely because most government officials had not yet compromised with what they feared were future trends—big guns, big ships, and big fleets. Whitney's programs seem less strange, less haphazard, less confusing when viewed in this light. Simply another step in the American naval "evolution," Whitney's programs reflected neither retrenchment nor revolution. But the time was right for a greater move forward.

When Benjamin F. Tracy crossed the White House grounds to the baroque State, War, and Navy Building, he could scarcely anticipate the strains and problems that awaited him in the next four years. Erect in carriage and vigorous in gait, the New Yorker at 59 appeared much the same as he had on that day thirty-five years before when he became the Empire State's youngest district attorney. He sported a matching mustache and beard, and although his hair was now grey, he carried his age well. A contemporary journalist, E. G. Dunnell, described the new secretary as "tall, strong, vigorous, dignified, graceful in manner without suggesting a particle of weakness for 'soft' manners . . . a face that can be grave or pleased without loss of a natural reserve of self-respect. . . ."[26]

Tracy unobtrusively entered Room 272, the office of the Secretary of the Navy. He was greeted by Whitney and soon all the officers and civilian clerks of the department were summoned and introduced to their new chief. Tracy took the oath of office during a lull at about 11:15 A.M. and then followed an hour's reception.

The new secretary no sooner commenced his duties than he began to set the pace which became quite familiar to reporters and the public for the next four years. Tracy's second-floor office overlooked the White House lawns to the east—reputedly one of the finest views in the capital. Portraits of former secretaries hung from the walls above glass cases which housed models of new navy vessels like precious gems—all testifying to the responsibilities of the room's occupant.[27]

The excitement and rush of the first week left Tracy anxious to depart for his Brooklyn home. By the afternoon of March 9 his thoughts had turned to mending political fences, future arrangements about his law practice, and of course, Delinda and the family who awaited his return from Washington. But a horde of reporters first greeted Tracy when he finally reached 148 Montague Street at 10:30 that evening. Tracy gave the newspapermen a story before retiring with his family. No, he would not be moving his family to Washington before the autumn; no, he would not go to the Brooklyn Navy Yard during that visit; and, most certainly, there was no danger of war with Germany over Samoa. Questioned about the Navy, the new secretary observed:

> Yes, we need a navy, a better navy, and the people are bound to have one, the best ships that art and artisans can construct. We need more and we shall build and have more. Within sixty days we shall advertise for proposals for contracts for several new vessels.[28]

Tracy returned to Washington early in the following week. The next nine months were to be almost like a shakedown cruise for one of the secretary's proffered ships. A full schedule of cabinet meetings, patronage interviews, and social obligations sapped his time and energy. According to Washington observers, Tracy arrived at his office at 9:30 and seldom left before 5:30 in the afternoon, hours simply unheard of in Washington at that time. But Tracy's main problem was that he wanted to see everything at firsthand—in Washington and at Eastern shore establishments to which he traveled in the spring and summer of 1889.

The financial sacrifice incurred by his acceptance of the cabinet post and the unsettled state of his family weighed heavily upon him. Tracy's income from his legal practice and investments had approached $22,000 annually at the time of his appointment. His salary as secretary was only $8,000 and what investments could be retained yielded scarcely $2,500 in additional funds. Tracy continued to participate in some cases for Tracy, Boardman, and Platt, but weekly trips to New York courts took their physical and financial toll during the early months of office. His expenses also rose precipitously, since government officials were expected to entertain freely and lavishly. Large living quarters were needed for guests as well as for Delinda, the two daughters, and a grandchild. In addition, the country property near Owego, managed by his son Frank, drained money.

Tracy's financial situation soon required sacrifice. He eventually

sold many of his beloved trotters at Marshland. A two-day sale
began on April 27 and proceeds from forty-nine horses reached
$59,950, although the famous Membrino Dudley brought only
$6,000, scarcely one-half his reported value, much to Tracy's dis-
gust. As he testily told one reporter:

> My reason for selling the stock is that I have about 500 head
> of horses and am about 500 miles away from them. I can't at-
> tend to them, that is all.[29]

Such was Tracy's sacrifice of personal matters to duty.

Spring of 1889 found Tracy engaged in house hunting in Washington accompanied often by his colleagues, Secretary of the Treasury William Windom, and Postmaster General John Wannamaker,
and on one occasion by his youngest daughter Mary. Finally, Tracy
and Windom found a suitable residence on the south side of "I"
Street facing Farragut Square. On May 8, Tracy deposited $500
toward the sale price of $40,000. The home had belonged to Don M.
Dickinson, Cleveland's Postmaster General, and newsmen declared
the section of the city around it to be "the most aristocratic quarter
of five or six years ago, modern fashion having moved a little
farther out."[30] It was convenient to his office and Tracy found that
he could add an extra story with five rooms where he might entertain. Not until autumn could the secretary and his family really
settle into their new home and place in Washington society.

The secretary's on-the-job training received a severe jolt toward
the end of March when the telegraph brought word of a naval disaster in the South Pacific. Reporters summoned Tracy from his
hotel room at 2:00 A.M. on March 30 with dispatches about a
Samoan hurricane which had destroyed the naval squadron representing American aspirations for a coaling station at Apia. Tracy
refused to confirm the report until later in the day. By then he had
received direct word from Rear Admiral L. A. Kimberly, the squadron commander, that only H.M.S. *Calliope,* a vessel of the British
squadron, managed to escape to open sea. Six German and American vessels fared less well, and when the storm cleared, the United
States possessed no warships in the Pacific worthy of the name.[31]

Following the initial shock of the calamity and official expressions of condolence, Tracy exonerated Kimberly and his officers
from any blame for the disaster. But he used the catastrophe and
the help of the press to dramatize the Navy's need for ships. Headlines screamed "Old Tubs for Samoa," and Tracy ordered wooden

replacements such as the *Alert, Adams,* and *Richmond* to the area. The newspapers also emphasized that Navy regulations prohibited American warships from maintaining steam power while at anchor and thus had hampered Kimberly in riding out the storm.

There were larger stakes in the Samoan situation than mere ships, for American and European diplomats had been locked in negotiations since 1878 concerning the island which lay astride the commercial route to the Southwest Pacific. European powers also noted the attraction of such a position, especially for coaling stations so vital to steam navigation. The United States, Great Britain, and Germany pursued a near collision course until the hurricane swept away the immediate danger and diplomats could peacefully arbitrate primary claims to the islands. With reports reaching Washington from Charles Denby, American representative in China, noting Chinese unrest and asking for naval protection for American interests, Tracy pressed the State Department to instruct its delegation at the Berlin conference to emphasize a coaling facility among its demands. Furthermore, Tracy's commercial ties with New York City enabled him to appreciate expansionist arguments. While the final pact gave the United States its claims to Pago Pago and weakened German influence, it also established a three-power protectorate over Samoa. Continued friction between the weaker nations—with the Samoans as pawns—hampered Tracy's attempts to establish a permanent naval base. The secretary sent Kimberly to survey appropriate sites, and he obligingly wrote that "the increasing commercial importance of these islands render it desirable to place this station as soon as possible on a permanent basis." But the impasse remained, as did Tracy's unquenchable thirst for overseas naval stations.

Before Tracy could press on with the building of overseas bases he wanted to evaluate his official domain at home. So, stirred by the Pacific disaster, a friendly public press, and his own natural inquisitiveness, the secretary isolated problems relating to departmental administration, shipbuilding programs, and the role of the naval service as an arm of the national government. Each area impinged upon another, but Tracy realizing that progress could not always be accomplished overnight, studied the problems, consulted with knowledgeable naval and civilian officials, and quietly formulated his own solutions during his first year in office. Only then did he move against the difficulties.

Tracy assumed supervision of the Navy Department in 1889 with all the liabilities of a politically appointed civilian. But, if he lacked the technical expertise required, he did have a sharp legal mind and good business sense. Finding his small staff unable to cope with the deluge of patronage requests, social invitations, and private correspondence, Tracy secured Henry J. Raymond's services as personal secretary. Disliking Whitney's desk arrangement because it severed the intraoffice communications system, Tracy moved the desk back to the middle of the room and reconnected the wires. Line and staff officers rejoiced that each of them regained direct communication with the secretary. But surely they could not fail to note the reverse logic in Tracy's decision either.

Actually, the no-nonsense Tracy moved quickly to counter any notions that he was being pocketed by bureau chiefs. Rumors floated about the department that this had been Whitney's difficulty and the senior admiral of the service made no secret of the fact that he believed Tracy would also be unable to harness the balky team.[32] Part of the problem lay in the nature of the navy which by late in the century conducted a most complicated business operation, cutting across a full spectrum of manufacture, naval architecture, steam engineering, scientific enterprise, education, the science and practice of war, naval and international law, diplomacy, medicine and surgery, finance and accounting, astronomy, and hydrography. Some of these functions were military in nature—the movement of ships, recruitment and assignment of personnel. But others like ship repair and construction and procurement fell into a civil category. A secretary needed to know something about political affairs, social duties, and the art of human relations.

A less energetic man like John D. Long (whose tenure included the Spanish-American War) found a simple solution: "What is the need of my making a dropsical tub of any lobe of my brain when I have at hand a man [a bureau chief] possessed with more knowledge than I could acquire, and have him constantly on tap."[33] But other secretaries like Whiteney, Tracy, and Hilary Herbert, had little inclination to default on their responsibilities. Yet, merely intending to be master of one's house hardly insured automatic success, as Tracy found out. Theorists such as Captain Alfred Thayer Mahan might contend that in American naval administration there was but one head with no division of responsibility. Still, theory and practice were often dissimilar in the Navy Department of the late nineteenth century.[34]

The problem focused quite simply on civil versus military control. The short-term nature of political secretaries, their own technical deficiencies, and an inadequate office staff for asserting their prerogatives, fostered overly powerful bureaus, the bane of both navy and war departments in this period. Tradition developed through the years whereby each bureau jealously guarded its little empire all the while pronouncing its own goals to be "for the good of the service." If the bureau chiefs did defer to anyone, it was only to the Chief of the Bureau of Navigation. As one analyst declared later:

> He, with the consent of the Secretary of the Navy, moves and removes the officers and controls the naval ships. In the naval firmament he is a star of the first magnitude and rivals the Secretary in brilliance. Until after the Spanish-American War, no other officer of the Navy compared with him in power, authority, and consequence.[35]

The bureau chiefs fought especially hard against any consolidation of their domains. They enjoyed well-placed support in Congress. Allies could also be found within the department among engineers fearing loss of status, employees fearing loss of jobs, even rival bureau heads fearing accretion of power in another's hands. The consequences were reflected in feeble departmental administration and became especially obvious in the designing and construction of warships, and the duplication of manufacturing, engineering, and procurement.

Yet Tracy was not to be pocketed, as his naval subordinates quickly discovered. Adept in the ways of political intrigue, he quickly dispersed corridor gossip by sharp cross-examination on official matters and energetic pursuit of responsibilities so that by the end of his first half year in office one Washington correspondent could recall that the secretary's disciplining a subordinate for neglecting an order ". . . showed me who is running the Navy Department, and convinced me that the Navy officers' clique has been no more successful in managing Secretary Tracy than it was with Secretary Whitney."[36]

Tracy struck at bureaucratic inefficiency on June 25, 1889. The need for coordinated planning and unity of action led him to promulgate General Order 372 which brought together on "The Board on the Design of Ships" all bureau chiefs concerned with the vital organs of a ship from design to engines and equipment. Responsibility for delay might now be placed where it belonged. "It is not possible," Tracy argued, "to say any longer that one bureau is waiting for another to reach a conclusion. Conclusions must be reached and promptly reached by the board." Furthermore, Tracy's action also rearranged the duties of the Bureaus of Navigation and of Equipment and Recruiting and the secretary declared:

> The fleet, including vessels, officers, and seamen—training, assignment, enlistment, inspection, and practice—falls under the Bureau of Navigation, while miscellaneous branches of equipment, and the supervision of subordinate officers connected therewith, or engaged in investigations not pertaining to administration proper, fall under the Bureau of Equipment.[37]

This dry dust of administrative reorganization received scant attention from the American public at the time. Naval reaction remained muffled despite old Admiral Porter's gleeful congratulations to his chief. At least one editor expressed fear of "empire building" in the Bureau of Navigation, but only time could prove the value of Tracy's efforts.[38]

During those early weeks in office, Tracy also showed concern for the efficiency of shore establishments. He realized that ship repair and construction, as well as training and education, would assume greater importance as those complex weapons systems— the vessels of the New Navy—increased in numbers and size. Mechanically intelligent and skillful workmen would be needed to service them and adept crews to man them. Intellectually broadened officers would be required not only for command but also in Washington for formulation of policy.

Tracy also faced one of the more glaring problems besetting the naval shore establishment—political patronage. In spite of the Pendleton Act of 1883 and its vigorous enforcement by Secretary Whitney, elections in some localities were made or lost on the Navy Yard vote. Tracy witnessed the patronage problem first in Brooklyn where many residents worked at the local Navy Yard. Their ranks rose and fell with the political tides, according to Civil Service Commissioner Theodore Roosevelt. Over 1,000 men were employed temporarily at the yard during the campaign of 1888.[39] When a fellow Brooklynite subsequently became Secretary of the Navy, they naturally expected appropriate emolument for their efforts on behalf of the Republican party in Brooklyn.

Early in March 1889, after Tracy finished reading the last congratulatory telegram, he turned to more onerous duties—the flood of politically motivated correspondence which followed. The usually patient New Yorker soon grew irritated with a deluge of requests for favors and jobs from Congressmen, local politicians, friends, and relatives. Tracy lost little time in announcing publicly his intentions regarding patronage in the shore establishments. He declared in mid-March at a testimonial dinner at the Hamilton Club in Brooklyn:

> I know how thoroughly intrenched is politics in the navy yards of the County . . . but I promise . . . that the navy yards . . . during my administration shall not be asylums for the inefficient, the incompetent, and the worthless mechanic. Whether they are Republicans or Democrats, I have a right to insist, and I shall insist, that they be skilful and efficient foremen and skilfull and worthy mechanics.[40]

Politicians and many navy yard workers failed to echo the enthusiasm of the Civil Service Reform Association and press for Tracy's reformist notions. He soon received the first complaints from House Speaker Thomas B. Reed, Congressmen Henry Cabot Lodge, and Boss Tom Platt, as well as from various groups like the Republican State Committee for Kings County and Brooklyn. Their outcries probably caused the new secretary to quietly retrench without completely ending his desire to pursue reform in the future.[41]

Tracy bided his time. He visited a number of naval facilities at Boston, League Island, and Newport, and his private scrapbooks are filled with clippings concerning their activities. While talking with workers, naval officers, and local politicians, the secretary quietly formulated plans. Newspapers praised his energy and enthusiasm.[42] Yet the real drama of his first six months in office took place off stage, away from public view. Behind the scenes he met with influential and persuasive men, concerned with larger policy. These individuals appreciated the navy's needs, and they understood the implications of sea power.

One group comprised the professional naval officers—bureau chiefs as well as ship and installation commanders, with old Admiral Porter at the top. Progressive younger officers as well as their more conservative seniors numbered among this group. Closest to Tracy were the bureau chiefs, who, although chary of their preroga-

tives, were able men who knew how to sail before the political wind.
They included Chief Constructor Theodore D. Wilson (Construction and Repair), Rear Admiral George W. Melville (Steam Engineering), Commodore Montgomery Sicard (Ordnance), Commodore Winfield Scott Schley (Equipment), and Commodore J. G.
Walker (Navigation). These officers were physically located where
they could influence the secretary's daily actions and their ideas
could not fail to leave a mark on a landsman like Tracy.

Furthermore, there were personalities affiliated with the strug-
gling young war college at Newport, men like Luce and Mahan,
sometime president of the institution and a brilliant intellectual
whose theories and writing became almost synonymous with the
era itself. James R. Soley, author and professor both at Newport
and Annapolis, also entered the group. If not located physically in
Washington, these three and other men like them in the field, had a
direct line to the secretary through Admiral Porter.

Tracy met still another group over brandy in the drawing rooms
of Washington as well as in their offices on Capitol Hill. This body
included Speaker Reed, and Charles Boutelle, Chairman of the
House Naval Affairs Committee, who numbered Admiral Luce
among his friends. In addition, the second-ranking member of
Boutelle's committee was Henry Cabot Lodge, and across the aisle
on the Democratic side of the chamber sat Hilary Herbert of Alabama and William G. McAdoo of New Jersey, both friends of the
navy. Senator Eugene Hale of Maine added his voice to the group,
and elsewhere, young Theodore Roosevelt of the Civil Service
Commission, Charles Dana of the *New York Sun,* and others
favored the sea service. They could be expected to comment and
advise, and Tracy undoubtedly drew upon this brain trust. Yet, in
the end, Tracy was independent both in mind and action. He listened, he learned, but he formed his own opinions as to the direction to be taken.

A major influence apparently came from that small group of
naval officers seeking to rehabilitate the war college. The institution experienced hard times after its founding in 1884, for, as
Mahan phrased it, the Whitney administration "had absolutely no
appreciation for the systematic study of naval warfare."[43] Tracy
probably did not either, at first. But Luce lost little time in briefing
him on the promise and activities of the effort at Newport. The war
college lay in Senator Nelson Aldrich's constituency—Aldrich was

CtR #16140

U.S. COASTAL DEFENSE
(late Nineteenth Century)
Army Shore Fortification; Civil War Era Monitor; Modern
Harbor Defense Vessel, U.S.S. *Arkansas*
[Courtesy National Archives]

a man of considerable influence—and it was not long before Tracy
wrote Luce the cheering note: "I can assure you that I consider no
matter of greater importance than the education of our officers in
the subjects which have been introduced at this college."[44] By July,
Tracy was able to break away from departmental chores in Washington's summer heat and visit Newport to see things for himself.
The secretary quickly realized that the educational facility provided
a sounding board for relevant information on modern naval warfare. He became a firm friend of the school and the men who staffed
it.

Other events in mid-summer pointed to a pattern in the secretary's
expanding interest and appreciation of American sea-power. The
July issue of *The North American Review* published an article by
Luce entitled "Our Future Navy."[45] Luce's writing pointed especially to the recent British announcement that the Admiralty would
construct seventy new warships, including ten battleships and sixty
cruisers, over the period between April 1889 and April 1894. Luce
proclaimed the United States Navy devoid of any comparable
"battle" vessels and cited the need to build them immediately.

Luce argued cogently that the country was re-constructing a navy
without the necessary constituents of a line of battle. Calling a navy
a sort of sea army, Luce went on:

> We are building cruisers of various sizes, which correspond to
> the cavalry and light artillery of the land army; and we have
> monitors for coast and harbor defense, which supplement our
> fortifications; but we have no battleships to correspond to the
> infantry of the line, which constitutes the main strength of the
> line of battle.

In short, the father of the war college felt that the battleship was
the very foundation of the navy. Since the United States had no
battleships, she really had no navy. The nation possessed merely
"the accessories only—the satellites, the cruisers, and the coast-
guard ships." Drawing upon historical precedent (thereby ante-
dating Mahan's published work), Luce clearly saw a navy's duty as
offensive. It should consist of balanced fleets, each fleet built around
twenty battleships and their auxiliary vessels, the cruisers, torpedo
boats, depot-ships, and hospital ships. Cruisers might still act inde-
pendently against enemy commerce and for protection of the merchant marine. Thus Luce laid great stress upon the role of the battle
fleets. Their number would be determined by geographical location

and the political situation. The seven or eight fleets which England promised to float, replete with battleships, seemed to verify Luce's thesis.

Luce concluded with a warning. Citing the earlier sea power of the nation—a squadron of ten ships of the line equal to any in the world—Luce thought the new steel navy could make no comparable claims. At least twenty years would elapse before the American navy could float twenty modern steel battleships. Indeed, it might take a mere decade before "we may begin to talk about 'rehabilitating' our navy without provoking a smile of derision." Meanwhile, said Luce, a solitary American steel cruiser, with "its delusive prefix of 'protected' represents the latent possibilities of a great country placidly awaiting some national disaster to generate its military forces."

Luce's article may have prompted Tracy to appoint a so-called "Policy Board" on July 16 to consider and recommend the policy which the department might follow in the next phase of the New Navy program. The secretary named Commodore W. P. McCann, commandant of the Boston Navy Yard, to head the board and charged it with answering certain basic questions. Tracy wanted to know, for instance, how many years should be allowed for the building of the fleet and what number and classes of vessels should be built "both for cruising and for coast defense purposes." He asked what size and general features should be reflected in each class of vessel and what proportion of the entire projected fleet might be constructed annually. Finally, he asked about the number and classes of vessels which should be requested from Congress in the next session, and most important of all, the annual and aggregate cost of the whole project.[46]

Navy officials and the press generally praised this unprecedented move to bring unity into policy planning. Only a minority complained about the lack of technical proficiency among board members, but as the New York Times explained: "It is simply to make recommendations to the Secretary . . . the actual designing is to be done, as heretofore, by the board of bureau chiefs."[47] In any event, the McCann board descended from the advisory boards of the Hunt-Chandler period. Neither the board, nor Tracy's questions particularly broke with traditional policy—or so it seemed on the surface. The board would take several months to arrive at a conclusion and shatter that illusion.

At about this same time, Secretary Tracy recalled Captain Mahan from his temporary duty on the Pacific Coast in search of navy yard sites and assigned him to Newport as president of the war college. Pressure from Luce and Porter, as well as his own interest in rehabilitating the institution, prompted the secretary's action, and probably Mahan's intellectual prowess seemed to the practical Tracy more useful closer to Washington. It appears doubtful that Mahan joined top naval advisory circles in the capital at first. But he had been working for several years on the manuscript which would emerge a year later as *The Influence of Sea Power Upon History.* Tracy may have become privy to the unpublished ideas which, while hardly new, having been a part of British strategy for centuries, strongly reinforced Luce's observations in the *North American Review.* Indeed, Mahan's writing reflected the refrain of some other navalists in the eighties—the key to seapower rested with a permanent fleet of powerful warships under unified command; such a fleet would necessitate acquisition of overseas bases for logistical support; and colonies would subsequently develop around these bases which would benefit commercial interests while serving as sources for raw materials and markets for surplus products. Mahan at this point needed official sanction for his manuscript. He found a receptive listener in Tracy who, in turn, realized that this eccentric naval officer could provide the codification and clarity of expression necessary for public understanding of the Navy's plans and policies.[48]

Building upon the foundations represented by establishment of the Policy Board, resuscitation of the war college, and advice from official and unofficial advisers, Secretary Tracy directed the Chief of the Bureau of Navigation to form the Navy's first "squadron of evolution" in the early fall. Commodore J.G. Walker received orders to take command of the squadron and give practical application to the strategic and tactical principles under study at Newport. The move, long anticipated by the press, grew out of an abortive attempt by Luce during the Whitney era to turn the North Atlantic Squadron into a training school. The idea had been premature but it found greater favor with the new Republican secretary.[49]

A crowd of dignitaries including Tracy and two of his predecessors, Whitney and Robeson, were on hand for the squadron's departure on November 18. They accompanied Walker aboard the flagship *Chicago* as it made its way out of New York harbor. A simple leave-taking occurred off Sandy Hook—no gun salutes, no tooting of whistles—Tracy's escort boat merely hoisted the signals, "Goodbye, Good Luck" and the flagship answered with the single word, "Thanks." With that the nucleus of a permanent American fleet made its way to sea. The simplicity of the event typified Tracy.

Tracy ended the initial phase of his reorientation of policy and submitted his first annual report to President Harrison that same month. This provocative document provided more than the usual commentary on the state of the navy. It also contained proposals which represented a radical shift in naval policy. The document was forceful, well organized, and calculated to codify the significant strands of new navalism as advanced by Luce, Mahan, Boutelle, Hale, and others.[50]

Tracy felt that despite eight years of progress the American navy enjoyed only nominal existence. "At no previous time in the present century has the country been so relatively powerless at sea," with makeshift wooden ships, useless monitors, and a fleet in-being of scarcely eight modern warships. The secretary rather bluntly proclaimed that the United States Navy had fallen behind not only Great Britain, France, Russia, and Germany, but even Turkey, China, and Sweden. The profitless program of building unarmored cruisers (for which Tracy unsympathetically criticized the Whitney administration) could not provide defense for an unprotected American coastline of 13,000 miles with its twenty centers of population, wealth and commercial activity. Tracy believed that a more powerful deterrent force was distinctly necessary.

He called for the creation of a fighting force composed, not merely of unarmored cruisers, but of "sea-going battle-ships," coast defense vessels, fast armored cruisers, torpedo boats, and other auxiliary ships. Capture or destruction of a few enemy merchantment was not going to prevent an enemy fleet of steel warships from shelling American cities or from exacting tribute. While Tracy spoke of fighting a defensive war, such a force would be necessary to raise blockades, beat off the enemy's fleet on its approach to American waters, and even to carry combat to the enemy's coastal waters. Tracy denied that such offensive operations reflected a policy of aggression. Rather, and here he tried to counter the spirit of business pacifism of the day and its antimilitary feeling, he argued that it was a practical economic question of protecting property and trade, not only for coastal centers of commerce but also for the production centers of interior America. To Tracy:

The annual increase of wealth in this country is estimated to equal that of England, France, and Germany, and before it can create an effective navy its population is certain to exceed that of any two of these powers combined. Such a nation can not be indifferent to events taking place in close proximity to its own coasts, threatening the freedom of its commerce and the security of its sea-ports.[51]

Tracy considered the security provided by such a deterrent force but a small price to pay for survival. He predicted that future naval wars would be short, fought with the force available at the beginning of hostilities and that ". . . to strike the first blow will gain an advantage . . . and inflict an injury from which [an antagonist] can never recover."[52] But, he warned, building these ships would take time—fifteen years because of the limited capacity of both private and government shipyards. Unless construction began immediately, the first six months of hostilities would not only find American cities susceptible to capture but every shipyard in the country destroyed, thereby the last hope of creating a navy to meet the emergency of war would be extinguished forever.

Having laid the theoretical base for his program, the secretary moved to specifics. He envisioned a balanced armored fleet of twenty battle-ships, twenty coast-defense ships, sixty fast, armored cruisers, a line of fast merchantmen for coaling and transport service and possible use as auxiliary commerce destroyers, and a large number of torpedo boats. England had large numbers of these craft—even the Brazilian navy included fifteen—and American naval planners worried that they lacked such a capability.

The real striking power of Tracy's program lay in the recommendation of two fleets of seagoing, armored capital ships. Twelve of these vessels would be assigned to the Atlantic and Gulf coasts, while the other eight would be the backbone of a Pacific fleet. The secretary stressed that these ships should be the best of their kind anywhere with respect to armament, armor, structural strength, and speed. Tracy thought the construction of at least eight of them should receive precedence over the cruisers and monitors. Private contractors should have a chance to build them, since, in Tracy's view, both political as well as national security questions were involved here.

The battleship clauses captured the attention of later naval historians, but contemporary newspapers heralded a number of other points in Tracy's report. In direct opposition to Whitney's policy, he had recommended the transfer of the war college to independent command at Newport where it shared a base with the torpedo station. He urged the creation of state naval militia in the absence of any well-trained federal naval reserve. He sought the transfer of the Revenue Marine from Treasury to Navy control. In addition, the navy yards, fabrication of ordnance, reform of enlisted personnel conditions, as well as further administrative changes in the main department also received Tracy's attention. He mentioned the impact of the Samoan disaster and pushed openly for the acquisition of naval bases to support his proposed Atlantic and Pacific fleets. Finally, Tracy made a subtle play for public support. He recommended naming his proposed battleships after states of the Union, cruisers for the nation's cities, armored coast defenders in honor of important events in the nation's history, unarmored coast defenders after rivers, and special service vessels according to their intended usage.

The Secretary of the Navy ended his first annual report with a quotation from President John Adams's message in 1800 calling for a well-prepared navy. Now, nine decades later, Tracy declared: "Until the United States has a fleet of twenty battle-ships with coast-defenders, cruisers, and torpedo-boats in suitable proportions for efficient defense, and an establishment in such working order, as to administrative machinery, officers, men, reserves, and vessels, that it can be brought without delay into effective action, the country can not consider that it possesses a Navy; and a Navy it can never afford to be without."[53]

President Harrison released the substance of the report in late November. Press reaction was predictably mixed, as most leading editorials and articles quoted Tracy generously without fully understanding the radical departure from previous doctrine. Nevertheless, editors across the land suggested that every American should read the report in full since it represented a pragmatic approach to a major national problem. Several eastern newspapers considered that the report vindicated John Roach's "ABCD" vessels. A St. Louis daily opposed Tracy's battleships on grounds that it was poor economy for farmers and laborers to pay for huge weapons of war. *The Army and Navy Journal* praised the secretary's ability but favored retention of the traditional monitor-raider doctrine. Still almost all newspapermen were inclined to agree with the *New York Daily Tribune* that:

Secretary Tracy's report is receiving marked and general approval. It is an exceedingly useful paper, strongly, and indeed brilliantly, written. It tells the country what it needs to realize— that it cannot afford to be without a first-class, adequate navy.[54]

Close associates of the secretary also found much to praise in the report. An ecstatic Mahan told Luce of his joy at Tracy's treatment of the war college and Tracy's brother-in-law observed that it was the first departmental paper that he had ever read from beginning to end. General Catlin added: "It will be a stolid Congress that shall dare to disregard the recommendations based upon the facts and reasoning you give." From the Squadron of Evolution came Commander French E. Chadwick's comment:

> I regard the report as the best state paper which has ever been issued from the Navy Department and I know of none from any Department of late years, certainly, which can compare with it in clearness of statement and in stating succinctly a policy. It is indeed the first which I have ever known which has given definitely a real policy of any sort.[55]

So Tracy's contemporaries praised or dismissed the document to their own liking and perhaps missed the point that the American navy had turned yet another corner in its history. Later historians realized slowly that Tracy's progressive report symbolized a new departure. It proposed to gauge the appropriate size of the United States Navy by comparison with selected foreign navies and it suggested for the first time the stationing of a fleet of substantial size in the Pacific as well as the Atlantic Ocean. If the report provided a model of insight and planning, it also indicated that Tracy was the first cabinet level official to modify the strategy of coast defense and commerce raiding, and to superimpose upon it the larger doctrine of control of the seas.[56]

The ex-Union officer, gentleman farmer, and sometime political worker took only nine short months to emerge as a forward-looking navalist. But could proposal be translated into action? By Christmas, 1889, Tracy was hard at work on the firing line with Congress.

CHAPTER 5

Implementing a Program with Ships

Secretary Tracy told a New York reporter late in 1890 that originally he had wanted no part of any cabinet job which entailed only routine tasks.[1] But he admitted that his job developed into something quite different as soon as the battles began with Congress over naval programs. The initial volleys were fired when a letter from Senator Eugene Hale arrived on Tracy's desk late in October 1889. Writing from his home in Ellsworth, Maine, the legislator asked the secretary to prepare four bills "to embody your ideas" for introduction in the new Congress, the first of which was to be "for the further increase of the Navy in ships."[2]

Hale introduced these proposals, incorporating Tracy's program for a fighting navy, on December 5, 1889. The first measure called for construction of eight battleships (7,500-10,000 tons displacement), as well as two monitors, three cruisers, and five torpedo boats. The second bill reflected Tracy's desire for a new procedure of naming and rating the vessels. The third proposal lengthened the term of enlistment and provided bounties for longevity of service—devices to attract superior enlisted personnel. Finally, the fourth bill called for a survey of the merchant marine to determine its value and availability as a source for auxiliary cruisers in wartime.[3] Six days later, Hale invited Tracy to appear before the

Senate Naval Affairs Committee to discuss his program. At this point, the Tracy–Hale proposal seemed certain of passage.

Unforeseen developments soon muddied the waters upon which the new naval program was supposed to float into effect. Much of the muddle reflected somewhat adversely upon Tracy's control of his own subordinates. The whole episode merely confirmed the fact that while the secretary might submit estimates of actual navy needs and suggest a national defense program, this did not guarantee Congressional acceptance. The Senate generally seconded administration requests, but the House had a mind of its own, often best expressed in reduced estimates and disregarded recommendations. As Tracy's sagacious advisor, Rear Admiral Stephen B. Luce, told the secretary three years later: "These two branches of government continue to this day, as they have in the past, to play at cross-purposes.[4]

Tracy's program first ran into trouble in January 1890 when Senator William E. Chandler (under whose supervision the "New Navy" first hit the waves) told the secretary of his opposition to battleships. Chandler believed that monitors could provide equally adequate and far more economical protection for the seaboard. Furthermore, the senator even protested Tracy's modernization of the old monitor *Puritan* by removal of obsolete turrets and installation of newer ordnance. Such criticism reflected isolationist America wherein battleships shocked peace-loving citizens and defied monitor tradition. Even to a New Hampshire native like Chandler, they smacked of imperialism and offensive warfare.[5]

Later that same month, as Tracy recovered from a brief bout with the grippe brought on perhaps by fatiguing dabblings in local Brooklyn politics, another bombshell hit official Washington. Commodore W. P. McCann's Naval Policy Board, after six-month's study, submitted its findings to the secretary. Tracy well knew the need for only gradual exposure of his program to a wary Congress and American people, but apparently McCann's people did not. Someone leaked the sensitive report, a number of Congressmen, heretofore friendly to Tracy's program, began to waver, and the cabinet official found himself with a *cause célèbre*.[6]

Naval officers had been building up a messianic zeal for a long time and the McCann board simply mirrored the restless spirit which pervaded particularly among younger officers. As one student of the period has concluded: "The Young Turks, in short, constituted a body of amateur, but aggressive, navy public relations men."[7] They saw new fields of opportunity for professional achievement as the New Navy expanded in size and purpose. McCann's people undoubtedly felt as the rest of the navy: it was high time to lay it on the line for the civilians.

How else may we explain the extraordinary stance taken by the board members? Their ideas corresponded certainly with those advanced by Luce and Mahan. The board attempted to provide for the future as well as the present by advancing an enormous building program. Yet, by so doing, they were out of step with a nation unprepared to challenge the world in a naval armaments race. Board members began with an analysis of America's international position. McCann and his colleagues foresaw no imminent danger of war because of the security of the Mexican and Canadian frontiers and the apparent national disinterest at that moment in overseas colonies. They believed, however, that the situation was potentially dangerous. Conflicting commercial imperialism of European powers might lead to United States' involvement; American moves to secure a larger share of the world's cargo trade could lead to a crisis; and finally, creation of an isthmian canal under American protection or ownership could place the nation under great responsibility without, perhaps, a commensurate naval deterrent. None of these observations was especially novel.

The Naval Policy Board then outlined those factors which governed its decision—the naval strength "of our possible enemies, proximity of coal and bases to possible areas of conflict, and finally the extent of the area to be attacked or defended." McCann's colleagues hinted that the first consideration alone indicated that America should maintain a navy at least equal to the most powerful navy in the world since she might have to fight such an opponent. But, they continued, the United States Navy would be operating in close proximity to bases of supply while the enemy would be quite distant from Europe. Thus the first condition would be modified by the second; the nation might need tactically offensive battleships but only to conduct a strategically defensive conflict.

The remainder of the report analyzed the intimate details of ship design, armor, armament, and funding. It amounted to a blunt recommendation for a fleet of ten "offensive" battleships having a 15,000 mile cruising range, to be supplemented by twenty-five "defensive" capital ships with a cruising range of not less than 3,000 miles. As a supporting force, the board proposed construction of twenty-four armored cruisers, fifteen light "torpedo cruisers," five miscellaneous ships for China service, ten rams, and three depot ships. Finally, one hundred small torpedo boats would round out the fleet. The total cost of this 497,000 ton armada would approach $281,550,000. Added to the tonnage already in service or authorized, the United States Navy would total 610,000 tons. If such a program went into effect, and barring any great change in foreign fleets during the construction period, the American naval force would then rank second only to Great Britain in tonnage and well ahead of France.[8]

News of this program provoked immediate reaction when it became public knowledge. Congress immediately asked for a copy of the report. Tracy's accompanying letter publicly repudiated the radical views of the board. Senator Hale agreed, declaring that it "would be difficult . . . to find a Senator" or for that matter any responsible government official who "in the least degree" endorsed the report. On the other side of Congress, Representative Hilary A. Herbert of Alabama suggested adamantly that Congress should officially turn its back on McCann's findings.[9]

Tracy's repudiation of the work of his own subordinates seems hypocritical at first glance, since he too requested numerous capital ships from Congress. But, the "leak" undoubtedly caught Tracy off-guard, a regrettable breakdown in departmental management and communications. The secretary planned to keep the report confidential and utilize it as a long-range planning document for constructing the fleet one step at a time. Commander C. M. Chester, an officer privy to many secrets in the department, later told Admiral Luce that Senator Hale indicated the disclosure seriously endangered naval appropriations for that year.[10]

Newspapers across the country quickly confirmed Hale's observation by decrying the board's report as overly aggressive. Even expansionist editors called it a product of "naval fanaticism," and Democratic partisans joined the chorus against the "wild dreaming." Moreover, during the winter and spring, members of pacifist groups flooded Capitol Hill with petitions demanding rejection of the navy's programs. Even moderate opinion in the land evidenced a strong desire to stay out of the naval race with other maritime powers. Tracy's entire program was clearly in trouble.[11]

The turmoil kept Tracy tied to his desk and in close contact with Congressional proponents of naval legislation. He told a New York client: "I very much regret to find that for the coming four weeks my time is to be so continuously occupied before the Senate and House Committees that it will be utterly impossible for me to be away from Washington."[12] Then, a great personal tragedy suddenly interrupted the secretary's official life. Fire swept through the Tracy home on "I" Street in the early dawn hours of February 3, while the family lay sleeping. Mrs. Tracy and Emma Tracy Wilmerding and her daughter Alys were trapped on the second floor and escaped only by jumping from a window. Delinda Tracy did not survive the fall although Emma and Alys escaped with only minor injuries. The second Tracy daughter, Mary, and a French maid also perished in the flames. Even Tracy was carried from the building unconscious and on the verge of suffocation.

President Harrison soon learned of the tragedy and made his way to the scene immediately. Finding Tracy still unconscious Harrison took his turn in administering the artificial respiration which helped to save Tracy's life. As the New Yorker regained his senses, he failed to recognize Harrison. Tracy dazedly inquired about his family and the President had to break the news of Delinda's and Mary's deaths. Harrison then ordered Tracy moved to the White House and as Attorney General W. H. H. Miller recorded later in the day:

> We are all in dreadful distress here today from the calamity to Gen'l Tracy this morning. It looked at first as if Gen'l Tracy might go too, but fortunately he has revived and the Dr. assured me a short time ago that he would get along alright.[13]

Official mourning descended over the nation's capital as the funeral of Mrs. Tracy and Mary took place in the East Room of the White House. Secretary Tracy recuperated slowly under the watchful eyes of the President and Mrs. Harrison. Their solicitations forged deep bonds of friendship and an unwavering loyalty in Tracy. Harrison's increased confidence in the New Yorker also sprang from the association. After all, Tracy was a fellow lawyer and ex-soldier, and his generally austere personality closely paralleled that of the Chief Executive. He rapidly emerged as the President's chief policy adviser and confidante in the months ahead. Tracy refused to indulge in prolonged grieving. The fire occurred

at a delicate point in negotiations with Congress. He returned to
work by Lincoln's birthday and buried himself in the details of
office. Soon Emma was able to reestablish a home for her father
and her own daughter in a new house on K Street between Vermont
Avenue and Fourteenth Street.

Tracy celebrated his first anniversary as secretary while convalescing. He felt that reconstruction of the double-turreted monitors *Puritan, Amphitrite, Monadnoch,* and *Terror* showed progress;
that Whitney's cruisers were performing creditably; and that the
Squadron of Evolution was back from a successful cruise in good
shape. Moreover, the Herreschoff Company of Bristol, Rhode
Island had delivered the torpedo boat *Cushing* for acceptance
trials and, elsewhere, departmental technicians were grappling
with tests of smokeless powder, projectiles, fuses, and Gatling guns.

There were snags, however, as private shipyards failed to keep
pace with Congressional ceilings on expenditures for ship construction, armor plate deliveries from Bethlehem Steel slumped, and
the *Maine, Texas,* and *New York* lay far behind their construction
schedules. Tracy received warm accolades for his theories and programs from the Philadelphia shipbuilder Charles Cramp, but by
March 1890 the secretary seemed restive. Cramp might well take the
stand that "the time has come when Congress ought to decide con-
clusively what kind of a navy we were to have."[14] But Tracy could
do little more than wait impatiently as springtime broke along the
banks of the Potomac.

The secretary's spirits remained high. He confidently told newsmen on one occasion that his proposed cruisers would ". . . catch
and whip anything afloat or that is likely to float within the next
ten years." He tried to advise Senator Joseph Dolph as to the
costs of a three-year cruise of a 10,000 ton battleship by chiding
that, since no type had been built, it was purely speculative to suggest costs approximating $17,000 to $19,000 per month for maintenance, $26,253 per voyage for coal, and $2,387 per quarter for
incidentals. Undismayed by the grounding of the U.S.S. *Dispatch*
on a Potomac sandbar during his first outing after the fire, the
secretary coolly observed: "If we had gone much further we would
have run into a farm house."[15]

Still Tracy's good humor hid his anxiety about developments
on Capitol Hill. The Republican party enjoyed majorities in Congress for the first time since 1875, albeit slim in the House of

Representatives. Tracy attempted to placate both parties by easing his stance on navy yard reform, praising the programs of his Democratic predecessor, and catering to the wishes of isolationists by ordering boards of survey for reconditioning as many of the old monitors as possible. Yet the fate of Tracy's battlefleet dreams lay not with the secretary but with agile politicians like Senators Hale, Chandler, and Aldrich, as well as Representatives Herbert, Boutelle, Lodge, and McAdoo. Certainly a variety of Congressmen scanned the expressions of popular enthusiasm for naval programs in the letters from constituents and they enjoyed Tracy's sociable appearances before their committees. But party managers such as Boutelle and Herbert held the key to steering Tracy's fleet through legislative passage. Even these legislators pursued an independent course as witnessed by Boutelle's solicitation of advice from naval authorities other than the secretary.[16]

Congressman Boutelle questioned David D. Porter and Stephen B. Luce as to the needs of the navy. He may have been unaware of the close liaison between the admirals and Tracy. Porter, for his part, advocated a policy similar to that of the McCann board report. He saw a requirement for no less than twenty-eight "line-of-battle ships", twenty-eight coast defense vessels, ten flagships, forty cruisers, forty gunboats, fifty torpedo boats, and five dispatch boats as part of a long range plan. He backed the secretary's program for meeting the immediate needs of the navy. The old admiral concluded: "These ideas may startle some members of Congress but they will be much more startled if within the next decade we should be involved in a difficulty with some foreign power, for no man knows when war is coming, and we might have a fleet of armor-clads steaming into New York and relieving the sub-Treasury of its surplus. . . ."[17] Luce proved no less positive that at least two battleships should be constructed each year.

Boutelle sent the views of the Committee on Naval Affairs to the full House of Representatives on April 1. After lengthy reflection, his committee had sanctioned only three sea-going coastline battleships designed to carry the heaviest armor and most powerful ordnance upon a displacement of about 8,500 tons with a coal endurance of about 5,000 knots. Boutelle told the House that his committee desired a simple defensive squadron, not a fleet of long-range capital ships. But these defensive vessels should be fighting ships, capable of standing out to sea against an enemy. The com-

U.S.S. *OREGON*, 1890
A "Coastline" Battleship
[Painted for Spanish-American War Service]
[Courtesy National Archives]

mittee report adeptly juggled the Tracy and Policy Board proposals with political reality. Boutelle obviously thought it unwise to request too many battleships in the initial legislation. The congressman felt that construction of "coastline, sea-going battleships," as they came to be called, might allay popular apprehension of naval jingoism. Winning Tracy's acquiescence to the compromise measure, Boutelle told one correspondent that such vessels could equal "foreign cruising battleships" in all but speed and fuel capacity.[18]

The debates which followed introduction of the naval appropriations bill proved that compromise was much in order. The battleship provisions became the focal point as Populists and westerners led by Congressmen Joseph Cannon of Illinois, Joseph B. Sayers of Texas (a one-time friend of the navy), Samuel Peters of Kansas, and William Holman of Indiana, archenemy of naval expansion, provided tougher opposition than anticipated either by Tracy, congressional navalists, or newsmen. New as well as traditional objections arose from several quarters. Some astute legislators rightly termed the bill a "new departure" and declined to strike out on an uncharted course. Other congressmen of the Chandler school remained wedded to the monitor; still others desired only smaller, cheaper cruisers; and some hard-line economists wanted only to construct land defenses for harbors. By the middle of spring, the anti-battleship clique seemed to be gaining the upper hand.

The political sagacity of Speaker Reed, the oratory of Boutelle, and the bipartisan support of Herbert and his Democratic colleagues won the day in the end. Key qualifying phrases—"seagoing, coast-line"—placated those members concerned with the defensive nature of the battleships. Even the erroneous but soothing remark of Henry Cabot Lodge that the battleship proposal introduced nothing new, but was "merely the continuance" of a policy "settled by the War of 1812, and followed consistently thereafter," had its desired effect. Navalists pardoned Lodge's inaccuracy as both chambers voted to build the warships.[20]

Tracy left Washington for a tour of shore facilities on June 30, the day that the naval appropriations bill became law. But he knew the act exceeded expectations concerning specifications for the three battleships. Although only slightly larger than the *Texas* and *Maine,* each of the new vessels would displace over 10,000 tons,

mount four 13-inch and eight 8-inch rifled guns. Secondary armament would include numerous rapid-fire guns and four torpedo
tubes. Two coal burning, triple expansion engines would drive each
ship at about 16 knots. The low freeboard and conspicuous turrets
would exude a monitor-like appearance, yet the battleships' price
tag far exceeded that of any monitor; $6,000,000 each.[21]

Before the year was over, Tracy could declare confidently
that: ". . . the United States will become possessed of three vessels
of the highest power, whose equal as fighting ships does not exist
at the present day." Designated the *Oregon* class and named for
the states of Oregon, Indiana, and Massachusetts, the much
vaunted warships compared reasonably well with Great Britain's
most powerful counterparts of the time, although smaller, lighter,
and slower. Tracy concluded that twelve of them would probably
be the equal of the original twenty he had asked for in his 1889
annual report and would permit retirement of the monitors to
reserve duty with state naval militia.[22] Other bonuses derived from
the Naval Act of 1890, including a protected cruiser, a torpedo
cruiser, and a light torpedo boat. Additional provisions concerned
naval administration (prohibition of duplicate purchasing by the
bureaus), the war college (a return to its original facility at the
Newport installation), and plans for an international naval parade
in home waters in conjunction with the Columbia Exposition. Altogether the Act signalled the debut of the United States as a
modern naval power.

Tracy's energy carried over immediately to the various bureaus
as they acted "with a promptness unexampled in the history of
naval administration in this Country"—according to the secretary
in his report for 1890. Early in July they presented plans for the
new vessels. The department immediately advertised for construction bids, but delays in completion of hold-over contracts from
the Whitney programs threatened to create a logjam in Tracy's
schedule. Not the least of his worries concerned purchase and
delivery of armor and ordnance from domestic contractors. In
fact, by the summer of 1890, the Navy Department found itself
with a near crisis in armor on its hands.

The search for armor and armament was by no means new to
Tracy. The secretary recalled later that he had first studied the sub-
ject early in his administration, indeed, as early as May 1889.[23]
Admitting complete ignorance in such matters, the secretary re-

acted characteristically by investigating the history of the navy's previous relations with the steel industry. The trail led back to the Chandler era and the "ABCD" ships wherein lay the seeds of later armor production difficulties—rigid naval specifications and inspectors, expensive experimentation by steelmakers, uncertain future benefits directly proportional to the fluctuations of naval rearmament, and Congressional desires to cultivate the growth of a domestic steel industry.[24]

Even Secretary Whitney searched almost a year for a contractor after Congress appropriated funds for ship construction. Prospects of the high navy rejection rate frightened away such men as Andrew Carnegie. The Cambria Iron Company and the Midvale Steel Company confined their bids entirely to gun forgings, and the Cleveland Rolling Mills bid for armor alone. Only the Bethlehem Iron Company expressed any interest in both types of work. Whitney awarded that firm a contract for $4,500,000 on the condition that Bethlehem promise to construct an armor forging plant at government expense. The agreement called for completion of this plant, capable of delivering 300 tons per month by December 1, 1889.[25] Tracy soon discovered that the company could not meet these contractual provisions.

His immediate interest in armor and ordnance developed from conversations with William Bisphan of the New York firm of William H. Wallace and Company in May 1889. Bisphan thought Whitney made a mistake in selecting all steel armor instead of the English compound armor adopted by the Royal Navy. Bisphan and Wallace served as agents of the English compound armor firms in the United States and they wanted another hearing on the matter. The secretary summoned his naval experts, despite their known opposition to the British product. Commander William H. Folger, sometime ordnance inspector at the Washington Navy Yard and later Chief of Ordnance, explained the weakness of compound armor. He pointed out that this type of armor was prone to cleaving at the point of welding, exposing the soft back. Folger told Tracy that the ideal plate would be a homogeneous substance, having a hard surface without any line of welding; but he did not suggest how such a plate could be produced in the United States.[26]

Tracy devoted much time in 1889 to examination of the various foreign competitive tests of the two varieties of armor, discovering "that the tests were very ingeniously planned to give the plate the victory over the gun." It mattered not whether the plate was steel or compound since neither was destroyed but merely damaged, leaving each party to claim that his particular plate was damaged least. He considered such tests inconclusive and decided that the Navy Department should hold its own competitive test in the United States as soon as possible.

Bisphan offered to furnish a compound plate free for an American competition if other steelmen would do likewise. Tracy immediately got in touch with Lieutenant Commander F. M. Barber, a former member of the Gun Foundry Board during the Chandler era, and now serving as exclusive agent in America for the Henri Schneider armor works at Creusot, France, while on leave from the navy, requesting cooperation from the French firm.

Other pieces of the armor puzzle began to fit together meanwhile as information came to light of a spectacular advance in the art of fabrication. This phenomenon concerned the addition of nickel to steel which produced a metal especially suited for naval armor. S. J. Ritchie, of Akron, who owned several Canadian nickel mines, first approached Tracy in July 1889 with news of unusual activity in the nickel market, especially with respect to so-called nickel matte. The mine owner could not understand the European interest but promised to investigate the matter. He gave Tracy a copy of a lecture by Professor James Riley, and English scientist who noted the greatly increased tensile strength of nickel-steel. The secretary became quite interested. Later conversations developed Ritchie's notion that Europeans might be employing nickel in the manufacture of naval armor. Tracy immediately offered the services of Lieutenant B. H. Buckingham, naval attache in London, in order to facilitate Ritchie's effort to gather information. The Navy Department learned consequently that European armor makers, notably Schneider's firm, were indeed experimenting with nickel armor, and had been so engaged for some months, perhaps as early as the spring of the year when Riley delivered his lecture in Great Britain.[27]

Tracy also learned that the Schneider Company had no particular desire to engage in competition with the compound armor men. The secretary lost his patience and informed Lieutenant Commander Barber:

> Commander, you undoubtedly understand that I know the relations that exist between Creusot and Bethlehem. I know

that your people are interested in the Bethlehem contract for
armor . . . there never will be a contract for a ton of armor
let by me until I have had a competitive test. They can coop-
erate voluntarily with it or not. I should like to have them do
so if they will, but the test will be made, and they may as well
understand it.[28]

Creusot's reply surprised both Barber and Tracy, for the firm
suddenly agreed to a competition. Noting its unqualified success
with nickel armor, however, the French wanted to use only this
variety, purchased by the United States government.

Tracy also felt pressure from another direction. He originally
thought that the time needed by Bethlehem for production design
and preparation would enable him to investigate and experiment
further before making a final decision on the type of steel for the
navy. Then December was upon him with his annual report spot-
lighting battleships, the Policy Board report about to emerge from
committee, and the Bethlehem people far from ready to fulfill the
1887 contract specifications by commencing production.[29] The
firm's failure to deliver armor plate soon affected completion of
ships like the *Maine*. Captain J. W. Philip, the naval inspector at
Cramp's yard in Philadelphia, informed Tracy that even the *New
York* faced delays in launching because of the lack of armor. The
situation worsened as Barber alerted Tracy to mounting opposition in the Senate to any new ship authorizations so long as the
country lacked sufficient armor. The moment seemed critical with
the new naval appropriations bill under consideration.

Tracy reacted to the growing crisis by contacting spokesmen
both at Bethlehem and Creusot, ordering a test armor plate from
the latter. Bethlehem representatives Joseph Wharton and W. H.
Jacques visited Tracy on January 22, 1890, and two days later
confirmed in writing that delivery of armor was to begin within
six months. They tried to rationalize delay by citing the difficulties
of purchasing and transporting an entire forging plant from England to the United States in 1887. They also cited conversion of
Bethlehem's hydraulic press from making gun forgings to steel
hammers for forging armor plate. The two representatives promised to deliver 1,500 to 2,000 tons during the last six months of
1890, and to maintain a rate of 8,000 to 10,000 tons annually thereafter.[30] But Tracy countered by pointing out the ease with which
the company had finished initial plant construction and delivered

gun forgings ahead of schedule. He could not understand why such distressing delays should occur with respect to armor plate.

The issue dragged on until May, when, finding that no armor was in the offing, Tracy directed Commodore Montgomery Sicard, Chief of Ordnance, to proceed to Bethlehem. Sicard inspected the plant thoroughly and reported on May 14 that the firm could not deliver any armor for another fifteen to eighteen months. The steelmakers rebutted Sicard's assertions but Tracy became impatient. All the uncompleted ships faced indefinite delays unless he moved personally to provide an additional supply of armor. He told a Senate investigating committee several years later ". . . having the authorization to build three battle ships and three large cruisers which would require about 14,000 tons of additional armor . . . I felt it necessary to found . . . a second armor plant, because at 300 tons a month for each establishment . . . they could only furnish armor enough to build about two battle-ships a year."[31] For this reason, in the summer of 1890, the armor-starved navy entered into negotiations with Carnegie, Phipps, and Company of Pittsburgh.

The man who helped Tracy and the Navy Department meet the armor crisis of 1890 was ambivalent about the tools of war. Andrew Carnegie, who later served in the front rank of anti-imperialists, maintained that he yielded unselfishly to the requests of his president and the nation in their hour of need. But his image as a voracious Captain of Industry left posterity to decide whether or not his patriotic response might also have been clouded by the profit motive. Carnegie was wary of the navy's strict inspection methods, despite his keen sense that "there may be millions for us in armor." Pushed by Tracy to "read up" on the subject in late 1889 or early 1890, Carnegie remained aloof and shrewdly told his factory representatives to study armor but to avoid commitment to nickel.[32] Carnegie learned of Tracy's renewed advances towards his firm while vacationing in Great Britain.

Tracy apparently told William L. Abbott, Chairman of the Board of Carnegie, Phipps, that he needed more armor, noting his preference for nickel-steel but stating that the decision awaited results from the armor trials. Even at this point, however, Tracy offered Abbott a contract for "a good quantity" of armor which might be either nickel-steel or even another variety. Abbott telegraphed this information to Carnegie and mentioned that he also understood the Bethlehem people opposed the nickel tests but were sending two men abroad to investigate the matter. He wondered if Carnegie should not again approach Le Ferro Nickel in order to reduce the exorbitant demands for use of their nickel-steel patent rights.[33] The crafty steelmaker won a concession from the French firm on June 16 and ten days later concluded an agreement, just at the time Tracy learned that the British government had successfully tested a nickel-steel plate for protective deck armor at Portsmouth.[34]

Negotiations between the Navy Department and Carnegie now entered an awkward phase. Both Tracy and Carnegie were shrewd and they applied all their bargaining talents to the subsequent maneuvers. Tracy was quite aware that the Bethlehem firm had gained extra incentives under the Whitney contracts because of the immense initial outlay of capital for construction of the armor plant. But he also realized that the Bethlehem experience provided future ways to avoid the expensive trial and error method. He assumed then that the Carnegie firm could profit from their competitor's wisdom and that Carnegie himself would accept a lower price than that given to Joseph Wharton by Secretary Whitney in 1887. Carnegie hid his feelings as he wrote candidly to Tracy about his European findings on steel, his doubts concerning the superiority of compound plates over solid steel plates, and his intention to provide the navy with either solid steel or nickel-steel plates for testing in about four to six months.[35]

Meanwhile, Carnegie traveled extensively, examining numerous facilities in Great Britain. He continued discussions with Le Ferro Nickel, while Lieutenant Commander W. H. Emory, Buckingham's replacement in London, supplied him with the latest European developments, gathered through naval intelligence. By July 18, Carnegie also had Tracy's first quotations on the amount and price for the armor. Tracy, in turn, received an idea of the long maneuvers which lay ahead when the steel magnate telegraphed the following day from Scotland:

> Wish to help you out with armor and will do best possible but Bethlehem prices being lowest offered under strong competition. We cannot risk taking one iota less . . . . Their prices almost if not quite as low as Britain pays. . . . If you give us five thousand tons Bethlehem prices shall order necessary tools and go ahead otherwise must decline . . . armour making no childs play.[36]

The Secretary of the Navy knew nothing of Carnegie's instructions to his lieutenants at Pittsburgh. Numerous telegrams in Carnegie's private papers indicate the hard bargaining which he demanded of Abbott. He expected his board chairman to remain firm concerning Bethlehem and European prices. By late July, negotiations broke down because of the rigid positions taken both by Carnegie and the Navy Department. Carnegie patronizingly told Tracy that he was disappointed by the navy's low offer, especially since it was obvious that the department expected the Pittsburgh firm to succeed where Bethlehem had not. He once again cited European prices and noted Bethlehem's fatal miscalculation about time required for erecting a plant. He bluntly told Tracy that it took much effort to train men to handle such masses of steel. Since his firm was well-supplied with work "it will not disappoint us very much if you decide to drop us as to Armour." But, Carnegie quickly added the tempting morsel:

> We could no doubt deliver finished plates a year before any other party in the United States. Any one else who tries to deliver in a year will just land where Bethlehem is.[37]

A fortuitous event happened at this stage which broke the Tracy-Carnegie impasse. The secretary received a vague and verbose letter from Robert H. Sayre, General Manager of Bethlehem Iron Company, on July 24. Sayre, noting the continuing technical difficulties and "unforeseen contingencies," considered that "Sicard's estimate of fifteen months from May, 1890 as the time . . . actual manufacture of hammered plates will begin, is more than ample." He hoped to anticipate that delivery date and he foresaw no difficulty in exceeding the rate of deliveries as fixed in the contract. But Tracy did not wish to hear of any fifteen-month delay at this point. By August 27, the Navy Department reached a verbal agreement with Carnegie, Phipps and Company calling for manufacture and delivery of some 6,000 tons of armor, at precisely the unit price promised Bethlehem in the 1887 contract.[38] Meanwhile, assured of a contract on his terms, Carnegie left the hair-splitting details to the home office while he undertook to locate and purchase tools for the new endeavor.

Tracy finally set up a competitive armor test as the department was concluding its negotiations with Carnegie, Phipps. The secretary appointed a board of ordnance experts headed by Rear Admiral L. A. Kimberly to evaluate the experiment. The Kimberly Board conducted the test at the navy's proving ground near Annapolis between September 18 and 22, 1890. Schneider's nickel-steel armor, treated with a new hardening process named for its inventor, August Harvey, competed with the English compound armor and simple all-steel armor. To the dismay and opposition of the manufacturers, Tracy insisted upon testing their plates using 8-inch projectiles fired at point-blank range. Nothing larger than 6-inch shells had ever been used before, but Tracy wanted definitive results.

The tests gave the secretary just that. The compound armor was demolished completely. The simple steel plate showed alarming cracks. But the "harveyized" nickel-steel armor completely blunted the test rounds. Even after prolonged bombardment, this particular plate evidenced a superior capacity for stopping penetration. This first decisive proof of the superiority of nickel-steel armor astonished international munitions makers and admiralties alike. Overnight, sages pronounced the vaunted armored fleet of Great Britain to be disasterously vulnerable and only eight days after the Annapolis tests, Congress, at the request of the Secretary of the Navy, appropriated $1,000,000 for the purchase of nickel by the United States Navy.[39]

Nickel developments paralleled negotiations with Carnegie's firm, for it seemed that while nickel-steel patents could be purchased, the metal itself was in extremely short supply. The demand was great even before the tests, because of excitement over the very possibilities of nickel-steel armor. Prices soared accordingly.[40] Carnegie's representatives knew S. J. Ritchie, the person who first told Tracy about the metal, but for some reason, perhaps the high prices, Carnegie held a deep distrust for the nickel market in general, and Ritchie in particular. He warned Abbott and others in Pittsburgh against the Canadian mine owner who "hitherto had always failed." Finally, just before the armor trials, the steelman told Tracy that he seriously doubted whether nickel would ever prove practical for armor, due to its scarcity and price. Carnegie, in fact, took the occasion to lecture the secretary again on the need for extensive experimentation. He advised that every type of plate had some weakness. One compound plate might do well and the next might be a failure. The solid steel plate of one American maker might prove unsatisfactory and yet the solid plate of the British

Vickers or French Creusot firms might be surprisingly good. Altogether, Carnegie tended to debunk the armor trials because: "This armour plate business is, so far all uncertainty."[41]

Heretofore Carnegie may have held the trump cards in the armor game, but Tracy now proved to have an ace of his own in reserve. He thought Ritchie, like Carnegie, was a loyal American as well as a shrewd businessman, and capable of supplying the navy with the scarce metal in its hour of need. The mine owner later stated that early in their association Tracy promised to pressure Congress to put nickel on the free list of the pending tariff bill if Ritchie's Canadian Copper Company retained their supply of the metal until the navy received permission to purchase it. Tracy apparently kept his promise, for he wrote to Congressman William McKinley in March noting that, since Ritchie's concern controlled three-quarters of the world's nickel supply, they "should be permitted to introduce their ore free of duty to be smelted in this country."[42]

Furthermore, as early as February 1890, Tracy and Captain William Folger both appeared before the House Naval Affairs Committee on behalf of a "nickel joint-resolution." This subject reappeared immediately following the Annapolis tests, when congressional backers quietly reintroduced the measure, citing only the immediate needs of the American navy. Tracy placated significant Senate opposition by meeting privately with Senator Arthur Gorman and indicating Carnegie's reluctance to buy the metal, the soaring market prices, and the extreme urgency for securing the supply before Canadian Copper sold it abroad. The measure passed smoothly and Tracy almost immediately contracted for nickel ore with Ritchie. The price proved lower than what it brought several weeks later and the protective McKinley tariff, which passed Congress in October, completely removed the duty on nickel ore.[43]

Tracy's initiative avoided a deadlock once more. The United States Navy now possessed an immediate supply of ore although Tracy, at first, rushed to purchase only $50,000 worth for experimentation purposes. But he told Abbott that the department was prepared to conclude negotiations on the armor contract and he soon implemented his new found power over the steel industry.[44] Late in September he called for a conference of steelmakers and shipbuilders to meet in his office on October 12. He wanted to expedite the delivery of all steel (armor plate and other forgings) for the construction program. The *New York Times* speculated that while little change could be expected in the steel inspection procedures, rigidly fixed by law, "it is likely that the Secretary will urge all steel producers taking naval contracts . . . to turn out a fixed amount of steel each day on such contracts, without regard to . . . private work they may have on hand at the same time."[45] But when the conference finally opened on October 16, Tracy was unaccountably absent and the meeting generated into little more than a name-calling contest. Shipbuilders claimed the steelmakers lagged in supplying finished steel plates. The manufacturers complained again of the navy's steel inspectors and their high rejection rate. The Navy Department held its ground, continuing to demand set specifications for material. The conference accomplished little. The final negotiations between Tracy and Carnegie, Phipps proved more successful if nonetheless prolonged. Apparently, Carnegie remained generally unmoved by the Annapolis tests and continued to oppose what he termed Tracy's "pet nickel." The secretary soon pressed Carnegie for complete clarification of his views.

The steelmaker assumed his usual patronizing stance, telling Tracy that his greater experience with alloys prevented his sharing the secretary's enthusiasm for nickel. "My position has been this throughout: 'We are manufacturers; we do not wish to have anything to do with nickel patents; we shall pay the royalty and charge it to the government!' " His plan, wrote Carnegie, was "first to permit us to make you the best solid steel plates we can . . . after this point is reached, you can try the next step—nickel, which I am as anxious as you are to make successful." He again advised Tracy to keep an open mind and to continue testing. He concluded this letter: "Yours for all-steel, compound, nickel, aluminum, chrome, or anything that will give us the best results." The two parties at last signed a written contract in November 1890, based upon the earlier verbal agreement reached in August.[46]

Carnegie's canny bargaining had caused the delay all along as he sought to inject several additional provisions into the agreement. For instance, the Navy Department ended up paying the royalty of two cents per pound demanded by the nickel-steel patentee, Le Ferro Nickel. Carnegie forced an additional concession similar to that which Bethlehem secured from Secretary Whitney in 1887, whereby Tracy implied that the contractor would be favored with work beyond the initial contract. Finally, Carnegie sought to avoid any penalty clauses for failure to deliver according to contract specifications.

Tracy soon learned from Sicard, who visited the works again, that Bethlehem's armor plant could not begin operation before June 1891. He estimated that the first 300 tons could be delivered by October 1, with total deliveries of 1,200 tons before January 1, 1892. Sicard thought that Bethlehem would be able to deliver 6,000 tons of armored steel in 1892, thereby fulfilling by late summer the terms of the 1887 contract. Much more encouraging word came in December 1891 from the Homestead works of Carnegie, Phipps that the first attempt to produce nickel-steel in the United States had turned out successfully.[47] In general, this report when added to the Naval Act of 1890, consummation of crucial armor contracts, institution of departmental changes to relieve some of the secretary's workload, and publication of Mahan's book on the influence of seapower upon history partially compensated for Tracy's family tragedy.

Tracy surveyed the year's activities in the autumn of 1890 preparatory to writing this annual report. He noted that the steel cruisers *Baltimore, Charleston, Philadelphia,* and *San Francisco,* the gunboats *Yorktown* and *Petrel,* the torpedoboat *Cushing,* and the experimental dynamite cruiser *Vesuvius* were all in active service. The *Baltimore,* in fact, carried the remains of John Ericsson back to his native Sweden in late August, thus dramatizing the progress since that inventor had first introduced the screw propeller and the *Monitor.* Yet Tracy's correspondence basket had filled also with memoranda concerning minor but time-consuming repair problems on the *Atlanta, Baltimore,* and *Cushing.* Insufficient manpower continued to bother naval officials, and as the secretary told Senator J. D. Cameron: "The new ships of the Navy are too complicated structures for each one to be without a mechanic specially acquainted with her requirements.[48] Elsewhere, twenty vessels, sixteen of them holdovers from Whitney's programs, lay in asssorted stages of construction. Logjams over armor and design plagued the *Texas* and *Maine,* ships which once caused Tracy to tell the Naval Senate Affairs Committee ". . . today the Department would build neither . . . the *Maine* has neither the speed of a cruiser nor the fighting or resisting force of a battleship." But in November, the *Maine* finally slid silently into the waters of the East River off New York City and began her way to destiny.[49]

Tracy could point more positively to increased departmental efficiency by individual bureau accounting (instead of Whitney's system of consolidated accounts). Then too, the position of Assistant Secretary ("moth-balled" since the Civil War), had been reinstated and his duties grew to include responsibilities for civilian personnel, housekeeping chores in the department, and the shore establishments. Systemization of ship repairs under departmental supervision had been set up instead of the divisive independence of previous bureau operations. Finally, Tracy gathered together a strategy team with his new Assistant Secretary James M. Soley, Commander William M. Folger, and Captain Alfred T. Mahan, charging them with development of operational war plans to be used in the event of European aggression.[50]

The Navy Department's preoccupation with building surface ships probably cost Tracy a superb opportunity to effect an additional technological advance with untold policy ramifications, in 1890. John P. Holland, a New Jersey inventor of a submersible craft, approached the navy originally when Whitney's administration advertised a contest for a submarine design. Whitney's successor reallocated the original submarine appropriation to complete the surface craft then under construction. Tracy's mind was on battleships and Congress did not replace the $200,000 originally allocated until the eve of Cleveland's second inauguration.[51]

Tracy showed more foresight in other areas such as increasing the efficiency of the naval constructor corps. In October he ordered five (later increased to six) young officers abroad for a special course in naval architecture. They studied at the Ecole d'Application Maritime in Paris and the University of Glasgow, and joined four other future Assistant Naval Constructors already in residence at the French school and the Royal Naval College, Greenwich.

The commotion of a busy year apparently served as a tonic for Tracy. His busy schedule left little time for any private life as numerous official trips to Eastern shore establishments were supplemented by hasty trips to Brooklyn and Owego, especially on the eve of the fall elections. He witnessed his son Frank depart on a venture to South America selling phonographs, and he effectively deflated rumors of a second marriage and possible appointment to the Supreme Court, election to the Senate, or even candidacy in the next gubernatorial election in his home state. The energy and spirit which showed in Tracy's life by the autumn of

1890 was evident in the order he gave to the bandmaster of the Marine Corps, John Philip Sousa, to compile a book of national and patriotic airs of all nations, and by his elaborate entertainment of Brazilian naval officials in Washington in December.

Tracy finally dispatched his second annual report to the White House late in November. After a detailed accounting of naval progress for the year, the secretary concluded his observations on the state of the sea services with a brief hypothetical attack on the country. He focused upon the American coastline from Hampton Roads to Boston and the utter defenselessness of the four commercial cities in that area. "There is no other instance in the world at the present time of so much wealth in so exposed a situation." To protect it would require a combination of guns afloat and guns ashore. Then Tracy pointed directly to New York and its environs. He painted a picture of an enemy fleet sweeping past the Army's forts, through the Narrows, sailing unobstructed into the East River. He derided the cast iron cannon shells of the seacoast artillery as making "no more impression on modern ironclads than hailstones on a roof." New York would lie naked to an enemy's navy.[52]

Calamity would not end with the payment of ransom and the surrender of American ships, said Tracy. He described the consequences in terms befitting later generations facing atomic holocaust. An enemy fleet would remain in the waters off New York cutting trade and communications; ferry boats would cease to run; the Brooklyn Bridge would be closed to traffic as the condition for its perservation. Rail lines with the rest of the nation would be cut and the food supply for 2,500,000 people would come to an end. Capitalists might afford to yield a ransom, but famine would fall first upon the homes of the poor. The ransom paid by that population would be anything which they could give and which the fleet in the harbor would accept as the price for its departure.

Tracy concluded that neither the military nor the naval forces of the United States were capable of handling an enemy—and that foreign powers knew it. The Gulf and Pacific coast cities only complicated the problems of defense. As in 1889, the secretary again preached: "Nothing short of a force of battleships, numerous enough to be distributed in the separate fields of attack and able to concentrate on any threatened point within their own field, will prove a complete protection."[53] But Tracy recognized the continued unpopularity of the battlefleet concept. He suggested an enlarged *Puritan* type of warship for purely local defense. Such craft, of light draught, with only twenty inches of armor and mounting eight 13-inch guns, would be less expensive than battleships and could serve as a rallying point, drill hall, parade ground, and naval school for the nascent state naval militia of Massachusetts, Rhode Island, and Pennsylvania.

Should the nation adopt such a plan, said Tracy; "it is reasonable to believe that Boston, New York, Philadelphia, Baltimore, New Orleans, San Francisco, and the cities on Puget Sound would become centers of naval strength instead of being, as they are today, conspicuous examples of maritime weakness, and inviting objects of maritime attack; while these local forces, organized in complete harmony with the spirit of American institutions, would be welded together and transfused with the spirit of naval discipline by the small but efficient standing force which the Country will always maintain."[54] Newspapers in coastal cities praised Tracy's words. But journals in America's heartland mirrored the *Memphis Commercial* which scoffed; "the man brought up in the woods—so to speak—of America and who knows nothing of her resources, is not scared by that bear."[55] In any event, the off-year elections in November 1890 tended to deflect much of the newest call for action from the Secretary of the Navy.

CHAPTER 6

Navy Yard Reform and Cruiser Diplomacy at Midterm

The congressional elections of 1890 shocked Republican politicians across the nation. They had captured the national government in 1888 by dint of hard work, party unity, and an appealing platform. Now, scarcely two years later, the Harrison administration found itself hard aground on the rocky shoals of the tariff issue and public disgust with Federal spending. The American voter returned only eighty-eight Republicans to face two hundred and thirty-five Democrats and fourteen Populists in the House of Representatives; in the Senate the GOP majority dropped to six. This tidal wave retired such notables as William McKinley and Joseph Cannon in the House, and John Ingalls in the Senate. Some observers blamed silver legislation, and stay-at-home voters, as well as predominantly local concerns such as temperance and parochial schools. But the result was that Republican spending programs like naval reconstruction were in trouble.[1]

Not all Democrats opposed a stronger navy. But they complained that some $432,820,762 had been lavished upon the fleet's overhaul since the Civil War with little positive result. Like the taxpayers they represented, these legislators felt that other programs demanded attention. Additionally, isolationist congressmen from interior America found it difficult to understand the great need for costly steel warships. Their farmer constituents were restless and Republican ranks had thus been especially decimated in key Midwestern states. The whole election year was a water-shed, at least in retrospect.

Probably all too few Americans understood how to communicate their feelings. On the one hand, domestic tranquility and prosperity provided laudable aims as the United States turned the corner into its second century of nationhood. The admission to statehood of Idaho, Montana, Washington, Wyoming, and the Dakotas reflected America's looking inward in traditional fashion at the very moment that publication of Mahan's book on sea-power, Tracy's battlefleet programs, and businessmen's search for new international fields in commerce and industry battled for headlines. The result confused many people. Cities like New Orleans, Galveston, Portland, and Portsmouth vied with one another for visits by the popular White Squadron, while citizens inland, who knew little of warships beyond atrocious sketches in their daily newspapers, registered disapproval of the huge expenditures despite the fact that they produced these symbols of national wealth and protection.[2] Economic expansionists stressed the necessity for new markets for absorption of the tremendous output of industrial America. But farmers continued to clamor about the plight of falling farm prices, often failing to realize that a main plank in the expansionist programs called for overseas outlets for agricultural products.

Trade depended upon naval protection in either case, and Secretary Tracy did not share rural America's fears of excessive naval spending. He suggested to a reporter in March 1891 the need for at least six to nine additional battleships, another cruiser like the *New York,* four to six harbor-defense vessels, and twelve more torpedo boats. Tracy considered an additional $65,000,000 might be needed to complete a navy befitting a first-class power. But he also knew that too many vessels remained incomplete and he took to heart the subtle remark of Senator Eugene Hale: "I do not believe that we need a great extravagant Navy."[3] Congress agreed wholeheartedly, for the naval appropriations bill enacted on March 2, 1891, provided funds for only one additional cruiser, although it did set aside $25,000 for arms and equipment for the 1,150 men in six state naval militia units and it encouraged the navy to provide warships for training these organizations—a move Tracy had long urged.[4]

Two deaths in 1891 confirmed the transitional nature of the

period in which Tracy held the reins of the Navy Department. Ex-secretary George Bancroft, who had established the Naval Academy before the Civil War, and Rear Admiral David D. Porter, salty senior admiral of the smooth-water navy days, both succumbed that winter and their passing pointed to the end of the days of wooden ships and iron men. To reinforce this transition, successful testing of a 10½-inch steel armor plate from the Creusot works, treated by the Harvey process, led to consummation of a contract between the Navy Department and Augustus Harvey, with Secretary Tracy declaring ". . . if the Harvey process can be applied to nickel steel, we have the ideal armor." Such success in the armor field won over still another skeptic. Within three months Andrew Carnegie capitulated and wrote Tracy:

> The favor with which you have regarded it [nickel] from the first is now in my opinion, fully justified . . . our nickel steel . . . excelled the Creusot plate . . . which proved even our French competitor is behind us.[5]

There was nothing the steelmaker admired more than success. From the spring of 1891 onward, the two canny individuals became complete friends as well as comrades in the armor business. Still, Tracy realized that Carnegie's operations needed observation; he sent a young naval officer to Pittsburgh to keep his department informed about the activities there and to provide advice as well.

Departmental interest in deck planking and paint for ship bottoms, public advertisement for contract bids, protests from domestic manufacturers of discrimination against American products, and continual reevaluation of skyrocketing costs in estimates of the new vessels probably best represented matters of daily concern for late nineteenth century secretaries, Tracy not excepted. Relations with private contractors such as Cramp's Shipyard in Philadelphia and the Bath Iron Works in Maine seemed especially touchy. Owners like Charles H. Cramp and T. W. Hyde took it upon themselves to dictate policy to Tracy simply because their construction of naval warships seemed to give them license to do so. Cramp was notably difficult in one case involving a naval officer assigned to inspect the construction of a cruiser in Cramp's yard and to report directly to the department. Cramp wrote testily to Tracy:

> In issuing his order you doubtless overlooked the fact—perhaps well known to those who recommended it—that the

effect would be to introduce into a private shipyard some of the most pernicious and harassing evils of the Navy Yard system; which, as you are all aware, is an awkward and clumsy effort to perform mechanical work under the restraints and embarassments of military etiquette and discipline. No shipbuilder wants anything of that kind and I protest against it with all the vigor I have.[6]

Tracy, impatient for progress, could never quite understand the construction delays on vessels even in government yards. Requests for extensions of time for repairs often received the department's icy response: "The Department cannot understand how a delay of this extent on an unimportant item of work should be permitted to occur. The Department also fails to understand why necessary work of this character was not done or reported long ago. . . ."[7] The problem festered and Tracy continually maintained that the fault lay with navy yard employees chosen by local political bosses. With the fall elections over and his building programs in drydock, Tracy by 1891 could afford to attack political patronage once again.

Public criticism of Speaker Reed's reputed introduction of extra workmen into the Kittery, Maine, yard just prior to the elections and President Harrison's favored extension of civil service rules and policies remained fresh in Tracy's mind. He also received petitions from civil service reform groups in Boston and Brooklyn, as well as from various clerks and officials in other shore facilities, asking for application of civil service rules to future appointments. Tracy's invitation to address the new Republican Club of Massachusetts in early April gave him the opportunity to make a major statement concerning the navy yards and patronage.[8]

The evening of April 8, 1891 found Tracy at the Boston Music Hall suffering from an attack of bronchitis, but anxious to make his announcement. Most of his lengthy remarks simply recounted, in somewhat partisan fashion, achievements of the administration. While denying any intention of dwelling upon naval progress at length, Tracy told of his appropriations battles with Congress and his search for armor and armament. Many prominent listeners probably sat dozing over brandy and cigars when the New Yorker got to his principal point late in the talk.[9]

Tracy believed that mechanics and workmen in the government shops had worn "the collar of the bosses who run the local political machine" for too long. He argued:

The practice is a source of demoralization to any party that attempts to use it, destructive to the Government service, and debauching local and national politics. It is an ulcer on the naval administrative system, and I propose to cut it out.

The secretary noted the Boston municipal employment system which he felt could be applied to national government service. Tracy then outlined the essential features of his plan. First, there would be the appointment at each yard of a registration board to examine three categories of applicants—unskilled, skilled, and foremen. Probationary periods would test each worker and the selection process would be highly competitive. Finally, declared Tracy, he sought three ends from this system: free and open competition; employment upon grounds of merit, as determined by non-partisan experts engaged in and responsible for the work; and absolute publicity for every detail. "I do not propose to stop until the principle of efficiency and worth is the only test of Navy Yard employment."

The Secretary of the Navy closed his address by observing that he did not know whether the Civil Service Act was the best in the world, but he did know from personal observation that persons appointed under it were unquestionably more efficient than those selected under pure patronage. Its extension to the navy yards would remove all machine politics from those facilities. The community might rest assured that the navy yard in their midst was not a place for political intrigue. Rather it "is the place of employment of a body of independent and self-respecting workingmen, whose only indolence or bad habits will surely lead to discharge."[10]

Public opinion once again approved overwhelmingly Tracy's unorthodox action. Newspapers such as the *New York Sun* cited his speech as "a notable public utterance." Civil Service Commissioner Theodore Roosevelt called it "the greatest step in advance that could be taken," and the ardent reformer, Seth Low, president of Columbia University, thought Tracy deserved the thanks of all patriotic citizens.[11]

A few editors tried to decipher Tracy's political tour de force regarding navy yard patronage. At least one observer thought he saw the stamp of Assistant Secretary James Soley and the bureau chiefs, while another attributed the reform to political expediency. The *New York Herald* guessed that Republican leaders brought pressure on Tracy to terminate patronage because they thought it lost more votes than it produced. The same editor pronounced the Democratic victories of 1890 had shocked the Republican hierarchy into believing that the way to assuage the reformers was to clean up government yards.[12]

Any doubts as to Tracy's intentions dissipated quickly when he returned to Washington. Soley was in fact already hard at work upon implementation of Tracy's announcement. As a preliminary move, the department dismissed all foremen at the yards. Then, on May 28, Soley, acting upon Tracy's orders, directed Captain F. M. Bunce to travel to Norfolk "to examine foremen or master mechanics" employed in that yard. Bunce became senior member of a special board "to make a general report on the efficiency of workers at Navy Yards and to examine foremen and master mechanics" for the whole shore establishment and he subsequently visited other installations at Portsmouth, Boston, and New York. His "Board on Navy Yard Organization" continued its work until December 18, 1891. It gave the secretary an overall view of operations and needed reforms in the navy yards as seen through the eyes of professional officers.

Tracy next established a local employment board in each yard composed of department heads and their assistants. The mission of these boards included classification of all applicants according to trade. When the head of a particular department in a yard wanted to fill vacancies he simply requisitioned a list of applicants from the yard's employment board. The department head then gave all applicants on the list a two-week trial and selected the most proficient for permanent employment. The registration board could classify and certify candidates but only the individual department heads could actually employ workmen.[13]

As time passed more and more politicians in both parties began to realize the potential dangers of Tracy's reform. The loudest opposition came from Republican leaders of districts surrounding the yards. Thomas Reed asked Tracy to reconsider the program. District ward captains in Brooklyn adopted a formal resolution in the autumn, after the dismissal of one of their supporters, to the effect that "the future success of President Harrison and the Republican party demands the immediate removal of Benjamin F. Tracy as Secretary of the Navy." Even Tom Platt sought in vain to change the course of his erstwhile political lieutenant.[14]

Tracy stood firm against the hot winds of political criticism. The

merit policy was his alone and the good of the naval service took
precedence above the whims of political opportunism. He directed
his staff to peruse newspapers and incoming correspondence for
reported violations of civil service rules, and he sent Soley on various fact-finding trips to investigate serious infractions as well as
the general progress of the program.

As Secretary of the Navy, with responsibilities not only for fleet
improvements, departmental management, and maintenance of
shore facilities, Tracy also possessed overall direction of vessels at
sea. Naval ships needed base facilities whether cruising singly on
station or operating in squadron. The secretary's appreciation of
commercial needs enabled him to stress repeatedly from the very
beginning of the Harrison administration "the necessity of es-
tablishing foreign coaling stations."[15] The usually moderate Tracy
in fact by the fall of 1891 had moved far beyond mere expansion
of trade when he uttered oft-quoted tenets, more closely aligned
with later spokesmen of American imperialism:

> The Sea will be the future seat of empire. And we shall rule it
> as certainly as the sun doth rise! To a preeminent rank among
> nations, colonies are of the greatest help.[16]

Tracy's transformation from 1889 to 1893 reflected the dawning
of America's "Empire Days," and his own participation in its arrival rose toward a crescendo midway through his stewardship of
the Navy Department.

Tracy appreciated the desires of President Harrison and Secretary of State Blaine to find opportunities for expansion of trade
particularly with Central and South America. Republican platform
promises in 1888, Blaine's pet scheme of Pan-American union, and
the possible construction of a trans-isthmian canal announced such
intentions and Tracy found himself actively sympathetic. The United States Navy naturally played a vital part in extending American
influence, prestige, and commercialism. But Tracy's incursions into
foreign affairs must be viewed as more than merely the traditional
ties of Navy and State departments. One cannot discount the New
Yorker's friendship with Manhattan commercial interests. His own
interpretation of seapower and commercial imperialism as advanced by Mahan and others, the temporary retardation of the
ship construction program by Congress, and Tracy's general service to the administration must be considered in an era when policy
advisers to the president were far fewer than today.

ONE OF TRACY'S "FLEET-IN-BEING"
U.S.S. *Boston*
[Courtesy National Archives]

The Secretary of the Navy played an active if not altogether impressive role in Harrison's cabinet even before 1891. Tracy was rebuffed on one occasion in 1889 when he supported unadvisedly the retention of the controversial James Tanner of Brooklyn as Commissioner of Pensions. Harrison dismissed Tanner and the following year he again rejected Tracy's advice, this time on economic matters, during a threatening financial crisis. But the secretary enjoyed greater favor with the president in the area of foreign affairs where the two men shared similar views. Here Tracy and Harrison, as well as Blaine, could agree on the goal of American hemispheric hegemony. Here also Harrison could turn to Tracy for prompt and energetic reinforcement of his own views on diplomacy at a time when Blaine presented a picture of political opportunism, failing health, and flaccid pursuit of the affairs of his post. In fact, Tracy represented a counterpoise to Blaine's quiet diplomacy.[17]

The dichotomy between Blaine and Tracy on upholding national honor appeared first in the summer of 1890 in the celebrated Barrundia case. General J. Martin Barrundia, the Guatamalan revolutionary, was killed in an attempt by officials of the legitimate regime to remove him from an American owned steamship while the USS *Ranger* placidly stood by. Blaine recalled the American minister because he intervened in the first place, not because he relinquished Barrundia. Tracy similarly removed the commander of the warship because that officer failed to protect the rights of refugees aboard ships flying the American flag. Some militant observers felt Blaine was more interested in the delicacy of international relations than in safe passage for travelers aboard American vessels.[18]

At times it appeared that Tracy and Blaine actually worked at cross purposes in seeking the same goal. One might even speculate that the president subtly played off Tracy's impetuosity against Blaine's popular appeal in order to discredit in some political quarters the "Plumed Knight's" success. Certainly Harrison and Tracy applied their knowledge of the tactics of machine politics in the area of foreign affairs. When crises developed over Haiti, Santo Domingo, and Chile in 1891, their forceful methods shattered the elaborate structure of traditional diplomacy which had been carefully constructed through Blaine's patient negotiation.

Latin America and the Caribbean figured highly in the plans of the Harrison administration. While Blaine dreamed of trade and Pan-American union, Harrison worked closely with the Senate Foreign Affairs Committee to strengthen the Maritime Canal Company of Nicaraugua (incorporated under the Cleveland administration) and Tracy sought a practical way to secure a base to service Atlantic naval units which policed trade lanes in the area as well as the eastern approaches to the potential canal. Together they singled out Haiti's Mole St. Nicholas as their first goal.

This prize was ostensibly offered to the United States during the Cleveland administration, but a fluid Haitian political situation hampered any firm agreement about what official Washington might expect in return for aid and comfort to a particular Haitian political faction. The Harrison administration inherited its predecessor's support of General Florvil Hyppolite's group, which openly cultivated American friendship against rivals led by Francois Legitime, a puppet of European interests. Soon after Harrison took office the State Department received reports from its lame-duck minister at Port-au-Prince that the presence of British and French warships in Haitian waters indicated European interference, possibly to the point where France might attempt to regain control of the country. Washington officials abruptly reacted against this imagined affront to the Monroe Doctrine and rushed into a suspicious intrigue in order to secure the Mole as a naval base, with coincidental American supremacy in Haitian affairs. Events over the next two years resembled a bungled, amateurish plot to coerce the Haitian government into bowing before blatant American power—with notable lack of success.[19]

Principal figures in the intrigue included Harrison's representatives led by Blaine and Tracy; the distinguished seventy-two year old Negro journalist-diplomat, Frederick Douglass, acting as Minister Resident and Consul General in Haiti; Rear Admirals Bancroft Gherardi and John Walker of the United States Navy; and Tracy's old friend and prominent New York shipping magnate, William P. Clyde. Haitian president, Florvil Hyppolite, and his astute foreign minister, Antenor Firmin, completed the roster. The surprise lack of coordination, differing philosophies of power diplomacy, traces of racism, and inability to control subordinates on the American side all combined with stubborn diplomatic poker-playing by the Haitians to thwart the aims of Harrison and his policy makers.[20]

Tracy at first ordered Gherardi in the USS *Yantic* to Haitian waters merely to reflect American interests in the face of European presence (while at the same time surveying the Mole). The secretary appeared content to rely upon normal State Department actions to secure a base. He told the admiral to avoid the mantle of diplomatic agent and to eschew especially any suggestions of an American protectorate for Haiti. He observed that no such convention was necessary to protect the Caribbean nation from European interference since enforcement of the Monroe Doctrine would furnish sufficient guarantee of protection. In Tracy's view ". . . all Hayti needs from the United States will be attained by closer commercial relations which will compel the United States to give its moral support to the government in power against . . . revolution and in favor of permanency of the government of Hayti to be changed not by revolution but by constitutional and peaceful methods . . . ."[21]

Such delicate delays of formal diplomacy soon irritated the action-prone Tracy. He decided to proceed on his own through Gherardi as well as through his friend and unofficial emissary, Clyde. None of the three trusted Douglass because of his sympathy for the Haitians.[22] Tracy also knew of Clyde's service to Hyppolite during the revolution when, aided by the U.S. Navy, the magnate's vessels had carried munitions and supplies to provisional government forces slipping through Legitime's "blockade." Tracy supposed, as did Clyde, that Hyppolite might wish to pay off his debt by rewarding the steamship company with lease of the Mole as a coaling station, a first step toward securing a similar concession for American warships. Tracy directed Gherardi to open negotiations with the Haitians on Clyde's behalf, and the admiral secured what was coveted in January 1890. Yet eight months later, when Clyde tried to expand his hold into a ninety-nine year lease for an exclusively American coaling station, Hyppolite balked and caught Clyde, Gherardi, and Tracy completely off guard. The Secretary of the Navy retreated quickly, once more leaving the diplomatic moves to Blaine and Douglass, but promising stronger action privately should the State Department not succeed.[23]

Blaine summoned Douglass, home on leave, to his office and told him to negotiate with Hyppolite for lease of the Mole. But Douglass knew little of the Gherardi–Clyde machinations. He sympathized with Haitian reluctance to yield territorial sovereignty to any foreign power and he assured the Secretary of State that continued presence of American warships at Port-au-Prince acted only to the detriment of positive negotiations. By this time Blaine was inclined to agree with Tracy's evaluation of Douglass' unaggressive attitude. The Secretary of State rejected the diplomat's position, turned to Tracy's advice for a more assertive replacement for Douglass, and thus effectively played into the hands of the American navy. Tracy immediately recommended Gherardi, and in January 1891 the admiral steamed into the harbor of Port-au-Prince as Blaine's special commissioner.

Gherardi, accompanied by Douglass, conferred with Hyppolite and Firmin and they expressed Harrison's ardent desire to acquire a coaling station at Port-au-Prince. The naval officer tempered a reminder of Hyppolite's indebtedness to the United States for past services with a lucrative promise of naval protection and commercial profits. But Gherardi told the Haitian president that similar favors at the Mole should not be granted to other nations. The American offer impressed Hyppolite, but Firmin remained uncooperative and reminded the president that popular unrest might result from territorial concessions to the Americans. Hyppolite resolved to put the proposal before his cabinet and to abide by its decision.

Four months passed while the cabinet deliberated the Mole question. Despite frequent meetings between Gherardi, Douglass, and Firmin, Tracy fretted back in Washington until, seeking to stir action, he directed the admiral to conduct gunnery drills aboard warships anchored at Port-au-Prince. Such psychological coercion produced absolutely no result and by the spring of 1891 both Tracy and Gherardi began to entertain seriously the idea of seizing the Mole by force. At this point Firmin inadvertently threw the scheme off schedule by questioning Gherardi's credentials. While the naval officer retired to Washington to secure credible documents of authority, Secretary Tracy acted with customary alacrity. He dispatched every vessel available to Haiti, including the White Squadron, in a massive show of force.

The situation became more involved after Rear Admiral John G. Walker's buff and white cruisers dropped anchor on April 18. Gherardi and Walker became enmeshed in a childish episode regarding who was senior officer. Then, just as Frederick Douglass feared, the overwhelming presence of American warships unsettled

the Haitian people, and Hyppolite wavered in his desire to continue negotiations. Meanwhile Blaine, fearing adverse press reaction at home, consulted hastily with Tracy. The two secretaries
cooperated by assuring newsmen that American naval aid was sent
to Port-au-Prince to help the provisional government against
impending insurrection. But few people accepted the explanation,
least of all the Haitians, and the Mole negotiations broke down
completely on April 22 when Firmin told Gherardi of his government's refusal to talk further. This news came to light only a day
after the admiral wired Washington asking for instructions concerning Walker's squadron. Three days later a thoroughly disgusted
Tracy solved the dilemma. A tersely worded telegram told Gherardi
to steam to Samana Bay, Santo Domingo, and survey that site for
a possible coaling station. Walker's steel cruisers received word to
return to Hampton Roads. Clyde continued to inform Tracy of the
local situation in Haiti during May but all of his letters noted the
impossibility of resuming negotiations while Douglass remained
accredited to the regime at Port-au-Prince. Neither Tracy nor
Blaine were interested any longer. They washed their hands of the
matter and the Mole affair was over.[24]

The Secretary of the Navy failed to find any other suitable site
for naval bases in the Caribbean. The Samana Bay plan foundered
in the same manner as the Mole. While the American minister at
Copenhagen alerted Washington officials to that country's desire
to sell its possessions in the West Indies, the State Department
counseled against acquisition. Tracy and Harrison showed enthusiasm, but Blaine contended that their lack of commercial value
and their strategic vulnerability rendered them unattractive. Besides, he observed, St. Thomas and St. John, the two islands in
question, ". . . are destined to become ours, but among the last
West Indies that would be taken."[25]

Blaine also vetoed yet another scheme to give the navy overseas
bases in the Azores. Whitelaw Reid, the American minister at
Paris, engaged in secret talks with Portuguese officials who offered
joint occupation of facilities in the Azores, although he realized
that the proposal held little chance of success.[26] Tracy favored the
project at first, then, learning of Blaine's determined opposition, he
reversed course. He advised the president against going beyond the
Western Hemisphere (in the Atlantic, at least) and, together with
Blaine, he suggested that only Cuba, Puerto Rico, and Hawaii pro-

vided truely logical candidates for acquisition. But diplomatic intelligence from Spain indicated the improbability of securing any
concessions from that nation in the Caribbean short of the use of
force. Harrison and his associates had recoiled from the overt use
of naval power against Haiti and Santo Domingo and the nation
as a whole lacked sufficient provocation in 1891 for any war to
acquire Cuba or Puerto Rico. By this time Blaine seemed genuinely
tired of haggling over naval bases, and Tracy appeared content
to avoid controversy. Close cooperation between the two cabinet
officials was often lacking in the cruiser diplomacy in the Caribbean,
although few clues appear as to genuine antagonism between the
two. Perhaps the problem was one of understanding, for despite
Tracy's legal acumen his ability to inject a decisive note of bellig-
rency at the least propitious moment in Blaine's delicate diplomatic
negotiations seemed uncanny.[27]

The major focus of American efforts shifted at about this time
to the Pacific slope and to the eruption of a major crisis between
the United States and Chile. Just when Blaine became too ill and
fatigued to actively conduct hemispheric diplomacy and at a time
when he began to search for agreement on a possible naval base
in Peru, his Pan-Americanism received its sternest test. However,
conduct of the Chilean crisis of 1891–1892 passed almost by default to Harrison and Tracy. The two stopped just short of war
in the Caribbean and perhaps only Blaine's steadiness also re-
strained them from plunging over the abyss of war in South
America.

Chile possessed no more desire to be bullied by American power
than did Haiti or Santo Domingo. While the immediate cause for
the Chilean-American confrontation arose from the famous *Baltimore* incident in the fall of 1891, deeper causes went back as far
as Blaine's first term as Secretary of State ten years before. Open
advocacy of Peruvian interests against her neighbor, flaunting of
Blaine's anglophobia when Great Britain largely controlled the
Chilean economy, and the evolving American search for markets
in South America in the face of European economic expansion—
all inflamed the Chilean situation. President Jose Balmaceda's
pro-Americanism and Harrison's appointment of an Irish nationalist immigrant as Minister to Chile further contributed to the
unrest, especially among the prominent British element in Chile.
Then, following the outbreak of civil war in January 1891, the

arrival of American naval vessels to protect American interests, as in the Caribbean, led to an international crisis.[28]

American warships steamed along the Chilean coast and observed the simmering revolution. Rear Admiral William P. McCann reported to Tracy at the end of March:

> I have visited Chilean ports to the north. No injury to American citizens or interests. . . . The British commander-in-chief has orders to remain on this station.[29]

Such news immediately aroused Tracy's and State Department concern, since foreign observers seemed to be paying undue attention to Chilean affairs. The insurgents thoughtfully seized the important nitrate beds and established a profitable trade with British and German buyers—hence European interest in events.

The situation may have appeared quiet to McCann, but American involvement rose gradually despite State Department desires to maintain neutrality. The American minister, Patrick Egan, displayed open support for the Balamaceda government, asserting that the regime protected American citizens and interests. Then, the arrival of a rebel steamer at San Diego in early May created a major headache for the Harrison administration. Not only was the steamer *Itata* stoked by coal from European ships, but her mission was procurement of munitions, and Tracy and Attorney General W. H. H. Miller immediately raised the question of violation of neutrality. Secretary of State Blaine was ill at the time, out of touch with developments, and Miller and Tracy carefully persuaded their cabinet colleagues to recommend seizure of the vessel. Meanwhile, the *Itata* slipped away from American officials sent to detain her and the chief executive, who was off on a political swing through the Far West, merely advised by telegraph:

> . . . we should make an effort to recover possession of [Itata]. I approve of sending the *Charleston* for that purpose but would not continue any pursuit far south.[30]

Tracy interpreted this mandate somewhat differently, for he ordered the navy to pursue and capture the rebel steamer by force if necessary—but he did not limit the distance for the chase. A thrilling but largely inept pursuit down the coast of Central America ended when the rebels handed over the munitions to McCann off the port of Iquique. McCann thought the "appearance of a squad-

ron of modern vessels on this coast" had effectively displayed
American naval power, and the Balamaceda government thanked
the State Department for American help. Tracy's stock as a man
of action rose with the American public and, all the while, the
Chileans became increasingly incensed about the whole affair.[31]

Further trouble was not long in coming, thanks to continued
American naval presence in the Chilean war zone. Tracy realized
the inherent dangers of American neutrality and issued specific
instructions to his naval commanders off Chile, Rear Admirals
McCann and George Brown. He told McCann at the time of the
Itata capture: "Your correspondence and other official acts must
proceed on the principle that the United States knows no provisional government and has not recognized those engaged in hostility
against Chile as a government or even as belligerents." He urged an
attitude of complete impartiality and specified that insurgent vessels be treated as foreign men-of-war unless engaged in piratical
ventures. In Tracy's view; "the obligation to receive political refugees and to afford them asylum is . . . one of pure humanity."
But in taking "whatever measures are necessary to prevent injury
by insurgent vessels to lives or property of American citizens, including American telegraph cables," it soon proved impossible
for American naval vessels to avoid incidents.[32]

The Chilean insurgents especially resented American protection
of Balmacedist refugees and their conveyance to Peru aboard U.S.
naval vessels, despite similar solicitude shown by German naval
commanders. Relations grew worse when insurgents accused the
American naval commander of disclosing the location of an insurgent landing force to Balmacedist shore batteries. The rebel
government protested McCann's disregard of their refusal to permit an American cable ship to re-lay the nautical cable of the Central and South American Telegraph Company. Tracy belligerently
asserted: "The act was in no way the act of the United States
government, but it was the act of the cable company in the execu-
tion of its lawful right to protect and make available for use its own
property."[33]

Judge E. M. Ross, presiding judge of the Southern District of
California, further inflamed the situation when he decided in August that no law had been violated in the *Itata* arms transaction
and dismissed all charges. It was official Washington's turn to
become difficult, resulting in a delay in recognizing the new Chilean

government which had finally wrested power from Balmacedist elements.

Harrison worried over the turn of events in the dehabilitating heat of Washington. Life in the capital from July through September could be unbearable. The president returned from his arduous five-week tour of the west to discover several other international questions demanding his attention. Moreover, his ailing arch-rival Blaine seemed to be soaking up the cool breezes of Bar Harbor, while the Second Assistant Secretary claimed poor health all summer, and the Third Assistant Secretary hovered on the edge of resignation. With admirable restraint the icy Harrison quipped to Blaine that these events made life in Washington rather unpleasant. Always testy, the president also decided that the trouble with the Chileans was that they knew nothing of dignity and moderation in victory, ". . . and sometime it may be necessary to instruct them."[34] In the absence of experienced advisers at State, Harrison turned to his loyal friend Tracy. When Harrison took a quick vacation at Cape May, New Jersey, he temporarily entrusted the work of the State Department to Tracy's care.

Newspapers quickly sensed Tracy's new role and wondered if he was destined to replace Blaine. Tracy avoided reporters and the fall and winter of 1891-1892 found him reading diplomatic dispatches from Valparaiso, plotting strategy with his navy advisers, and unifying the administration behind the President's hardening line toward Chile. Blaine may have remained Secretary of State in name, but Tracy was at least the principal foreign policy consultant in Washington.[35]

By the middle of autumn the new Chilean government consolidated its powers, Balmaceda committed suicide, and even American naval officers advised Washington that it was time for them to come home. Yet Tracy deemed it propitious to leave Commander Winfield Scott Schley and the *Baltimore* in Chilean waters for a time. As it turned out surface events hid a volcano. It erupted on October 16 when a shore party from the *Baltimore* got into a normal shore-leave brawl with local rowdies. Unfortunately, the American group emerged with two of its number dead, seventeen injured, and Chilean-American relations seriously damaged.[36]

Harrison and Tracy immediately demanded investigation both by Schley and Chilean authorities. Meanwhile American reaction ranged from press demands for a war of vengeance to the soothing advice of Andrew Carnegie: "Chile very weak and sorely tried. Her giant sister should be patient and forbearing." The President and his Secretary of the Navy were not so sure. Harrison fumed "almost to the point of distraction and exhaustion" and Tracy regarded the incident as an insult to the uniform of the United States. Blaine, still ailing, remained more relaxed and advised that precipitous action might hamper his plans for Pan-American harmony.[37]

When Pedro Montt, the Chilean representative in Washington, protested that the investigations were internal matters, both Harrison and Tracy lost their composure. The legalistic Tracy even insisted Montt's position ". . . might almost have been a cause for war itself. It sought to justify the assault on the sailors and dodged the issue in every way possible."[38] Tracy and Harrison wanted nothing less than a formal apology from the South American republic.

The controversy simmered on into November and December with Harrison threatening action in his annual message to the country, the sickly Blaine masterfully restraining Tracy's and Harrison's bellicosity, while Chilean diplomatic notes continued to exacerbate the controversy. Some observers thought they saw a subtle struggle for power within Harrison's cabinet. W. R. Grace told his agent in Valpariso that the president desired war, Tracy was preparing for the same, and that Blaine, who wanted war only under certain conditions, could not overcome the belligerent tide. Chile held the key to the impasse. Blaine may have realized that his months of convalescence enabled Tracy to become the chief adviser on foreign affairs in the cabinet and even a possible contender for the presidency in 1892. When a New York editor expressed these thoughts in January, he possibly mirrored what was in Blaine's mind all along:

> A war with Chile would certainly develop one name as a compromise candidate between Blaine and Harrison. And that dark horse might be the horse marine, the alert, active, and accomplished . . . Benjamin F. Tracy, who would have more to do with the immediate making of war with Chile than all the rest of the cabinet combined.[39]

Greater certainty surrounds Tracy's preparation of the navy for war. Preoccupied with construction of the fleet and with administrative reforms, not to speak of the search for bases, he had been caught unprepared a year before by a brief crisis with Italy.[40] He resolved then that his department should not be similarly embarrassed in the future. So in September 1891, as he assumed a greater role in Harrisonian foreign policy, he ordered Mahan to the capital to join a secret strategy board. Mahan was by now an old hand at strategic formulation having been involved earlier in drawing up contingency plans in case of conflict either with Spain or Great Britain. He joined Captain William Folger, Assistant Secretary Soley, and various naval intelligence officers in planning fleet operations against Chile. But Tracy kept quiet about most of his intentions, as Mahan observed to his old mentor, Rear Admiral Stephen B. Luce. In fact, the secretary worked arduously behind the scenes—ordering a seven-day work week at all navy yards, directing every operational vessel made ready for battle, and manipulating plans and directives in a manner reminiscent of his earlier steel negotiations with Carnegie.

The best American naval expeditionary force which could be mustered at this time numbered scarcely twenty warships, mounting 199 guns in main batteries, 240 guns in secondary batteries, and served by about 4,000 crewmen. Moreover, Tracy's "battlefleet" would have to conduct an operation far from base facilities or the protective shorelines of the United States. Unable to secure a Peruvian coaling station, Tracy ordered large coal purchases in London, New York, and California, negotiated a refueling site at Montevideo, and chartered coal colliers from among such "principals" as Collis P. Huntington, president of the Southern Pacific Railroad.[41]

Tracy also directed naval vessels in Chilean waters to report on the condition of the prospective enemy's fleet, coastal defenses, strategic harbors and land areas as well as on shipping movements. Using sources of intelligence from the naval attache in London, Tracy ordered surveillance of Chilean agents in England and on the continent. His advisers in the department warned especially of sveral warships under construction in England for sale to Argentina, but which might emerge in Chilean hands.[42]

The secretary also pushed the preparations of the bureaus at home. The Bureau of Steam Engineering prepared plans to outfit four Floating Repair Shops to repair a "fleet of about fifty vessels." Various Civil War era monitors came out of reserve status. One particular transaction by Engineer in Chief George Melville illus-

trated the earnestness of Tracy's preparations. The secretary authorized the Steam Engineering Bureau (and it may be assumed other
bureaus as well), to purchase stores on the open market in advance
of approved requisitions. Only a national emergency would have
prompted the rigidly proper Tracy to depart from naval regulations.

Harrison was astonished when he finally learned of the extent
of Tracy's activity. Even the secretary feigned amazement at reports of his desire for conflict. As he told reporters rather irately
in late January, when the situation reached its zenith:

> I did not know I was a war man; I rather thought I was peace-
> ably inclined, but I am also inclined to maintaining the dignity
> of the United States government and its power to protect its
> civilians, soldiers, and sailors when abroad. If that leads to
> war, then I am for war; if it leads, as I believe it will, to peace,
> then I am for peace.[43]

The sands of patience were running out in Washington as a new
year dawned with continued Chilean intransigence. Blaine again
forestalled the president's dispatch of an ultimatum to Chile, but
according to Cecil Spring-Rice, secretary at the British legation,
war clouds hung over the city. Late in January came a Chilean call
for Egan's removal, and the Secretary of State finally bowed to
pressure by dispatching Harrison's ultimatum demanding either
immediate apologies or severance of diplomatic relations. Harrison made a final challenge when no reply came—a plea for Congress to consider declaring war. Within hours of this action, on
January 25, Washington received word of Chile's unequivocal
acceptance of American terms.

Speculation continued as to the cause of Chilean acquiescence
long after the crisis was over. Unknown to Harrison and his advisers, the Chilean president decided to yield fully just as news of
Harrison's request for war went out from the White House to Congress. Contemporary newsmen and many later historians accorded
Blaine the honor of cooling the hot temperatures of officials in
Washington. Yet observers immediately after the event also held
that the strong stand of Tracy and the Navy Department effectively
blunted Chilean belligerence. Tom Platt thought Harrison ". . .
must divide honors with the Secretary of the Navy who built and
armed cruisers between nightfall and morning of two weeks after
the Chileans were down on their knees in abject apology, and with

Commander [Robley] Evans, whose martial demeanor gave the Chilian Admiral a terrible cramp." Even one naval officer in London wrote a colleague a year later:

> For all those at home who are glad that war with Chile has been avoided—they have to thank the able administration of the Navy Department. That at least is the opinion here of the few Chileans and their sympathizers in this country. Here they were bent upon war, and were astonished at the activity the Navy Department showed, as well as the strong forces it disposed so strategically. I hear this straight from the Chilean Headquarters. Nothing but the able disposition of our forces brought them to their senses.[44]

American involvement in the Chilean fracas can be interpreted as a response to a European threat to carefully planned American pretensions for dominance in South American affairs. Disengagement resulted from Blaine's adroit management of an energetic president and his honor-conscious Secretary of the Navy.[45] Yet, if Tracy's cruiser diplomacy once again led the country nearly to the edge of war, the nation could point to his naval preparations which apparently brought the issue quickly to a satisfactory conclusion. In any event, Tracy's naval officers could settle back to study Mahan's offering, "Naval Lessons of the Recent Naval War in Chile" at the war college without either nation having suffered the agonies of open conflict.

At the height of the Chilean crisis, Spring-Rice suggested rather ungraciously the reasons for the Harrison-Tracy belligerence: ". . . one to get re-elected, the other to see his ships fight and get votes for more."[46] There was some truth in the assertion about Tracy, at least, for the naval official radiated great pride in the navy's progress in 1891. Early in that year two English experts, J. H. Biles and John White, praised Tracy's *Oregon* class battleships and the newer cruisers in public statements, although both privately chided the Americans on inferior coal capacity and poor operating radius for their capital ships. Even Tracy took to the printed page with an article on "Our New Warships" in the June 1891 issue of the *North American Review*. Therein he repeated the remarks of

Biles, White, and other European experts, once more illustrating the great reliance at this time upon European judgment and experience. But Tracy also told his readers that the "novel American designs," as the British termed them, represented adaptation to purely American conditions. "What is a good ship for England or France," he observed, "is not necessarily a good ship for the United States." In a spate of Yankee bravado, the secretary concluded:

> If our European friends insist upon underrating the qualities of our naval vessels, it is a thankless and unnecessary task to undeceive them. Some of them have made similar mistakes before, and have found out their error only after bitter experience. But it is important that the operations of the Navy Department, inviting the intelligent scrutiny of every citizen, should not be misconstrued by our own people through an inaccuracy of statement.[47]

Tracy may have secretly desired to test his new vessels in defense of national honor. Ships like those in the White Squadron certainly caused expansionists to flex their muscles thinking they now possessed military power to underwrite diplomatic ventures. Naval reviews such as the one in August at Bar Harbor gave the public a sense of national strength as they viewed the gleaming ships shimmering in the sunlight off shore. But at the same time events in the Caribbean and Chile injected a sobering note of realism into the celebration. The United States might itself overawe smaller hemispheric nations in 1890 and 1891, but the Northern giant lacked sufficient naval strength to force any issue which could flare into a conflagration involving possible European intervention.

In a sense, the three American statesmen simply played the game of diplomacy according to rules which they had gleaned from the arena of domestic politics. Tracy and Harrison were products of the maneuvers, intrigue, and pragmatism of machine politics. Certainly Tracy, for all his ethics and honesty, had learned his lessons well at the knee of that arch-boss, Tom Platt. He saw nothing illegal or immoral in scheming to take either the Mole or Samana Bay. When it came to defending America's national honor in Chile, both Tracy and Harrison understood the political maneuver of applying coercive force to achieve an objective. Perhaps only Blaine really appreciated the finesse of diplomacy, because of his longer service in the field of international relations. Yet, in the end, all three knew perfectly well that the law of nations prevented overt acquisition of territory or trade concessions from less powerful countries at the point of a sword. The American eagle might bluster and strut but at this hour it still hesitated to apply the full force of its talons to achieve expansionist dreams.

Negotiation and acquiescence proved the better part of valor for Harrisonian diplomacy. The United States was not yet ready for empire. Spring-Rice had told an English friend in 1887 that while he enjoyed the life in the American capital; ". . . there is very little experience of Foreign politics to be got here—in fact, none."[48] Five years later the situation was changed—Tracy, Blaine, and the President had seen to that.

CHAPTER 7

Defeat at the Polls Cuts Short a Program

The Chilean crisis broadened the experience of Secretary Tracy. Always an ardent navalist, he now had evolved into an outspoken expansionist, as he became caught up in the heady atmosphere of Harrisonian diplomacy. He spoke of growing threats to the United States as extension of European commercial interests into the Caribbean and the Pacific threatened American trade. Seeking increases for the navy in his annual report in 1891, Tracy stated: "With the great maritime powers it is only a step from commercial control to territorial control." The lessons of the Chilean crisis seemed clear. He saw distinct advantages in building a trans-isthmian canal, since the establishment of total commercial supremacy by a European power in any nation in the western hemisphere would mean the end of American influence, if not even subjugation of the victimized country. Since the construction ways promised to be free from previously authorized vessels within two years, Tracy thought it advisable to prod Congress for the next installment of the new battlefleet.[1]

Tracy noted happily the commissioning of the cruiser *Newark,* the monitor *Miantonomah,* and the gunboats *Concord* and *Bennington* during 1891. Other vessels like the *Raleigh* and *Cincinnati* showed progress, he reported, but he also confessed that more than a dozen vessels from Whitney's programs remained incomplete. The secretary wanted two additional *Oregon*-class battleships, a second armored cruiser like the *New York,* replacements for the navy's obsolete river craft on the China station, and a torpedo cruiser and a flotilla of torpedo boats. Development of a domestic capacity to produce the Whitehead torpedo now permitted such a request, Tracy said. Furthermore he sought to pacify isolationist congressmen from the Midwest by explaining that the latter craft might be constructed on the upper Mississippi River. As he saw it: "Not only the type of vessel, but all the smaller craft of the New Navy . . . torpedo cruisers . . . light-draft vessels . . . should be the subject of competition by the numerous shops . . . at Pittsburgh, Cincinnati, Louisville, St. Louis, New Orleans . . . and every establishment that acquires the plant for building a naval vessel in these waters makes a distinct and important addition to the naval resources of the country."[2]

The secretary declared enthusiastically: "The old wooden ships of the Navy have now practically passed out of existence." But Tracy knew better, that this assertion was deceptive. Fifty-one of the 109 vessels on the 1891 Navy list were constructed of wood. Moreover, an additional thirteen were ancient monitors and at least twenty-five other ships remained in some uncompleted state of construction. Only the cruisers *Chicago, Philadelphia, Newark,* amd *San Francisco* mounted twelve modern guns or more; only the monitor *Miantonomah* possessed sufficient armor. Tracy's navy was a "paper navy" and he knew it.[3]

Still, his energetic and enthusiastic programs garnered support. President Harrison realized Tracy's problems and in his third annual message to Congress commended Tracy's dedicated work while requesting additional appropriations for the "best modern type" of fleet, one large enough to protect American lives and property anywhere in the world. Harrison declared his support of the Nicaraguan canal scheme and observed: "We shall probably be in the future more largely a competitor in the commerce of the world, and it is essential to the dignity of this nation . . . that its Navy should be adequate . . . upon the . . . Atlantic and . . . Pacific."[4]

Other Americans like William C. Whitney and J. P. Morgan shared Harrison's feelings. Whitney congratulated the Secretary of the Navy not only for his department's work but also for the "lucid exposition which you have made of it." Morgan waxed poetic about the steel ships, declaring them to be "almost as far in advance of the European standard as our Wooden Clipper ships were ahead of the world in 1850."[5] Yet Tracy realized that he faced an antagonistic Congress. One observer contended that the new navy was at its most critical stage since ". . . the new Congress which is to assemble in a little more than two months, has in its lower branch almost a three-fourths majority which the friends of the New Navy, if they are prudent, will reckon as initially hostile to its development on existing lines."[6] When these legislators considered the next naval appropriations bill just after the beginning of 1892, Tracy dutifully supplied information to committee members and consulted closely with both houses. At this time Tracy undoubtedly agreed with a suggestion from his adviser and friend, S. B. Luce that what was really needed was a blue-ribbon commission composed of naval and military officers, Congressmen, and eminent civilians all appointed by the President—with the Secretary of the Navy as president. Such a panel might formulate international as well as wholly military and naval policy, and its report would reflect the views of both legislative and executive branches.[7]

Luce cited France and Great Britain as exemplifying the type of policy-planning needed. England considered it essential to maintain a fleet equal to that of any two European opponents. France built her own navy on the basis of having two battleships to England's three, but, Luce asked: "Who can state in as few words the naval policy of the United States? No one. It has not yet been formulated." He thought his proposed commission could reflect the naval views of all concerned. It would avoid the problems of the past whereby Congress and the military services held widely divergent ideas about the military needs of the nation.

Congressional debates in April reflected the very point of Luce's advice to Tracy. As the discussion progressed, Congressman Charles Boutelle, no longer chairman but still an influential member of the House Naval Affairs Committee, wired Tracy on April 12 that an early vote impended on the navy's needs and he wished to receive the department's draft proposal incorporating the program in Tracy's annual report. The secretary enthusiastically complied and even accepted the substitution of two gunboats for the torpedo cruiser, perhaps a move suggested by Boutelle to appease antinavalists.[8] Still, the measure experienced great difficulty before final congressional approval in July. The Navy Act of 1892 authorized only one battleship, reintroduced by Senate conferees after their House colleagues deleted from the measure all provisions for capital ships.[9] The economy-conscious legislators also removed everything except a single additional armored cruiser. Perhaps they feared shallow-draft gunboats would accelerate American involvement in the internal affairs of other powers in South America and Asia.

Tracy now resigned himself to the whims of Congress. But he was not wholly displeased, since the new act removed certain previously imposed restrictions on American warships. Either inadvertently, or perhaps through the shrewd conference room maneuvers of navalists (the record remains unclear) Congress provided funds for constructing warships superior to any sister ships in the fleet; they set no limit on fuel capacity or cruising range. The new battleship was to have a designated displacement of 11,340 tons, a main battery of 12-inch rifles, and a secondary battery of eight 3-inch rifles and six 4-inch rifles. If the *Iowa* (as she was designated) possessed a smaller battery than the *Oregon*-class, her coal bunker capacity exceeded her sister battleships by two hundred tons. This factor, declared Tracy, would ". . . render her design as a sea-going battle-ship a marked improvement over that of the three coastline battle-ships." Even the new cruiser, the *Brooklyn,* was to have a fuel capacity which, supposedly, could carry her from New York to San Francisco without refueling. By 1892, Congress clearly was moving abreast of planners in the Navy Department to meet the expanding needs of national defense in quality if not in quantity of ships.

Actual progress on construction of the fleet continued to seem phlegmatic to Tracy. The second-class battleship *Texas,* and the cruisers *Raleigh, Columbia,* and *Marblehead,* as well as the gunboat *Castine* and torpedo boat *Bancroft,* all reached the launching stage by fall. The cruisers *Olympia* and *Cincinnati* followed before the end of the year. However, much of the secretary's time continued to be spent in prodding subordinates concerned with repair and fabrication as well as dealing with continued delays in the delivery of armor from Bethlehem and Pittsburgh.

Tracy had toured the Bethlehem works in October of 1891 and witnessed at first hand the facilities for armor production. Addi-

U.S.S. *IOWA*, 1893
One of Tracy's Improved Sea-Going Battleships
[Courtesy National Archives]

tional tests on six armor plates provided by the steelmakers vali-
dated the superiority of harveyized-nickel-steel once and for all,
and only the Schneider executives seemed to be distressed about
the American navy's utilization of Creusot test plates in direct
violation of their rights. Shipbuilders like Charles Cramp acknowledged the "uniform excellence" of the product and Andrew Carnegie busily dispatched demijohns of refreshment to Tracy's residence, as well as offering special trains in which the secretary might
travel to the Pittsburgh works, in honor of their shared success.[10]
Thus the new year opened on a note of promise for successful delivery of quantities of armor.

Labor unrest, known to history as "The Homestead Strike,"
shattered that promise in the summer of 1892. The details have
been amply recounted so often that they require no elaboration.
But as early as January Tracy learned of labor-management
troubles at Carnegie's Homestead works near Pittsburgh where
much of the new armor was being fabricated. Armor mill workers
demanded, in part, a hundred percent raise of pay on all nickel-
steel work, alleging that the material was much harder to fabricate
than other steel and the chances of its rejection were much greater.
Actually the workers' unrest over wages and working conditions
went farther than the issue of steelmaking for the navy, but the local
labor union thought that it could win its demands because of
government pressure upon the management to complete the armor
contract. In turn Carnegie shrewdly directed his lieutenants on the
scene to stockpile unfinished plates in advance of any strike, and
labor saving machinery, introduced to manufacture the armor,
undercut the position of the workers. Tracy meanwhile gained the
impression that a general strike was in the offing for the whole
steel industry. Adding to the unsettled conditions at Pittsburgh, the
Bethlehem firm demanded an additional $150 per ton on turret
armor for the *Maine, Amphitrite, Monadnock,* and *Puritan.* Finally,
the outbreak of open violence at Homestead on July 6 caused all
deliveries from Carnegie Steel Company to drop precipitously.[11]

Tracy's concern related less to the labor dispute itself than to its
impact on the delivery of armor. He told Congress at the end of
June that the steel firms had supplied over 1,100 tons of armor
thus far. Then, with word reaching Washington that resumption of
casting and rolling work at Homestead could not begin before late
September, the secretary even shuffled work, perhaps illegally, be-

tween Carnegie's plant and Bethlehem in order to keep the program moving. To complicate matters, the Bethlehem management lagged farther and farther behind on their contract.[12]

Finally Tracy laid it on the line to Bethlehem officials. The secretary pointed out that Bethlehem deliveries had not approached 600 tons all told and at their present rate of delivery an additional three years appeared necessary to complete the contract. This was not satisfactory and the continual promises that increased facilities would yield increased armor dividends by fall had produced no results. Writing to Bethlehem managers in October, Tracy bluntly stated:

> These promises like many others made by your company have not been kept, and now you ask me to extend your contract. This I cannot do. Any extension of your time must be connected with conditions with adequate penalties attached to be imposed in case of failure on your part.[13]

Contemporary journals concluded that the Secretary of the Navy spoke with some justification. Apparently neither Carnegie Steel nor Bethlehem Iron showed concern because their companies lagged behind contract schedules. Tracy's discussions with M. Hunsicker and Lieutenant C. A. Stone from the Carnegie firm produced reassurances of a speed-up in shipment despite the Homestead troubles, but as the *Philadelphia North American* saw it: "Secretary Tracy has about reached the conclusion that he has been played with, and it is the impression that he is about to enforce the penalty clauses to bring the contractors to time."[14] The secretary carefully refuted reports that he planned anything as drastic as complete revocation of contracts, but he promised intensive review. Immediate shipment of 350 tons of armor from Bethlehem and personal consultation with Henry Frick of Carnegie in November eased relations between the navy and the steel industry.[15]

Tracy's almost fanatical concern with completing the fleet reflected America's continually growing concern over international matters. Navy tasks included expansion of intelligence-gathering efforts of its ships on station in the Indian Ocean, off western Africa, and in the Far East, as well as patroling Latin American waters. A special squadron of the newer cruisers kept an alert eye cocked toward British incursions in the boundary dispute between Venezuela and British Guiana. Furthermore, the navy was equally in-

volved in the Bering Sea where several years of diplomatic controversy concerning seal fishing threatened to reach a crisis for Canada,
Great Britain, and the United States. Tracy took a personal interest in this controversy because of its legal challenges and intricacies.[16]

Seal fishing, long a lucrative pursuit in the Bering Sea, had advanced to such proportions by the late 1880s that the herds were
in danger of extinction. Hunters from Canada, Australia, and
Hawaii had pursued the brutal practice of pelagic sealing—killing
seals as they approached their mating grounds in the open sea—
long after the larger nations had outlawed such practice. The United States had directed its Revenue Marine cutters to seize Canadian sealers operating beyond the three-mile limit off the Pribilof
Islands, hoping to prevent the extermination of the seals. Great
Britain had reacted customarily with vehement protest on behalf
of her Canadian subjects. Secretary Blaine and the State Department had made little headway with Britain's foreign minister, Lord
Salisbury, and Sir Julian Pauncefote, British ambassador in Washington. President Harrison then asked Tracy to apply his legal
experience to a study of the issue.

Tracy immediately approached Professor H. W. Elliott of the
Smithsonian Institution, an ardent student of the seal's life habits.
Tracy was not a naturalist but he joined with Elliott in an effort to
help the fur seal.[17] Blaine used Tracy's legal knowledge to secure
an agreement with the British by early 1891 which included joint
patrol and enforcement of a one-year cessation of sealing. Three
of Tracy's warships, *Thetis, Mohican,* and *Alert* set a course for the
north as the American contribution, but the controversy's turning
point in 1890 and 1891 was hardly a firm and permanent agreement.
Continued negotiations seeking a final solution produced only additional stalemate and the adolescent nationalism spawned by the
Chilean affair even led one British observer to wonder:

> . . . what will the U.S. be like when their fleet is more power-
> ful, if the administration acts in a similar manner? I can't help
> thinking that serious difficulty may yet spring from the Bering
> Sea matter, or something else, during this critical year, unless
> good temper is shown on both sides, which doesn't seem
> likely.[18]

Indeed, Britain and the United States had not yet arrived at the
stage of rapprochement which obtained in the following decade.

The possibilities of conflict with the United Kingdom and other European powers had already prompted Tracy to direct his secret strategy board to broaden its scope of war plans. Mahan recalled later that he exhausted much time and effort on schemes to thwart the Royal Navy. The Bering Sea affair contributed to the need for such measures, and it seemed no closer to solution in 1892 than it had two years before.[19]

The late winter of 1892 found the opposing sides adamant. Salisbury, now Prime Minister, especially enraged Washington late in February when he declared himself against restrictions on two consecutive sealing seasons and he rejected outright Blaine's arguments for a continued conservation of seals. Harrison, perhaps prompted by Tracy, then took a more belligerent position. As numerous observers suggested, in 1892 as well as later, a war to secure renomination ahead of Blaine and reelection in the autumn, whether with Chile or Great Britain, was necessarily abhorrent to the President.[20]

Meanwhile, the Secretary of the Navy busily prepared for the possible extension of an Anglo–American compromise. Tracy met with Rear Admiral F. T. Ramsay, Chief of the Bureau of Navigation and Assistant Secretary of State John W. Foster (in Blaine's absence) in March and planned a combined fleet of Revenue Marine and naval vessels to enforce any possible agreement. But, when he learned of this development, Blaine feared the ramifications of Tracy's enforcement squadron. He protested to Harrison on March 6 that sabre rattling and unilateral dispatch of warships to the Bering Sea would only lead to Salisbury's reelection; since key northeastern states like New York and Massachusetts wanted to avoid war with Britain, Harrison himself would suffer politically from such action. Pauncefote also urged caution to his superiors and then, just as Tracy brought the enforcement squadron to a state of operational readiness, Salisbury's agreement to extend the compromise made its way by trans-Atlantic courier to Washington. Once again Blaine's deft tactics diluted the strong stand of Harrison and Tracy and, combined with Britain's alert statesmanship, averted war.[21]

The United States Senate approved unanimously an arbitration treaty on March 29 whereby Great Britain and the United States promised to submit the whole difficulty to an arbitration court in Paris. Meanwhile, Tracy directed Commander Robley D. Evans to take charge of the special American enforcement squadron and together with warships dispatched by the Salisbury government, to aid in keeping all sealing vessels out of the Bering Sea until the fall of 1893. The American force vigorously performed its assignment, patroling 63,000 miles of ocean, warning ninety-eight American and Canadian sealers, and capturing numerous poachers and violators.

Secretary Blaine suddenly resigned from the Harrison cabinet on June 4, 1892, and the burden of the preparation of the American case for the Paris tribunal passed to other hands. Foster succeeded Blaine officially and together with Tracy, Elliott, and Secretary of the Interior John W. Noble, succeeded in rounding the rough edges of the American presentation. Apparently Tracy's interpretation of international law pleased some of Harrison's officials more than the stand Blaine had taken.[22]

Tracy based his own argument upon Roman, Danish, Saxon, and English legal precedents. He quoted from Coke, and Blackstone, and stood firmly upon two premises. First, he asserted, such legal precedents upheld the rudimentary right of a landowner to wild animals frequenting his land. This right of ownership ceased only if the landowner could not properly identify the animals formerly on his land. Tracy then applied these precedents to pelagic sealing. His second premise held that it did not matter whether the United States could legally exclude certain ships from the Bering Sea. Indiscriminate killing of seals on the high seas by people not owning the land upon which reproduction of the species took place constituted an invasion of property rights. But the key to the secretary's case lay in proper identification of the seals. The distinctive coloring of the Alaskan seals made their identity especially easy. Since the United States claimed no ownership of other herds, her agents might conveniently distinguish those seals while on the shores of the Pribilof Islands or in adjacent waters. Hence these seals would be subject to American property rights. Furthermore, the consistency with which the herds gathered in the area at certain seasons firmly established the boundaries for such property rights.

The Secretary of the Navy observed that the seals left the Pribilofs and Bering Sea and dispersed into the northern Pacific at the beginning of each winter. Identification of Alaskan seals on the high seas outside the Bering Sea was then impossible. In the spring, however, the seals returned to their mating grounds where American agents could ascertain American property. Finally, Tracy advanced the cause of conservation of this natural resource based on the dictates of common morality. Killing of pregnant seals was barbarous, if not wasteful, in Tracy's view. He concluded: ". . . there are few who will deny the justice of the assertion that any pursuit which must inevitably result in the total destruction of an animal of such valuable qualities to mankind as the fur seal, is an evil . . . the encouragement of which is, from the nature of things, immoral."

The American cause appeared doomed from the start when the international tribunal finally convened in Paris in the spring of 1893. Foster originally planned to use Tracy's property rights argument but his resignation from the State Department in order to act as agent for the United States in the proceedings cost him control of the ultimate presentation of the American case. American representatives first maintained Blaine's rather untenable basic premise concerning the immorality of Canadian sealing, then later retreated to Tracy's stand on property rights. But the final decision of the tribunal rejected American claims of exclusive rights in Bering waters. It ordered sealers to operate outside of a sixty-mile radius from the Pribilof Islands, but it declared illegal the American seizure of Canadian sealing vessels on the high seas and awarded $473,151.26 in damages to Canadian citizens.[23]

Both Foster and Tracy expressed disappointment over the outcome, the former especially deploring certain Russian diplomatic intransigence at Paris—the Russian arbitrator having refused to sustain American claims to exclusive jurisdiction over the Bering Sea based upon similar Russian assertions made prior to the cession of Alaska. Foster also contended that the tribunal failed to appreciate Tracy's argument about property rights because of its novelty and because it conflicted with the doctrine of free navigation. Throwing the onus back to Blaine, who had recently died, Foster decided that: "Had the American authorities based their action in the seizures and during the negotiations and correspondence [with the British from 1890 to 1892] on the right of property in the seals and in the industry, they would have been much stronger before the Tribunal and might have gained their case."[24]

Tracy's displeasure at the time probably approached that of a good lawyer failing to carry a point in court. As he had told Harrison much earlier, in August 1890:

Reflection and study have satisfied me beyond all doubt that the position indicated by me . . . as to our rights in the Bering Sea is sound. Our right to protect the seals while feeding in the waters adjacent to the Islands of Saint George and Saint Paul is absolute. No one acquainted with the habits and instinct of the seal, and familiar with the principles of the civil and common law applicable to analogous cases can doubt it.[25]

Avid imperialists like Theodore Roosevelt saw the whole episode as a disaster for American foreign policy. Tracy's impetuous fellow New Yorker confided to Foster in 1895 that: "I have always agreed with Secretary Tracy about that arbitration; once in it, our people did the best they could, but I don't believe we ought to have had the arbitration."[26] Tracy said little in public about the course of events. His sentiments may have been summarized best in the conclusion of his article for the *North American Review* in 1893:

> Such is the question which the United States, strong in the justice of its cause, and controlled by that spirit of forbearance and adherence to order and law which should always give in both domestic and international controversies, has now submitted to an impartial arbitration. It had no other alternative but to appeal to the God of battles.[27]

Possible war with Chile was one thing, but with Great Britain, something else. Tracy advised Harrison on the seal question much as he did with regard to Chile, but with considerably less belligerence. The secretary's course in international disputes always combined militance, perception, and justification of the American position. But Great Britain possessed naval power in being which could not be matched by the United States. Tracy perceived that national prestige could be maintained just as realistically in an international tribunal as on an international battlefield, but only if the United States bargained from a position of strength.

Tracy's final excursion in the expansionist diplomacy of the Harrison years came toward the end of his tenure. Undaunted by failure to achieve a permanent naval station in the Caribbean, the secretary also cast covetous glances toward the Pacific. But other American expansionists had preceded him in their commercial-strategic quest. Businessmen wanted Hawaiian rice and sugar and navalists saw the islands as the key to the Pacific world. Located on trade routes to the Orient, the island's proximity to Central America afforded additional promise as a western outpost for guarding an isthmian canal. The United States controlled Hawaii through reciprocity agreements after 1876 and certain naval privileges were accorded in the early eighties. Thus one senator could claim that Americans had planted a Gibraltar in the Pacific "which is stronger and better and more useful than the Gibraltar that commands the Mediterranean sea."[28] Yet the possibility always remained that someone else might desire this second Gibraltar. Great Britain, Germany, even Japan, could see advantages in preempting the strategic location despite Blaine's assertion that Hawaii comprised part of the "American system." American expansionist leaders could never be content until the Hawaiian kingdom moved completely and solely under the protection of the United States.

When viewed beside Tracy's evolving strategic consciousness, shipbuilding programs, and growing imperialist tendencies, it seems only natural in retrospect that he would join in the drive for an Hawaiian protectorate. Still, prior to 1892, the moving force lay with Blaine and the State Department. Tracy's office provided naval vessels to underwrite Blaine's ideas of protectorates, or to support the American minister, J. J. Stevens, in Hawaii, whenever that arch-annexationist asked for naval units to guard American citizens and property. The secretary read the thoughts of Mahan on the lure of the islands and he considered with certain alarm the dispatches of Captain G. C. Wiltse and Rear Admiral George Brown from Hawaiian waters which expressed fears of European "bogeymen" and other imagined threats to American interests. But Tracy remained in the background, at least until the spring of 1892.[29]

Harrisonian expansion rested mainly on the old "have the cake and eat it too" approach, as witnessed in the Latin American realm. Protectorates might provide American tutelage without the accompanying daily problems of political control. However, success evaded Blaine and the President on this count, not only in the Caribbean, but also in Hawaii in 1890. Anti-American and native elements successfully resisted American overtures quite similar in their demands and premises to those rejected by the Hyppolite regime in Haiti. Spectres of foreign influence (in this case Canadian railroad interests) and unstable political conditions in the islands clouded the issue throughout 1890 and 1891. Meanwhile, an annexationist group in the islands prepared for the proper moment for outright revolution and assumption of American control over Hawaii. The frustrated trio of Harrison, Blaine, and Tracy were quite ready by 1892 to consider outright annexation of Hawaii as the only expedient means of bringing both stability and American control. Thus they displayed unusual hospitality when early in that year, Lorrin A. Thurston, representing the dissidents, arrived in Washington seeking American aid.[30]

Blaine and Tracy expressed enthusiastic sympathy with the dissident cause. They gave Thurston the clear impression that annexation of the islands would not be denied, should proper preliminary steps be laid for it. Blaine left the State Department within the month, thereby removing any restraining hand from his impetuous naval colleague. Whether or not Tracy then became the leading figure urging a firmer grasp on Hawaii remains a question, but his true feelings certainly emerged by the end of the year. He told Rear Admiral J. S. Skerett, who was about to depart for Hawaiian waters, that the United States would be very glad to annex Hawaii if ordinary legal methods could induce the people to accept such annexation.[31] By this stage, the Harrison administration had lost the election of 1892 and its leaders may have desired one last attempt to encourage revolution and assumption of American suzerainty over the islands.

In any event, the scheme ended in failure although pro-annexationist revolutionaries staged a successful coup d'etat (under the watchful guns of the U.S.S. *Boston*) and Harrison sent a treaty of annexation to the Senate by mid-February 1893. A badly divided Senate refused to absorb Hawaii immediately as a new American dominion, in spite of administration enthusiasm, personified to a large degree by Tracy. President Cleveland later withdrew the treaty from consideration and the Navy's hopes for a permanent Hawaiian base temporarily became a dead issue.

Harrison and his subordinates naturally received partisan criticism from their Democratic opponents early in 1893 because they ostensibly possessed prior knowledge of the revolution and then intrigued to establish a protectorate before formal annexation. While Foster denied complicity and Washington officials probably did not know exactly when a revolution was scheduled to break out or whether it would be successful, there is reason to suppose that neither Tracy nor Foster exercised much restraint over their representatives in the islands, Stevens and Wiltse. As in the Caribbean, higher authority, that is, Foster and Tracy, sanctioned the Hawaiian developments of early 1893. In addition, both men served Harrison who observed to a friend on February 3 that no foreign power should be permitted to take Hawaii, since "such a possession would not consist with our safety and with the peace of the world."[32]

The Senate's refusal to bear the cross of empire and the conclusion of the Harrison administration stopped Tracy's search for overseas bases as well as his participation in America's expansion. Four separate attempts to gain coaling stations ended in failure. Tracy's over-zealous, perhaps even tactless, employment of cruiser diplomacy enraged foreign governments and undoubtedly frightened many citizens at home. Whenever Blaine's steadying hand was absent, Tracy blundered toward chauvinism and possibly detracted from Harrison's programs for a new manifest destiny. The indications are that had Harrison been given a second term an aggressive foreign policy supported by the energetic Tracy might have been a principal feature of administration programs.

Tracy's good intentions may have been detrimental in other ways to the Republican political cause in late 1892. Newspapers proclaimed a political kickback from the steel industry on the eve of the elections due mainly to a controversial decision regarding turret designs on the *New York* and *Monterey* which supposedly profitted the steelmakers, traditional supporters of the GOP. The topic stirred conversation in fashionable Washington club rooms during the late summer and autumn. Tracy remained aloof from reporters while vactioning at Bar Harbor and, when finally cornered later on, refused to reopen a subject which he considered closed officially. The *New York Herald* charged him with suppressing a scandal until after the November elections but he only admitted: "We are constantly changing our plans. Ship building is a progressive science. There can be no progress where there is no change."[33]

The secretary's national prominence proved particularly serious politically to the Republicans in New York. The apogee of Boss Tom Platt's disgust had come with Tracy's defection to the arch-enemy, Benjamin Harrison, as well as with the imposition of the merit system to the navy yards. Of course, Tracy was a national official, not merely the parochial henchman of a New York State political boss—a fact apparently lost upon Platt. Tracy refused to become embroiled in the internal politics of the Empire State. New York newspapers speculated on Tracy's future role, possibly as Secretary of State, Vice President, or even as a "dark-horse" compromise candidate for President. As Archibald Gordon,

an associate editor of the *New York Gazette,* pointed out to the
secretary:

> It has probably not occurred to you that today you are, be-
> yond all question, the most available candidate the Republi-
> can Party can put forward for the Presidency in 1892 . . . all
> the kudos of the Chilean affair belongs to you. Had it not been
> for the extraordinary rapidity of your executive action in the
> Department the Presidential ultimatum would have been im-
> possible. . . . you have demonstrated your remarkable execu-
> tive ability without having to go through the senatorial and
> gubnatorial [*sic*] phases which weaken, as often as they
> strenthen, a presidential candidate. Further, you have not
> been involved in the intestinal divisions of our party. There
> is nobody who can go before the people with a simpler or
> broader qualification than yourself.[34]

Tracy's reply was simple and straight to the point; he could not
conceive of any circumstances which would permit his name to be
used as a candidate. He reminded Gordon that his words were not
for publication "as I do not wish to appear publicly declining a position which it is very certain will not be offered me."[35] Tracy stood
for the renomination and reelection of Harrison. Yet rumors persisted, or as one editor put it: "Secretary Tracy intimates that he
wouldn't be a candidate for the presidency if he could be. The
Secretary should tell that to a company of his Marines."[36]

After the Republican National Convention determined upon a
ticket of Harrison and Whitelaw Reid, Tracy's task became one
of binding up Harrison-Platt wounds. It probably never dawned
on Tracy that his attempts would founder merely because of his
own prominence in the party. The press detected the impossibility
of the task, for, as one Philadelphia editor declared: "The attempt
to 'placate' Mr. Platt while Mr. Tracy remains in charge of party
politics [in New York] is about as promising as an effort to make
a horse eat shavings by placing green spectacles over his eyes."[37]

Platt actively supported Blaine at the convention and Harrison's
renomination, in his view, "caused a chattering of the teeth among
the warm blooded Republicans of the East. . . ." Tracy could do
little, as it turned out, for even he had to admit finally, ". . . the
trouble is Mr. Platt. The President has been friendly to him always.
. . . Notwithstanding the bitter fight at Minneapolis I do not be-

lieve that the sentiment of the President toward Mr. Platt was
changed . . ."[38] This failure to secure Platt's support for Harrison
caused the Secretary of the Navy to assume a back seat during the
campaign, hoping such a move might win over the petulant Platt.
Tracy confidently predicted Republican victory in November, but
he consistently refused all invitations to get out on the hustings,
telling newsmen of the pressure of work in Washington. He may
even have sensed the futility of the cause by early September when
he announced his intention to retire to private life once more after
March 1893.[39]

If the absence of Tracy from among Harrison's campaigners was
calculated to preserve New York for the Republicans, it did little to
stave off national defeat in November. Tracy had warned previously that the tariff would beat the party in 1892, but he was greatly
astonished at the size of the setback on his home ground in Brooklyn. There the Democrats rolled up a 29,000 vote margin instead
of the predicted 10,000. Tracy was especially shocked when several
friends suggested that his civil service reforms added measurably
to the Brooklyn defeat.

Tracy defended himself by pointing to the economic measures
netting profit to Brooklyn, including ship repairs and the construction of the *Maine* and *Columbia.* Furthermore, the civil service reforms should have given the public "extra confidence in
President Harrison's administration, through the evidence . . .
that it was the intention to conduct affairs at the Yard on strictly
business principles."[40] Yet Tracy's political enemies in the city
argued that the election merely confirmed the stupidity of the civil
service rules. One disgruntled Republican ward heeler exclaimed:

> [Tracy] has acted with no more political foresight than a head-
> strong mugwump who sees nothing good in party principles
> and whose only desire is to destroy. When Secretary Tracy
> leaves Washington he will probably fall to the level he should
> properly occupy. Certainly he can ask for nothing more from
> Republicans. Perhaps he will follow the example of his brother-
> in-law and join the Democratic party. It would be a blessing
> to us if he would.[41]

Routine matters, except for the Hawaiian issue, filled the final
months of the Harrison administration. Rumors circulated that
the president might appoint Tracy to the Supreme Court, but such

ripples hardly disturbed the more mundane aspects of Tracy's
final housekeeping chores. He granted Lieutenant R. E. Peary a
three-year leave of absence for arctic exploration, put the final
touches upon the large naval review scheduled for spring in connection with the Columbian Exposition, and negotiated two additional contracts with steelmen as a parting gesture toward continued progress in armor development. The contract with Carnegie
Steel called for delivery of 3,000 tons of harveyized nickel steel
armor and a similar agreement with Bethlehem involved 3,500
tons. Prices varied in these contracts from $515 to $725 per ton
for armor, $325 to $650 for armored appurtenances, and $500 for
splinter bulkheads, averaging out at $561.86. The Navy Depart-
ment furnished the nickel and paid an average of $57.54 a ton
extra for the harveyizing process.[42] Tracy could leave office in
March with the firm knowledge that he would bequeath a well-
established and progressive armor program to his successor.

One of Benjamin Franklin Tracy's more important parting works
proved to be his final report to the president and the nation on the
state of the United States Navy. This document developed into an
exhaustive summary of naval progress since 1889.[43] Tracy's statistics impressed Harrison when he saw them. The secretary pointed
out subtly that apart from a few "old ships, long since obsolete and
fast going to decay," the fleet of 1889 comprised only three modern
steel vessels, aggregating 7,863 tons, and mounting thirteen 6-inch
and four 8-inch guns, forgings for which were purchased abroad.
In comparison, the Harrison administration gave the country nineteen additional vessels, commissioned by the Republicans, with an
aggregate tonnage of 54,812 tons, mounting altogether two 12-
inch, six 10-inch, sixteen 8-inch, and eighty-two 6-inch guns, all
but five of these guns being of domestic manufacture.

The secretary also cited the fact that eighteen more vessels, in
process of construction and certain to be completed within the
following year, "should their armor be delivered," would aggregate an additional tonnage of 93,497 tons. They would mount some
twelve 13-inch, six 12-inch, sixteen 10-inch, thirty 8-inch, thirty-
two 6-inch, thirty-eight 5-inch, and thirty-four 4-inch guns, all of
domestic manufacture. Tracy declared that: ". . . of all the new
ships the construction of which has been begun during the present
administration, only two will remain on the stocks on the 4th of
March next." He even included a table which showed that while

U.S.S. *COLUMBIA*

Armored Cruiser of the Tracy Period

[Courtesy National Archives]

more tonnage was authorized under the Cleveland-Whitney administration, the Republicans were far ahead in tonnage commenced, commissioned, and constructed.

Table 3 — Tonnage of the New Navy 1881-1893[44]

March 4—	New Vessels Author- ized	New Vessels Begun	New Vessels Commis- sioned	Tonnage upon which work has actually been done
	TONS	TONS	TONS	TONS
1881-1885	23,076	12,363	. . .	12,363
1885-1889	67,183	34,814	7,863	69,197
1889-1893	66,616	108,018	54,832	169,564

Tracy explained that the authorizations during the first period
included five cruisers and three gunboats. Two battleships second-
class, one armored cruiser, one armored harbor-defense ship,
nine cruisers, four gunboats, one practice vessel, one ram, one
dynamite-gun vessel, one torpedo boat, and three tugs were authorized in the second period. Congress authorized in Tracy's period,
four first-class battleships, one armored cruiser, two protected
cruisers "of extreme speed," one torpedo cruiser, and one torpedo
boat. Tracy's administration had in fact essentially completed the
authorized but unconstructed navy of his predecessors and, to him
at least, "all of the above, with perhaps one or two exceptions, are
essential components of a fully developed naval force. . . ."

The secretary recommended for the next year an additional sea-
going battleship of the *Iowa* class, several torpedo cruisers, four
river craft for use in the Far East (recommended in 1891 but
dropped by Congress) and thirty small torpedo craft. Lest future
policy-makers identify Tracy's tenure with battleships only, the
secretary reiterated the views about construction programs which
he espoused in his initial annual report:

> The policy then advocated, which was a radical departure from
> any view previously presented in this Country, consisted in
> the production of the three principal types. First, the armored
> battleship of 10,000 or more tons; second the armored cruiser
> of from 8,000 to 9,000 tons; and third, the commerce pro-
> tecting and destroying cruiser, of extreme speed, of 7,500
> tons.[45]

Tracy saw no cause to depart in the future from his concept of a balanced battlefleet.

Tracy thought that his tenure witnessed equally progressive developments in the field of armor and armament. The manufacture of modern high-powered guns made rapid strides through the diverse efforts of the West Point Foundry, the South Boston Iron Works, and the Bethlehem Iron Company, as well as at the government-owned gun factory in Washington, D.C. The secretary pointed with pride to 214 pieces of heavy ordnance completed while he was in office. The previous two administrations contributed only 46 guns to the statistics while Tracy boasted of actually mounting 116 pieces aboard ship. Most of this ordnance still comprised small calibre weapons, although 12- and 13-inch guns for his battleships also lay in various stages of manufacture. He attributed the overall development of naval ordnance to improved breech mechanisms and fixed ammunition for medium calibre weapons, improvements in gun mountings for larger pieces, and application of nickel to gun as well as to armor manufacture.[46]

Tracy called attention to other important armament developments. Less sanguine about torpedo production in the United States than about gun construction (despite an 1891 contract for production of Whitehead torpedoes), he touted the manufacture of improved brown and smokeless gunpowder by the Dupont and California Powder companies, and the extension of facilities for making gun-cotton. Tracy bragged about overcoming "the most serious defect in our naval armament . . . the want of armor-piercing projectiles." He observed, further, the great strides in domestic manufacture since the projectiles ". . . are today the product of eight different firms, in as many different localities, none of which had manufactured a single projectile prior to . . . 1889."[47]

Tracy also spoke proudly of his other major success, the reform of navy yard employment. He reported to Harrison: "Today the policy outlined nearly two years ago is an accomplished fact, and its results are patent to all the world." To buttress these statements, Tracy included results of an independent survey conducted by the New York Civil Service Reform Association in the autumn of 1892 and a testimonial from the commandant of the New York Navy Yard which claimed that the reforms had reduced the cost of work in that facility by 25 percent in the previous year. Additionally, the secretary thought that the recent election was "the first within the memory of the present generation, in which the yards have not been used as a political machine." He could see no reason why the work force should change with each administration and he advocated legislation making the reform a permanent one. Tracy ended his comments on the note that the navy "has become a great national interest, which should receive the support of patriotic men, whatever their political faith."[48]

On other matters, Tracy reported defense of the Naval War College against its opponents during his term and that "its usefulness may be expected to increase in the future." Yet successful support of the navy's top educational institution did not hide Tracy's disappointment over his failure to secure other needed reforms in the new age which demanded increased proficiency and intelligence among both officers and seamen. To the end of his administration, Tracy still called for improvements such as four-year enlistments, reenlistments bonuses, pensions comparable to the army scale, and doubling the number of naval apprentices to 1,500 boys. He could point only to the establishment in 1891 of a school of application for enlisted Marines at the Washington Marine Barracks as a sign of progress in the procurement of abler enlisted personnel for the navy.

Equally frustrating was the continued defeat of plans to merge the Revenue Marine with the United States Navy and the development of a federal naval reserve. Tracy secured Congressional aid to state naval militia and the granting of mail subsidies in return for use of private steamships as "auxiliary vessels" of the navy in wartime. But such "half loaf" measures hardly pleased the demanding secretary. At the very top of Tracy's list of unfulfilled aims while in office stood his efforts to secure overseas bases. Then too, he had failed to reform the naval officer corps. In fact he battled for three years to substitute merit for seniority as the criterion for officer promotion from ensign all the way to captain. Congressional opposition, carefully stimulated by the officer caste, blunted the secretary's schemes completely and Tracy concluded wearily:

> The present system cannot endure much longer. With the new ships we must have a personnel whose efficiency is beyond question; and whose excellence is on the increase and not on the wane. No country could afford to keep up such a system and maintain a body of officers such as the line of the Navy

will become in a few years under existing conditions. No country could afford to pension in the higher grades officers whose whole time in these grades has been too short to enable them to perform any actual duty, and who hurry one after another, as admirals of a few months' service, to a constantly increasing retired list with constantly increasing rapidity.

Tracy finished his report for 1892 with a warning that the nation should not let down its guard: "The aggressive policy of foreign nations has continued, and this Country, whether it will or not, will soon be forced into a position where it cannot disregard measures which form a menace to its prosperity and security." With that, Tracy heartily endorsed the views of fellow navalists in Congress who had announced earlier: "Our true naval policy for the future is to construct hereafter, principally if not entirely, only first-class cruisers and first-class battleships, with their accessories."[49]

Certainly foreign authorities such as Lord T. A. Brassey, renowned British naval analyst, began to take more notice of the United States Navy by the end of Tracy's tenure. Greater coverage was given to the details of American war vessels and intricate statistical comparisons were made between the American battleships *Indiana, Massachusetts, Oregon,* and *Iowa* and their British battleships *Centurion* and *Barfleur* as well as between the cruisers *Columbia, Minneapolis, Royal Arthur, Blake,* and *Blenheim.* While value judgments on such ships varied considerably, the American vessels generally matched or even exceeded their English counterparts. If Brassey's comparative tables continued to reflect British concern primarily with continental competition from France and Russia, the noticeable addition of American statistics from Tracy's period reflected a rapidly expanding, modernized seapower being forged in the United States by 1893 which would increasingly affect European naval considerations in the future.

A glittering climax to Tracy's phase of the naval renaissance of the late nineteenth century took place later, in May 1893, in New York harbor. Warships gathered there from Argentina, Brazil, France, Great Britain, Holland, Germany, Italy, Russia, and Spain, to join Rear Admiral Bancroft Gherardi's American squadron in a great international naval review. Planned and arranged by Tracy,

TABLE 4—RELATIVE STRENGTH OF NAVIES BUILT OR BUILDING—1893

Class	Great Britain	France	Russia	United States
Battleships				
1st class	37 (395,300 tons)	16 (175,648 tons)	11 (111,857 tons)	1 (11,286 tons)*
2nd class	13 (89,000 tons)	14 (105,694 tons)	4 (21,172 tons)	3 (30,683 tons)
Lookout Ships	19 (36,390 tons)	6 (7,740 tons)		15 (22,840 tons)#
Torpedo Gun Vessels	32 (27,110 tons)	13 (6,835 tons)	8 (3,600 tons)	4 (2,598 tons)
Coast Defense Ships	12 (47,720 tons)	20 (66,947 tons)	28 (69,626 tons)	19 (47,802 tons)
Armoured Cruisers	18 (137,050 tons)	13 (68,766 tons)	12 (88,546 tons)	4 (30,348 tons)
Protected Cruisers				
1st class	15 (105,550 tons)	8 (44,941 tons)	1 (5,000 tons)	3 (20,450 tons)
2nd and 3rd class	54 (195,811 tons)	19 (54,480 tons)	2 (5,900 tons)	17 (49,838 tons)
TOTAL	200 (1,033,931 tons)	109 (531,051 tons)	66 (305,701 tons)	62 (215,855 tons)

* The U.S.S. *Iowa* slightly exceeded the qualities of the 2nd class battleships of Great Britain but did not compare with H.M.S. *Ramilles, Royal Sovereign, Royal Oak, Repulse, Resolute, Revenge,* and *Empress of India* (each 14,150 tons) or *Renown* (12,350 tons), all classed as 1st class battleships. Also equal to French *Jaureguibery* (11,818 tons) and Charles *Martel* (11,882 tons); Russian *Gheorghy Pobyedonosets* (10,280 tons).

Does not include 2 paddle steamers (2,055 tons total) in Far East, or 10 screw steamers, wood, (3000-5,600 tons total).

Source: Brassey's *The Naval Annual, 1893,* pp. 271-275, 402-403.

his Democratic successor, Hilary A. Herbert took the honors. Yet public response to the event justified Tracy's belief in publicizing the "New Navy."

Moreover, the massive impact of twenty-seven powerful warships of the foreign squadrons was not lost on American officials as they watched from the rail of the U.S.S. *Dolphin*. As colorful pennants flapped in the soft May breeze, they could recall Tracy's parting words; ". . . it is imperative to the welfare of this Country that the policy of naval reconstruction so successfully carried on in the past should suffer no interruption in the future . . ."[50]

CHAPTER 8

A Distinguished Citizen
in Active Retirement

Washington gossipers reported that President Benjamin Harrison and his Secretary of the Navy would become law partners in New York after they left office early in 1893. But such rumors proved untrue. Harrison returned to Indianapolis and several days after Grover Cleveland's second inauguration, the tall rapidly graying Tracy briefed his successor, paid his respects to helpmates in the department and left the baroque State, War, and Navy building as unostentatiously as he had arrived in that blustery March four years before. Ahead lay a return to the practice of law.

Tracy secured a house on East 30th Street in Manhattan for his daughter, granddaughter, and himself. His son Frank came down from the Apalachin farm for a brief visit, and before long the pace of the new life blended nicely with Tracy's desire for rest and financial recuperation. Seeking rapid recovery of his depleted estate, the ex-cabinet official became an energetic partner in the firm of Tracy, Boardman, and Platt, specializing in estate management cases. His former assistant, James Russell Soley, joined the firm, and Tracy's experience with steel negotiations as Secretary of the Navy led him directly into the field of patent law. The loose ends of family life, his summer property at Babylon on Long Island, and the Marshland horse farm soon vied for his attention.[1]

Tracy's resettlement in Manhattan rather than in Brooklyn lends a clue to his rather slow return to New York politics after 1893. His position in national politics as Secretary of the Navy and his vigorous prosecution of public morality through patronage reform had eroded Tracy's political credibility in the City of Churches. Even Emma once reprimanded her father, "you have not done much at the request of your family or friends."[2] Tracy slowly regained his position in the Platt organization, although hardly without penance for defection to Harrisonian ranks. Perhaps their long friendship, or his retirement from office in Washington, may have rendered Tracy harmless in Platt's eyes. In any event in the mid-nineties the two men emerged arm-in-arm once again during the campaign for initiating a charter for Greater New York—possibly because Platt sensed Tracy's usefulness in dealing with Governor Levi P. Morton, late vice-president under Harrison.

The Greater New York movement dated to 1865 when Andrew Green discerned an advantage in unifying and extending New York City to include Brooklyn, Long Island City, Staten Island, and the outlying towns and villages. But the success of Green's scheme was not assured until the fall of 1895. At that point Green convinced Platt of certain political advantages in the consolidation plan and Platt in turn promised to press Morton to support the bill, then pending in the state legislature, which would create a commission to draft a charter for a Greater New York. Platt, accompanied by Tracy, met with Morton and told the governor that he would withhold support from the latter's presidential aspirations at the upcoming Republican convention in 1896 unless Morton signed the legislation. Properly intimidated, Morton named a board of commissioners to frame a Greater New York charter and, in due course, Tracy's name appeared beside those of such notables as Judge John P. Dillon and President Seth Low of Columbia College as commission members.[3]

The charter which later emerged displeased a number of factions, and Mayor William E. Strong vetoed it early in 1897. Commentators thought it favored Brooklyn, granted too much power to the people, or simply should have been accomplished other than through a formal constitution. Tracy possibly saved the proposal by declaring that it was a law rather than a constitution and therefore could be rescinded with relative ease. The charter was finally signed into law on May 4, 1897, to become effective the following New

Year's Day. As one New York editor trumpeted on January 1, 1898: "The sun will rise this morning upon the greatest experiment in municipal government the world has ever known—the enlarged city. . . ."[4] Tracy had contributed much to its creation.

Meanwhile, Tracy now appeared very much in favor with Tom Platt. Thinking that he might further exploit his old lieutenant's rising tide of popularity, Platt asked Tracy to become the regular Republican nominee in the mayorality election of 1897. Tracy hesitated, leaning toward a reformist candidate, but finally consented because of an ardent desire to defeat Tammany Hall, the city's scandalous Democratic organization. Reformist Republicans had already solicited Platt's support for Seth Low only to have the political boss decline adamantly. Thus, as one authority suggested, Tracy's candidacy was only "Thomas C. Platt (by proxy)."[5] Yet the Democrats were equally blatant in running a little-known party regular, Judge Robert A. Van Wyck, as proxy for Tammany boss Richard Croker. Only Low and fourth-party candidate, Henry George of single-tax fame, provided any real choice to the voters and George's premature death narrowed it to a three-way race on election day.

Tracy expressed his trepidations from the very beginning. Having "reached a time in life when the promptings of ambition have largely lost their power to move me," he told the official nominating meeting, "two considerations have induced me after most anxious thought to accept the nomination." First, was the gravity of the corruption and graft for the people of New York. Secondly, so many party members and friends of good government had urged Tracy's acceptance "in the hope that in the present state of division I can contribute somewhat to bring into harmonious action and to unite under me banners of all the opponents of Tammy Hall." Tracy noted that no pledges had been asked for and none given, his obligation would be solely to the people. He promised to unite with all anti-Tammany forces and "if, the spirit of harmony and conciliation which we thus invoke does not prevail, I propose, having accepted this nomination, to make a fight to the end."[6]

Tracy's good intentions for conciliation and party unity ran counter to partisan politics. Most prominent Republicans desired Tammany's defeat, but many of them doubted Tracy's independence from the Platt organization, and even Platt seemed to prefer the election of Van Wyck to that of a reformist candidate. Thus, the

WEDDING OF EX-PRESIDENT BENJAMIN HARRISON
Tracy as "Best Man" at the Right
[From the collections of the Library of Congress]

picturesque campaign developed into a hard-fought and bitter battle. Torchlight parades, gaily dressed marchers and colorful bands heralded each candidate's following. Newspapers devoted numerous columns to exposure of a deal between Platt and Croker and the hint of a sell-out of Tracy's candidacy was often mentioned. Before ten o'clock on election night it was obvious that Tammany had triumphed, for Van Wyck won by a vote of 233,997 to Low's total of 151,540. Tracy finished a poor third with 101,864 votes.[7]

The mayorality contest of 1897 ended Tracy's aspirations for elected office. In only one instance—and that prior to the Civil War —had he won an election. On other occasions his identification with Platt's organization had contributed to his defeat. Platt may never have really forgiven Tracy for his close association with Harrison. Tracy's service as Harrison's best man at his wedding to Mary Lord Dimmick in April 1896 and a small ground swell in New York to place Tracy's name in nomination for the presidency that year certainly did not escape Platt's notice. In any event, Tracy's defeat in 1897 removed him as a possible threat to Platt's political control of New York.

Meanwhile, Tracy tried to stay abreast of national and international events and naval development while no longer having any role in either. Surging imperialism of the decade pointed directly toward a future naval armaments race although Great Britain had already reacted to the threat in 1889 when she announced a "two power standard" whereby the Royal Navy was to be kept at a level to match the combined strength of the next two maritime powers. Thus, she continued to be the benchmark of progress. In 1890, at what seemed to be the peak of her power, Britain lost first place as the leading industrial nation. The United States replaced England as the world's greatest iron producer, German industrial capacity was closing rapidly, and offered direct competition, and Japan was developing a rival textile industry to further challenge Great Britain's commercial supremacy. Deceptive complacency in the Admiralty at Whitehall hid a growing concern over energetic American, German, and Japanese naval power.

Tracy merely stood on the sidelines and studied events as a bystander. In August 1893 he wrote on the financial crisis of that year. He watched Secretary of the Navy Herbert battle the Populists in Congress over continued naval expansion, while the rest of the nation focused upon a depression and the fight over free silver. Tracy undoubtedly sympathized with the hard-pressed Herbert, since the latter's policies directly reflected the New Yorker's own reformist tendencies. Herbert praised Tracy's stewardship of the department at a dinner in New York in March 1893 declaring his work to have been "masterful, original, and progressive." Tracy in turn assured the same audience that there was no danger that the Navy Department would retrogress during the Alabamian's tenure.[8]

Many of the accomplishments of Herbert and his Assistant Secretary, William McAdoo, paralleled those of Tracy and Soley. After all, the two Democrats had viewed the Republican efforts from the House of Representatives and reacted by themselves becoming dedicated navalists before entering the Cleveland administration. Herbert continued Tracy's efforts to correlate and unify the work of shipbuilding bureaus and he announced agreement with Tracy's proclamation that politics held no place in the navy yards.[9] He further concentrated the work of purchasing for the navy; he added assistants to help bureau chiefs in Navigation and Supplies and Accounts; and he continued Tracy's progress toward providing the navy with better trained and more efficient personnel through establishment of medical training schools, as well as a permanent staff and broadened curriculum at Newport. Herbert pushed Congress for additional support of state naval militia and watched the first group of militia officers participate in a summer program at the war college. He cheered the authorization by Congress to give obsolescent naval vessels and their equipment to the militia for training purposes. On the other hand, the usual party politics and intra-departmental jealousies between bureau chiefs forced modifications in his programs, and Herbert suffered the same reverses as Tracy on such matters as reform of the officer corps. Moreover, congressional opposition stymied accomplishment of plans for further construction of warships for over two years. Herbert, like Tracy, focused his attention on capital ships and the Alabamian's proposals to Congress echoed Tracy's call for an armored fighting fleet.[10]

Herbert attempted to push his fellow Democrats further along the navalist path but even Cleveland admitted that large numbers of unfinished vessels and the depleted condition of the Treasury mitigated against more ships at the time. Only the return of the Republicans to control of Congress after 1894, coupled with increasing concern for overseas markets for surplus American goods and jobs for depressed American laborers, revived the naval programs. The timely appearance of foreign issues such as the Cuban Revolution of 1895, disturbances in Turkey, and the ever-present commercial and territorial rivalry with Great Britain (seen notably in the Venzuelan boundary crisis) also reawakened America's concern with its navy. Herbert's battles with balky Populist Congressmen recalled Tracy's similar difficulties with earlier isolationists but, by the end of the Cleveland administration, Democrats joined increasingly with Republicans in uniting behind ambitious naval proposals.

The United States Navy rose from ninth to sixth place among the world's navies between 1893 and 1897 in terms of capital ships launched, building, or authorized. Herbert's tenure saw completion of many of the vessels which had worried Tracy for so long, including the battleships *Indiana, Oregon,* and *Massachusetts;* the cruisers *Columbia, Minneapolis,* and *Brooklyn;* the defense monitors *Monadnock* and *Terror;* the armored ram *Katahdin;* the gunboats *Castine* and *Machias;* and the small torpedo boat *Ericsson.* Herbert persuaded Congress to authorize funds for five battleships, nineteen torpedo craft, one submarine boat, six gunboats, and a training vessel. Tracy's program was admittedly broader in scope and included authorizations balanced between battleships, cruisers (armored and unarmored), gunboats, and torpedo boats. Moreover, Herbert and McAdoo both owed their conversion to the capital ship school in large part to Tracy, since even in 1890 the Alabamian preferred cruisers and commerce destruction to battleships, and his New Jersey colleague merely wanted the less costly defense monitors. Mahan's numerous publications certainly had their effect upon Herbert's doctrinal development after that year, but could scarcely eclipse Tracy's preeminent contribution at a crucial point in the Democrat's career. So in this additional way, Tracy had set in motion the fleet which was to emerge victorious in battles with the Spanish in 1898 and thereby open the door to American empire.[11]

The paths of Tracy and Herbert crossed more than once during the next few years, somewhat unexpectedly in one instance regarding the armor program of the navy. When Tracy left Washington in 1893, he did not realize at that point that his efforts to find armor for the new ships would be the basis of controversy for the next decade and one-half. The national fires of Populist and Progressive

TABLE 5. EFFECTIVE FIGHTING SHIPS (BUILT AND BUILDING)—1898

CLASS	GREAT BRITAIN			FRANCE			RUSSIA			ITALY			GERMANY			UNITED STATES		
	A	B	C	A	B	C	A	B	C	A	B	C	A	B	C	A	B	C
Battleships																		
1st class	29	9	38	14	6	20	6	6	12	8	2	10	4	3	7	4	5	9
2d class	7		7	8	1	9	4	1	5	2		2	4		4	1		1
3d class	18		18	7		7	5		5	3		3	6		6			
Total—	54	9	63	29	7	36	15	7	22	13	2	15	14	3	17	5	5	10
Coast Defense Ships	14		14	16		16	13	1	14				18	1	19	19		19
Cruisers																		
1st class	23	11	34	8	14	22	6	4	10		4	4	1	1	2	5		5
2d class	47	6	53	13	2	15	3		3	5		5	3	5	8	6		6
3d class	34	10	44	9	3	12	1		1	9	1	10	9	1	10	10		10
Total—	104	27	131	30	19	49	10	4	14	14	5	19	13	7	20	21		21
Torpedoboats	34		34	19	2	21	8	1	9	15	2	17	4		4			20*
Total Effective Fighting Ships			242			122			59			51			60			70

A—Built   B—Building   C—Total
*not specifically listed by Brassey
Source: Brassey's *Naval Annual*, 1898, p. 63.

reform, stoked by economic depression, made armor profits a political issue. Congress returned to Tracy's record on three separate occasions in an effort to investigate the costs of steel armor and armor plants in the United States. The reputed Carnegie frauds of 1893 and similar investigations in 1906 drew upon records of the Tracy era. Tracy himself appeared on Capitol Hill as a star witness in the celebrated inquiries of 1895-1896.[12]

Background events for these particular investigations began in 1894 when Herbert uncovered remarkable similarities between the contract prices and size of orders placed with Bethlehem and Carnegie steelmakers. He concluded that the two firms had conspired against competitors and immediately asked the two to reduce prices. Their subsequent refusal sparked Congressional hearings with stormy Populist members like "Pitchfork Ben" Tillman trumpeting accusations of fraud. The Populist critics charged that contractors supplied defective armor (notwithstanding exoneration by previous congressional hearings on the subject), and had hoodwinked the Cleveland administration into reducing the penalties demanded by the Navy Department. Especially thorny were insurgent claims that Bethlehem people contracted to forge armor for the Russian government at $250 a ton, or less than half the unit price being paid by the United States Navy.[13]

The hearings dragged on and, while Herbert reported to the House of Representatives that harsh government treatment would permanently frighten steelmakers away from naval contracts, the Senate refused to relax its investigation. Additional factors were soon introduced into the hearings, including the involvement of naval officers with contractors, departmental interference with patent decisions, and the question of government establishment of its own armor factory. These matters led Tracy to offer testimony on January 18, 1895, on two points; the royalty fund on nickel provided in the Carnegie contract of 1890, and his own role in expediting the Harvey patent case the following year. As it turned out, the ex-secretary touched upon a great deal more under the intense cross examination. Senators Tillman, William Chandler, and Eugene Hale questioned him about the whole armor issue during the Harrison years and Tracy went into intimate detail in recounting the crisis in warship production which had beset the navy. He specifically denied knowledge of any conspiracy between Bethlehem and Carnegie managements and he stressed how the urgency for armor absolutely prevented competitive bidding.

Tracy's sharp testimony showed that he had considered nothing unethical or exploitative about the prices and manipulations of Carnegie and Bethlehem representatives. He freely admitted to acting, after leaving office, as counsel for the Carnegie company in litigations with the Schneider firm over nickel patents. Then, with typical Tracy aplomb, he contended:

> I always had assumed that when the United States asked a firm to found a plant, without any guarantee of a specific amount of business to justify it, they would have to pay necessarily a larger price for that quantity than they would have to pay if they were giving a guarantee of continuous business from that time on.[14]

Tracy also testified to the honesty of his former Chief of Ordnance, Commander William Folger, under fire for reputed favoritism toward certain projects and inventions of private citizens. Augustus Harvey was one such inventor, and while Tracy noted the practice whereby naval officers worked for government contractors while in positions of authority, he found no suggestion of Folger's misconduct in the Harvey matter. The intensive congressional interrogation also developed Tracy's "guidance" of the Harvey patent through the Patent Office. He recalled that in June 1891 he requested special treatment from the Secretary of the Interior since Harvey's requests were rejected twice before. Tracy claimed to have followed well-established precedents in the Navy Department, and he further observed: "I have always regarded the development of that armor as marking a new epoch in the history of naval development in this country."[15] Unorthodox methods seemed hardly very strange in an era when vested interest, patriotic and selfish motives were mixed together in negotiations, especially in the business community.

Congress responded by praising Tracy's contribution in procuring armor but not his methods. The Senate committee recommended an average price for armor between $300 and $400, nearly half that paid by Tracy and even Whitney. Other critical recommendations pointed to erection of a government armor plant "in case the armor manufacturers decline to accept such prices as may be fixed by law" and continuation of the June 1896 enactment which prohibited naval officers from employment by contractors having large dealings with the Navy Department. Finally the Senators took a retroactive slap at Tracy's maneuvers on Harvey

when they declared: "The Committee believe that Government officials ought not to promote a monopoly of the business of making
armor through patents issued to the use of the combined manufacturers while using the power of the Government to destroy
patents held by foreigners."[16]

Tracy's retirement from public office certainly did not diminish
public recognition of service to the nation. He received an unex-
pected invitation from Herbert to be a guest of the Navy Department at the opening of the North Baltic Sea Canal at Kiel in 1895.
President Cleveland planned to send four of the newest warships to
the international review. Herbert noted that all four ships—*New
York, Columbia, San Francisco* and *Marblehead*—were associated
with the Tracy era and he added in his invitation: "Certainly you
are entitled, if anyone is, to be upon those ships when they are being
exhibited to the world."[17] Tracy could not resist the opportunity,
and accompanied by his daughter and granddaughter he set out for
Europe. The Tracys received a warm reception in Germany, and his
granddaughter, Alys Wilmerding, later remembered the Kaiser as a
dancing partner.

While Tracy was abroad, his brother-in-law, Brigadier General
Isaac Catlin, approached the Secretary of War, Daniel Lamont,
about a Medal of Honor for his relative and sometime comrade-in-
arms. Declaring that he "had no disposition to make any 'fight' for
it," Catlin merely outlined Tracy's valorous service in the Wilderness in 1864. He noted that "no denial or criticism of [my] words,
or the act described . . . ' has ever been breathed." Whether
prompted by Tracy's prominence at the Kiel ceremonies, his record
as Secretary of the Navy, his war record alone, or a bipartisan
spirit, the Cleveland administration agreed to Catlin's request. Lamont announced on June 15, 1895, the award of a Medal of Honor
to "Brevet Brigadier General Benjamin F. Tracy . . . for distinguished gallantry in action at the Battle of the Wilderness, May 6,
1864."[18]

The gathering clouds of conflict with Spain gave Tracy another
opportunity to enter the national limelight. Speaking before the
Middlesex Club of Boston on Lincoln's birthday in 1898, he once
more unabashedly advocated Hawaiian annexation. He saw annexation as a way to preserve peace and avoid war, since possession of
the islands was vital to the security of the West Coast and the
growth of peacetime trade in the Pacific. He criticized those who

felt that national expansion should cease. In a ringing conclusion, he spoke of possible Hawaiian annexation and a trans-isthmian canal as crowning achievements for the century. "I see," said Tracy, "one vast confederation stretching from the frozen North in unbroken line to the glowing South, and from the wild billows of the Atlantic westward to the calmer waters of the Pacific,—and I see one people, and one language, and one law, and one faith; and over all that wide continent, the house of freedom, and a refuge for the oppressed of every race of every clime."[19]

Tracy's speech placed him in the front rank of imperialists when war with Spain developed late that spring. Ideological bedfellows like Theodore Roosevelt corresponded with the senior statesman and their letters ran the gamut from conversations on strategy during the war to a spirited exchange of ideas on the speed of naval preparations for the conflict, the Schley-Sampson controversy, and later on, Tracy's help for Roosevelt's election campaign in 1904. Then, too, Tracy could look with pride at the performance of the American navy as ships with strong attachment to the Tracy era smashed the archaic Spanish squadrons in Manila Bay and off Santiago.[20]

Unfortunately Tracy's interest in the events of the war might have been more intense had he not become involved with ex-president Harrison in arbitration of the Venezuelan boundary dispute at this same time. Representatives of that South American republic approached Harrison early in 1898 about serving as chief counsel in their country's deliberations with British Guiana. Harrison persuaded the Venezuelans to retain his old friend Tracy for $50,000 and they were joined later by Tracy's partner, James R. Soley, and the brilliant international lawyer, Severo Mallet-Prevost. Tracy's own interest in the case was reflected at the time Great Britain and Venezuela signed an arbitration treaty in 1897 when he declared:

> I thought it one of the greatest triumps diplomacy had ever achieved and that its notification would mark an epoch in the progress of civilization. But since reading with more care . . . I am led to doubt whether we do not by this Treaty agree to submit to the arbitration of a European monarch the whole question of the Monroe Doctrine and our right to enforce it.[21]

Such reawakening of Tracy's old concern with national honor and the defense of American hemispheric interest mirrored nation-

wide fears that Great Britain might be showing unusual interest in
what even President Cleveland chose to call the "most distinct of
home questions."[22] The Chief Executive and his advisers moved to
the edge of war over the issue in 1895 and 1896. Britain then backed
off and agreed to arbitration with Venezuela. It was for that reason,
perhaps, that the South Americans looked to their northern neighbors for help at the international tribunal.

The four American attorneys took two years to prepare their
brief, with Harrison, as chief counsel, carefully guiding the activities of his hard-working associates. Tracy's business schedule apparently prevented him from completely satisfying Harrison's rigor-
ous demands for speed and complete dedication to the task.
Nevertheless, by the end of 1898, the four had managed to prepare
one printed volume stating the Venezuelan position, two volumes
of appendices, a one-volume atlas, in addition to a counter-case of
two volumes, "or about eight hundred pages of primary argumenta-
tion."[23]

The formal adjudication began in Paris in mid-June of 1899, in
the same rooms of the Foreign Office where both the Bering Sea
Tribunal and later the Spanish-American Peace Commission had
met. The snail's pace of the deliberations infuriated Harrison and
the verbosity of the English attorneys as well as the brevity of their
position astonished the American group. Despite Venezuela's well-
prepared arguments, the tribunal of two British, two American, and
one Russian judge confirmed Great Britain's possession of most of
the disputed land except some territory at the mouth of the Orinoco
River. Harrison declared irritatedly: ". . . law is nothing to a
British judge . . . when it is a matter of extending British dominion." Mallet-Prevost continued to claim skulduggery between
British and Russian judges until his death in 1948, but Tracy remained silent, perhaps reflecting privately on the earlier Bering Sea
decision when in American eyes principle and right were sacrificed
for European unity.[24]

The Venezuelan case was Tracy's last real association with Harrison. Harrison died of pneumonia on March 13, 1901, and the
news drew the New Yorker to Indianapolis for the funeral. There he
met once more with friends and colleagues of cabinet days; but
their ranks were thinning with the passage of time. Tracy too had
aged, and after the turn of the century he became increasingly one
of the "grand old men" of the New York scene. He affiliated with

the law firm of Coudert brothers after 1900, while continuing to maintain ties with Tracy, Boardman, and Platt. The new firm dealt with the lucrative field of estate liquidation, and Tracy's bonds grew even tighter when his granddaughter married Frederick R. Coudert, Jr. A rough evaluation of Tracy's financial position in 1908 showed some $95,000 in cash and securities, extensive real estate investments primarily in Newark, New Jersey, and an annual income from legal fees, stock dividends, and property of about $25,000.[25] He belonged to a number of socially prominent organizations such as the Union League, Metropolitan, Brooklyn, and Hamilton Clubs, and the Navy League, the New York County Lawyers Association, and the New England Society of New York. A staunch conservative Republican, Tracy supported Taft both in 1908 and 1912, working actively for the regular Republican candidate in the latter election. Tracy's versatility as a lawyer prompted the New York Supreme Court to appoint him as a referee in the New York City debt investigations in 1908; he served as member of the board of directors of the Metropolitan Life and United States Casualty companies; and he became a member of the Saratoga Springs State Reservation Commission in 1910.[26]

Tracy celebrated his eightieth birthday in 1910 and he decided to spend the rest of his years in semi-retirement. Then living at 14 East 60th Street in Manhattan, he increasingly divided his time between the New York home and the Marshland farm, run by his son. Old General Catlin resided near the country place and implored Tracy to return to the country air to end his days. But Tracy continued to appear spry and snappy even in his upper years, despite a slight touch of gout. He told a *New York Sun* reporter in 1912: "I am in better health today than when I was 25 years old. I expect to continue in active practice for a great many years more, and if the Lord spares me, I don't see why I should quit until I am at least 100."[27] Still, he worried about his son's numerous business schemes, and the outbreak of war in Europe in 1914 caused many anxious moments, for Emma was abroad. Finally, the State Department assured him that she was safe in San Moritz.[28]

After the turn of the century Tracy had only occasional contact with the navy. In a rare public appearance in early 1908, Tracy welcomed Rear Admiral Robley D. Evans upon his return from the successful world cruise with the Great White Fleet. The two aging figures probably chatted at great length during the evening at

Carnegie Hall about the events of the Chilean crisis of 1891-1892 in which they both figured so prominently. Tracy also answered letters concerning his role in building the "New Navy" and in 1913 he must have noted sadly that the *Texas* and *Indiana* became mere target ships for the heavier guns of newer dreadnaught-type battleships of the fleet. Other contacts with the Navy Department were limited to developing opportunities for friends and even for his son, who in 1914 busied himself constructing gasoline powered trucks in an Owego garage.[29]

Newspaper reporters spasmodically took time to interview the sprightly Tracy, perhaps because his alert mind and sharp comments provided good copy. At the height of the Mexican crisis in April 1914 he told one newsman that he considered Woodrow Wilson all wrong in not recognizing the Huerta government and thereby avoiding the continuing chance of war with a Southern neighbor. Espousing the cause of "Preparedness" the following year, Tracy declared: "Our navy hasn't kept up with the smaller details, airships and submarines, although we are building excellent battleships now."[30] When pressed by one eager reporter as to whether or not he would have employed the submarine had that type of vessel been in existence during his years in office, Tracy responded affirmatively. But he readily admitted that the sinking of the *Lusitania* was inexcusable; ". . . to torpedo a ship that is not a war vessel, and to give non-belligerents no chance for their lives—inhuman, inhuman."[31]

Tracy never reached his centenarian goal. The automobile carrying Tracy to a GAR parade in Brooklyn on Memorial Day, 1915, collided with a peddlar's cart. He suffered head injuries but "desiring not to disappoint the boys" went on to the parade. The extent of his injury remained hidden until later that night. Several weeks later he seemed to be recovering when a paralytic stroke occurred. He died on Friday afternoon, August 6, as Emma and Frank stood by his bedside. Two days later funeral services were held at Trinity Church in New York City, and Tracy was buried beside his wife across the East River in Greenwood Cemetery in Brooklyn. Heading the list of mourners were Tracy's old colleague in Washington, ex-Postmaster General John Wanamaker, as well as Major General Leonard Wood, and Rear Admiral Nathaniel Usher. A guard of honor comprised of Marines and Coast Artillery troops led the cortage.[32]

Obituaries pointed to Tracy as a prominent soldier, jurist, and statesman, and specifically called him "Father of the Fighting Navy." They recounted the fullness of his life from boyhood on the Southern Tier to retirement in Manhattan. The Navy commemorated Tracy's contributions by giving his name to a destroyer in 1919, and a *New York Times* editorial observed at the time of his death: "It is unfortunate that he never wrote down his observations and conclusions."[33] Yet neither the interviews while Tracy still lived nor the obituaries after his death did justice to the variety of his accomplishments as Secretary of the Navy.

The press highlighted Tracy's query when he first entered upon the secretaryship: "What's the use of building a ship that can't run away from a ship it cannot whip?"[34] It also focused upon Tracy's response to his own question, and his lasting contribution in this regard, when he told an interviewer in 1915:

> The types of war vessels as I designated their nomenclature were battle-ships, armored cruisers and protected cruisers. They are the basic types of ships to do battle just as they exist today. Bigger yes, but with the same objects in view as when the divisions were taken on in my time.

Reporters stressed his introduction of nickel armor, a development which ". . . stripped the armor protection from the British fleet," and they cited his navy yard reforms. Full attention, too, was given to his surprising response to President Harrison when the Chief Executive enjoined him to prepare the navy for war at the height of the Chilean crisis. "Mr. President," Tracy reputedly said, "I have been thinking of war with Chili [*sic*] for several months past—all the while, in fact, since our State Department has been voicing our sentiments to the State Department of the South American republic." But no journal mentioned Tracy's contribution to the continued existence of the Naval War College, his patronage of Mahan's works on seapower, his departmental reorganization, or his participation in expansionist diplomacy.

It remains difficult in retrospect to separate Tracy's actions as nationalist, navalist, and imperialist. Obviously aware of the economic arguments for overseas markets because of his associates in New York, Tracy was really less economically oriented than Blaine with his Pan-Americanism. Like Harrison, he was more concerned about projecting national power. The New Yorker was certainly a

Social Darwinist, an expansionist, and an imperialist of much the same persuasion as Charles Boutelle, Stephen B. Luce, Henry Cabot Lodge, and of course, Alfred Thayer Mahan, and Theodore Roosevelt. He wanted the nation to take its place alongside the other great powers in the world. The United States Navy was the instrument for fulfilling such an ambition.

Yet as Secretary of the Navy, Banjamin Tracy worked with accepted talismans of machine politics of the era—hard bargaining, loyalty, and personal honor. Hard bargaining was the price to pay for securing the best steel armor to gird the symbol of strength—the battlefleet. The new technology demanded loyalty and professional proficiency from all in the navy, and in turn Tracy gave the same, unflinchingly, both to his subordinates and to his superior in the White House. His personal code of honor quickly translated into national honor when bumptious America faced either an unrepentant Chile or a stubborn United Kingdom. Through it all, Tracy projected an image possessed by most men of stature in this period—a quiet, certain sense of mission and national right.

Perhaps the American battlefleet itself in 1915 formed the most tangible proof of Tracy's contribution as one of the naval secretaries who built up American seapower. The United States Navy now ranked fourth in the world in terms of total tons of warships built or building. Her 894,889 tons (187 ships) ranked behind Great Britain's 2,713,756 tons (485 ships), Germany's 1,304,640 tons (304 ships), and France's 899,915 tons (368 ships), but well ahead of Japan, Russia, Italy, and Austria-Hungary. Moreover, the Americans possessed more battleships and coast defense vessels than France, and that was the standard gauge of superiority in those days.[35] The United States had clearly taken its place among the top naval powers of the modern world, and Tracy had been a paramount contributor.

Tracy lived in an era that was flowery in its eulogies. While he too could deliver a garrulous speech on occasion, the soldier, jurist, and cabinet official was generally direct and sparing with words. The letter he received from Secretary of the Navy Josephus Daniels some three months before his death probably contained all the words that Tracy cared to see accorded his memory.

> Since I became Secretary of the Navy, my whole time and thought has been centered in trying to measure up to the high standard set by my predecessors who, like yourself, have left the Navy better and stronger than they found it.[36]

Notes

Notes to Chapter 1

1. Tracy family history may be found in Genealogy Folder, Box 30, BTLC and in Charles Fitch, *Encyclopedia of Biography of New York* (Boston, 1916), III, 277.

2. Fitch, *Encyclopedia*, III, 278; W. R. Herrick, "General Tracy's Navy" (Unpublished Ph.D dissertation, University of Virginia, 1962), 37.

3. H. R. Stiles, *The Civil, Political, Professional, and Ecclesiastical History and Commercial and Industrial Record of the County, and the City of Brooklyn, N.Y. from 1683 to 1884* (New York, 1884), 1222; Miscellaneous unpublished biographies, Box 30, BTLC.

4. Edward Hungerford, *Men of Erie, A Story of Human Effort* (New York, 1946), 11-12 and Edward Harold Mott, *Between the Ocean and the Lakes, the Story of the Erie* (New York, 1901), 325, 326, 354.

5. Unpublished statement of life of General Benjamin F. Tracy, written by himself, 15 Apr. 1910, Box 30, BTLC.

6. H. F. Gosnell, *Boss Platt and His New York Political Machine* (New York, 1924), 66.

7. Miscellaneous unpublished biographies, Box 30, BTLC; Fitch, *Encyclopedia*, III, 278.

8. Ibid.; Stiles, *History of Kings County*, 1222-1223.

9. *Owego Times,* 2 May 1889, Newspaper Extracts, I, Box 34, BTLC.

10. Fitch, *Encyclopedia,* III, 278; Gosnell, *Boss Platt,* 67; and William B. Gay, *Historical Gazateer of Tioga County, New York* (Syracuse, 1906), 351-352.

11. Miscellaneous unpublished biographies, Box 30, BTLC.

12. Fitch, *Encyclopedia,* III, 278.

13. Gay, *Gazateer,* 86.

14. Address by Isaac Catlin, July 4, 1891 in Souvenir Program, "Dedication of the Soldiers Monument at Owego, N.Y., 4 Jul, 1891," Box 27, BTLC.

15. Sidney David Brummer, *Political History of New York State During the Period of the Civil War* (New York, 1911), 180.

16. Ibid., 181, *Brooklyn Eagle,* 7 Aug. 1915.

17. Miscellaneous unpublished biographies, Box 30, BTLC; Stiles, *History of Kings County,* 5; and Fitch, *Encyclopedia,* 279.

18. *New York Herald,* 27 Apr. 1862, quoted in Brummer, *Political History,* 186.

19. *Journal of the Assembly of the State of New York,* 85th Sess. (Albany, 1862), 279, 353, 391, 480-481, 528, 733, 1074.

20. Ibid., 763-764; Brummer, *Political History,* 173, 188-191, 279, 353, 391, 506, 528, 651, 733.

Notes to Chapter 2

1. Frederick Phisterer, (comp.), *New York in the War of the Rebellion* (Albany, 1912 ed.), I, 33.

2. Tracy–L. L. Livingston, 25 Jul. 1863, Regimental Descriptive, Letter, Order, and Casualty Book, 109th New York Volunteers, (RDLOCB–109), RG 94, AGO, NARS; *Binghamton Standard,* 23 July 1862.

3. Ibid., 30 July 1862.

4. Tracy–Livingston, 25 July 1862; *Binghamton Standard,* 13 Aug. 1862.

5. Ibid., 27 Aug., 3 Sept. 1862; also *Owego Times,* 28 Aug. 1862.

6. *Binghamton Standard,* 3, 19 Sept. 1862.

7. Major General John Wool–Secretary of War, 2 Sep. 1862 in U.S. War Department, *War of the Rebellion: A Compilation of the Official Records of the Union and Confederate Armies* (Washington, 1880-1901), Series I, Volume XII, Part III, page 806 (hereinafter cited *OR* with appropriate series, volume, part, and page).

8. Tracy–Wool, 17 Sept. 1862, RDLOCB–109, RG 94, AGO, NARS.

9. Tracy–J. H. Taylor, 29 June 1862, *OR,* I, XXVII, 406; and various orders in RDLOCB–109, RG 94, AGO, NARS.

10. Tracy—Morgan, 19 Apr. 1863, ibid. and Morgan-Tracy, 27 Apr. 1862, Copybook VII, 49, E. D. Morgan papers, New York State Library, Albany.

11. Morgan–Secretary of War, 24 Mar. 1864; Assistant Secretary of War–Morgan, 26 Mar. 1864, in T 408 (US) 1863), RG 94, AGO, NARS.

12. Tracy–Taylor, 19 Oct. 1863, RDLOCB–109, RG 94, AGO, NARS.

13. Edward Steere, *The Wilderness Campaign* (Harrisburg, 1960), 44; Herrick, "General Tracy's Navy," 49 citing recollection of Mrs. Frederick C. Coudert, Tracy's granddaughter, that in her youth her mother, Emma Louise Tracy Wilmerding, told of meeting Lincoln during a visit to the regimental camp near Washington. The president supposedly congratulated Tracy upon having a lovely little daughter.

14. Steere, *The Wilderness Campaign,* 325.

15. Remarks, Isaac Catlin, Souvenir Brochure, Dedication of Soldiers Monument at Owego, New York, 4 Jul. 1891, Box 31, BTLC. Details of the award appear in Chapter 8. The official reports of division and brigade commanders failed to mention Tracy's exploit despite Catlin's later allusions to recognition by his superiors.

16. Fitch, *Encyclopedia,* III, 279; Phisterer, *New York in the War of the Rebellion,* IV, 2382. Regimental losses totalled 23 killed and 55 wounded in the Wilderness and 46 killed and 71 wounded with 22 captured at Spotsylvania.

17. Examination of Regimental Surgeon, 14 May 1864, Compiled Service Record, Benjamin F. Tracy (Tracy CSR), RG 15, VA, NARS.

18. Tracy–Assistant Adjutant General, IX Corps, 14 May 1864, ibid.

19. Regimental Description Book Card, 127th U.S. Colored Troops, ibid.; *Owego Times* 15 Sept. 1864.

20. Raymond–E. M. Stanton, Tracy–Stanton, both 10 Sept. 1864, Tracy CSR, 127th USCT, RG 15, VA, NARS; Post Order 51, 20 Sept. 1864, General and Special Orders Book, July 1863–January 1865, RG 110, PMG, NARS.

21. C. W. Holmes, *The Elmira Prison Camp: A History of the Military Prison at Elmira, N.Y., July 6, 1864 to July 10, 1865* (New York, 1912), 12-26; also James I. Robertson, Jr., "The Scourge of Elmira," *Civil War History,* VIII, (June 1962), 185.

22. John R. King, *My Experience in the Confederate Army and Northern Prisons* (Clarksburg, West Virginia, 1917), 33.

23. Two modern works treating the Civil War draft although not the draft rendevous administrator are Eugene C. Murdock, *Patriotism Limited, 1862-1865; The Civil War Draft and Bounty System* (Kent, Ohio, 1967) and Leonard L. Lerwill, *The Personnel Replacement System in the United States Army* (Washington, 1954), especially Chapter II.

24. Tracy–H. C. Wood, 17 Jan. 1865, Letters Sent, Elmira Draft Rendezvous, June 1864–Jan. 1865 (LS 64-65), RG 110, PMG, NARS.

25. Various camp inspection reports, general orders, and correspondence, Elmira Draft Rendezvous letterbooks and Box 43, Letters and Telegrams Received 1864-1865 (LTR 64-65), ibid.

26. Tracy–AGO, 17 Oct. 1864 (LS 64-65); Memorandum 15 Nov. 1864, Letterbook 89, District of Western New York, ibid.

27. Tracy–AGO, 4 Jan. 1865, (LTR 64-65), ibid.

28. Tracy–Secretary of War, 15 Feb. 1865, (LS January 1865-February 1866), ibid.

29. Tracy–Wood, 10, 14 Dec. 1864, (LS 64-65); Assistant Adjutant General to Commanding General Elmira, 21 Dec. 1864, (LTR 64-65), ibid.

30. DuBarry–Benjamin C. Card, 11 Oct. 1864, ibid.

31. Tracy–Wood, 10 Dec. 1864, (LS 64-65), ibid.

32. Assistant Adjutant General–Quartermaster, New York City, 21 Feb. 1865, (LTR 64-65), ibid.

33. Notation on bottom of letter, Commanding General X Corps–Assistant Adjutant General X Corps, 2 Nov. 1864, Tracy CSR, 127th USCT, RG 15, VA, NARS.

34. Eastman—William Hoffman, 17 Aug. 1862, OR, II, VII, 603-604.

35. Elmira Advertiser, 29 Sept. 1864.

36. OR, II, VIII, 207-1004, passim.

37. Statement of Prison and Parole Camp Funds, 1864, William Hoffman papers, Box 1, RG 249, OCGP, NARS.

38. Tracy–Hoffman, 1 Dec. 1864, Box 87, Letters Received, 1864 (LR 64), ibid.

39. See for example Tracy's endorsement, 30 Sept. 1864, OR, II, VII, 1004.

40. Hoffman, H. W. Wessells–Tracy, 15 Oct., 12 Dec. 1864, Ibid., 989-990, 1217.

41. Wessels–Tracy, 6 Dec. 1864, ibid., 1195.

42. Tracy–Hoffman, 26 Oct., 1864, Box 87 (LR 64), RG 249, OCGP, NARS.

43. "E"–Editor, 2 Jan. 1865, The Army and Navy Journal, 7 Jan. 1865, 308. The original editorial appeared in the 17 Dec. 1864 issue, 265.

44. Hoffman–Tracy, 25 Feb. 1865, Letterbook, Letters Sent, 1865, I, 568, RG 249, OCGP, NARS. See also Tracy's third endorsement, 25 Feb. 1865 to enclosure Henry Palmer—J. Simpson, 15 Feb. 1865, OR, II, VIII, 232.

45. For the 1876 controversy see U.S. Congressional Record, 44th Cong., 1st Sess. and Special Sess. Senate, IV, 1, 5-24 Mar. 1875 and 44th Cong., 1st Sess., 6 Dec. 1875-10 Feb. 1876, 347-348, 385; Haywood J. Pearce, Benjamin H. Hill: Secession and Reconstruction (Chicago, 1928), 266-268, 272, 274, 278; and David S. Muzzey, James G. Blaine: A Political Idol of Other Days (New York, 1939), 79.

46. Compare the Holmes and Robertson accounts for example.

47. Herrick, "General Tracy's Navy," 42.

48. Tracy–Adjutant General, 5 June 1865; AGO Special Orders 300, 13 June 1865; Special Orders 19, Elmira, 17 June 1865; all Tracy CSR, 127th USCT, RG 15, VA, NARS.

Notes to Chapter 3

1. Gosnell, Boss Platt, 16; J. Lang (compiler and editor), The Autobiography of Thomas Collier Platt (New York, 1910), 11, (hereinafter cited Lang, Platt Autobiography).

2. Harold C. Syrett, The City of Brooklyn, 1865-1898: A Political History (New York, 1944), 16; Stiles, History of Kings County, 1225.

3. Fitch, *Encyclopedia,* III, 280.

4. Tracy–Weed, 21 Sept. 1865, Appointment Papers, Eastern District of New York, B. F. Tracy 1866-1873, Box 495, RG 60, Justice, NARS.

5. Stiles, *History of Kings County,* 1225; Miscellaneous unpublished biographical sketches, Box 30, BTLC.

6. "The Father of the American Navy," 6, unpublished biographical sketch, ibid.; "An Act to Amend Existing Laws Relating to Internal Revenue, and for other Purposes, March 2, 1867," in George P. Sanger, (ed.), *The Statutes at Large, Treaties and Proclamations of the United States of America, from December 1865 to March 1866* (Boston, 1868), XIV, 484.

7. "The Father of the American Navy," 7; Sanger, *The Statutes at Large,* 125-168.

8. Annual Report, District of Eastern New York, 1871, Box 495, RG 60, Justice, NARS.

9. Tracy–President, undated, enclosed, Tracy–A.M. Terry, 21 Dec. 1872, Box 1, BTLC; also Attorney General to District Attorney, Eastern District of New York, 14 Dec. 1872, Box 495, RG 60, Justice, NARS; Tracy–President, 10 Feb. 1873, Roll 46, Series 2, 17 Dec.–10 May 1882, BHLC.

10. War Department General Order 67, 16 July 1867, Compiled Service Record, Benjamin F. Tracy, RG 15, VA, NARS.

11. *Owego Times,* 31 Mar. 1889.

12. For details of trial see Paxton Hibben, *Henry Ward Beecher: An American Portrait* (New York, 1927), 248-271; Stiles, *History of Kings County,* 1220; Chester L. Barrows, *William M. Evarts: Lawyer, Diplomat, Statesman* (Chapel Hill, 1941), Chapter 18.

13. One of Tracy's subsequent legal associates wrote in 1889: "Standing by the old man [Beecher] did not harm any of us, in spite of the boasted power of the press, which was used to crush you. . . ." T. G. Shearman—Tracy, 5 Mar. 1889, Box 1, BTLC.

14. Hibben, *Henry Ward Beecher,* 333.

15. Syrett, *Brooklyn,* especially Chapters II, III.

16. Donald B. Chidsey, *The Gentleman from New York: A Life of Roscoe Conkling* (New Haven, 1935), 284; various unpublished biographical sketches, Box 30, BTLC.

17. Gosnell, *Boss Platt,* 66-67.

18. Unpublished biographical sketches, Box 30, BTLC; Fitch, *Encyclopedia,* 280.

19. Ibid.; Stiles, *History of Kings County,* 1226.

20. W. W. Phelps–Whitelaw Reid, 10 Nov. 1890, quoted in David J. Rothman, *Politics and Power: The United States Senate 1869-1901* (Cambridge, 1966), 164; Gosnell, *Boss Platt,* 25; Lang (ed.) *Platt Autobiography,* 184.

21. Platt suggested in his autobiography that one of the greatest disappointments of his life was his failure to become Secretary of the Treasury; Lang (ed.), *Platt Autobiography,* 184, 206-208. E. I. Lambert, *Stephen Benton Elkins* (Pittsburgh, 1955), makes no mention of any promise to the New York boss.

22. Harry J. Sievers, *Benjamin Harrison; Hoosier President–The White House and After 1889-1901* (Indianapolis, 1968), 6-7.

23. Ibid., 13.

24. Harrison–Elkins, n.d. [Jan. 1889], Series I, Reel 24, BHLC.

25. On the various theories as to who first suggested Tracy to Harrison, see: Sievers, *Hoosier President*, 21, n. 78; Walter R. Herrick, Jr., *The American Naval Revolution* (Baton Rouge, 1965), 42; Elkins–Harrison, 29 Jan. 1889; Reid–Harrison, 6 Feb. 1889, Reels 16 and 17 respectively, and Tracy–Harrison, 2 Jan. 1889, Reel 16, all Series I, BHLC.

26. Quoted by Sievers, *Hoosier President*, 21.

27. *Brooklyn Eagle,* 10 Mar. 1889.

28. Lang (ed.), *Platt Autobiography*, 208; *Brooklyn Eagle,* 10 Mar. 1889.

29. John H. Grow–Harrison, 2 Mar. 1889, Reel 18, BHLC.

30. *Brooklyn Daily Times,* 6 Mar. 1889.

31. *Albany Daily Argus,* 6 Mar. 1889; *The Negro World* (Knoxville), 9 Mar. 1889.

Notes to Chapter 4

1. James D. Richardson (compiler), *A Compilation of the Messages and Papers of the Presidents, 1782-1902* (Washington, 1904), IX, 10.

2. The problems of the post-war navy receive attention in F. M. Bennett, *The Steam Navy of the United States* (Pittsburgh, 1896); Harold and Margaret Sprout, *The Rise of American Naval Power, 1776-1918* (Princeton, 1939); George T. Davis, *A Navy Second to None* (New York, 1940); and Herrick, *American Naval Revolution.*

3. *Revised copy, unidentified speech accompanying Tracy-Thomas S. Moore, 31 Jan. 1890, Box 24, BTLC.*

4. *Sprout, Rise of Naval Power, 165.*

5. *Annual Report, Secretary of the Navy, 1864,* 38 Cong., 2 Sess., House Ex. Doc. No. 1, VI, 23; *Annual Report, 1870,* 41 Cong., 3 Sess., House Ex. Doc. No. 1, III, 3, 55; ____, *The Statistical History of the United States from Colonial Times to the Present* (Stamford, Conn., 1965), 718, 738-739; Tabular statements Chief Yeoman R. M. Bonham, attached to Superintendent Naval Records and Library–C. S. Atkinson, 16 May 1916, Box VN (1), U.S. Navy Dept. Policies, Folder, Statistical Statements, RG 45, NRC, NARS.

6. A recent provocative analysis of the Reconstruction Navy is Lance C. Buhl, "The Smooth Water Navy; American Naval Policy and Politics 1865-1876," Unpublished Ph.D dissertation, Harvard University, 1968.

7. Revisionistic works include: Milton Plesur, *America's Outward Thrust: Approaches to Foreign Affairs, 1865-1890* (DeKalb, Ill., 1971) especially Chapter 1; Healy, *U.S. Expansionism;* Paul S. Holbo, "Economics, Emotion, and Expansion: An Emerging Foreign Policy," in H. Wayne Morgan, ed., *The Gilded Age: Revised and Expanded*

Edition (Syracuse, 1970); Kenneth Hagen, "Protecting American Commerce and Neutrality: The Global Diplomacy, 1877-1889," Unpublished Ph.D dissertation, Claremont Graduate School, 1970.

8. Illustrative of differing opinions are Holbo, "Economics, Emotion, and Expansion . . ." and John A. Garraty, *The New Commonwealth, 1877-1890* (New York, 1968), both of which seek to moderate the stress laid upon economic determinism found in Walter LaFeber, *The New Empire: An Interpretation of American Expansion 1860-1898* (Ithaca, 1963), especially Chapter 1.

9. American historians have tended to muffle the impact of European naval developments upon the American service during the Gilded Age. Useful, however, are Arthur J. Marder, *The Anatomy of British Seapower: A History of British Naval Policy in the Pre-Dreadnought Era, 1880-1905* (New York, 1940), Parts I-III and John A. S. Grenville and George B. Young, *Politics, Strategy and American Diplomacy: Studies in Foreign Policy 1873-1917* (New Haven, 1966), 5-6. On the broader question of European expansion, see D. K. Fieldhouse, *The Colonial Empires; A Comparative Survey from the Eighteenth Century* (New York, 1967 edition).

10. David M. Pletcher, *The Awkward Years: American Foreign Relations Under Garfield and Arthur* (Columbia, Mo., 1962), especially Chapter 7; and Robert Seager II, "Ten Years Before Mahan: The Unofficial Case for the New Navy, 1880-1890," *The Mississippi Valley Historical Review*, XL, (December 1953), 491-512.

11. Thomas Hunt, *Life of William H. Hunt* (Brattleboro, Vt., 1922). The board also recommended an eight-year construction program for ninety-one additional cruisers, twenty-one of which were to be armored, and twenty-five additional torpedo boats. See Report of Advisory Board in U.S. Navy Department, *Annual Report, 1881* (Washington, 1882).

12. On Chandler's administration see L. B. Chandler, *William E. Chandler, Republican* (New York, 1940); on construction of the "ABCD" ships, Leonard A. Swann, Jr., *John Roach, Maritime Entrepreneur* (Annapolis, 1965).

13. Sprout, *Rise of Naval Power, 190-198* portrays the difficulties.

14. See Mark D. Hirsch, *William G. Whitney, Modern Warwick* (New York, 1948), Chapters X, XI.

15. Herrick, *American Naval Revolution,* 36.

16. U.S. Navy Department, *Annual Report, 1888* (Washington, 1889), viii-ix.

17. Ibid., xlv.

18. Quoted in Sprout, *Rise of Naval Power,* 197, n. 54.

19. U.S. *Congressional Record,* 48th Cong., 1 Sess, XV, 1453-1454, 1484-1486.

20. Grenville and Young, *Politics, Strategy, and American Diplomacy,* 6.

21. Marder, *The Anatomy of British Sea Power,* especially Chapter VIII.

22. See for example, U.S. Navy Department, Office of Naval Intelligence, *Recent Naval Progress, June 1887* [General Information Series, No. VI, Information From Abroad] (Washington, 1887), and various issues of *The Proceedings of the United States Naval Institute, 1881-1889,* (USNIP).

23. Sprout, *Rise of Naval Power,* 198; Grenville and Young, *Politics, Strategy, and American Diplomacy,* 5-10.

24. Stephen B. Luce, "Our Future Navy" reprinted from *North American Review* in *USNIP*, XV (1889), 4, 541-559, and Butler's comments appear in U.S. *Congressional record*, 49 Cong., 2 Sess., XVIII, 1807, and 50 Cong., 1 Sess., V, XIX, 6720.

25. Herrick, *American Naval Revolution*, 38; Sprout, *Rise of Naval Power*, 189, alludes to traditional Democratic neglect of the navy.

26. E. G. Dunnell, "Secretary of the Navy, Benjamin F. Tracy," *The Epoch* (New York), V, #122, 7 Jun. 1889, 285.

27. *The Negro World* (Knoxville), 9 Mar. 1889; *The Maritime Reporter* (New York), 14 Mar. 1889; also, Memorandum, 12 Mar. 1913, Folder, Description of Private Office of Secretary of Navy, Box 8, Subject File, VA, Administration and Organization, RG 45, NRC, NARS.

28. Quoted in *Louisville Courier-Journal*, 10 Mar. 1889.

29. *Brooklyn Daily Times*, 17 Apr. 1889. Tracy almost resigned later in his tenure due to financial strain with expenses exceeding $15,000 a year. See *Philadelphia Press*, 4 Dec. 1892. Secretary's salary appears in U.S. Navy Department, *Annual Report, 1890* (Washington, 1891), Appendix A; and Tracy's decision to "give regular days to . . . professional practice," was quoted in Platt to Tracy, 2 Dec. 1890, Box 7, BTLC.

30. *Portsmouth* (NH) *Chronicle*, 12 Nov. 1889.

31. Kimberly's report appears in U.S. Navy Department, *Annual Report, 1889* (Washington, 1890), Appendix IV, 95-123; public reaction can be measured in Washington *Chronicle*, 31 Mar. 1889, and *Brooklyn Daily Times*, 30 Mar. 1889.

32. Porter–Luce, 14 Mar. 1889, SLLC. Porter also told Luce that Tracy promised to confer with him adding "but I have a strong friend in the President who will express to the Secretary his wishes that he shall consult me." A letter to the editor of the *Philadelphia Evening Bulletin*, 7 Jun. 1889, intimated that line officers were about to capture Tracy through Lieutenant T.B.M. Mason's installation as "naval secretary" to the cabinet official. The *Portsmouth Chronicle*, 27 Aug. 1889 hinted that Commodore Walker had Tracy in his pocket.

33. John D. Long quoted in Leonard D. White, *The Republican Era: A Study in Administrative History, 1869-1901* (New York, 1958), 166.

34. A. T. Mahan, "The Principles of Naval Administration," in *Naval Administration and Warfare: Some General Principles with Other Essays* (Boston, 1908), 7. Tracy may have been aware also of Stephen B. Luce, "Naval Administration," *USNIP*, XIV, (1888), 46, 561-588 and 47, 725-737.

35. Charles Oscar Paullin, *Paullin's History of Naval Administration 1775-1911* (Annapolis, 1968), 328.

36. *The Republic* (Washington D.C.), 20 Oct. 1889.

37. U.S. Navy Department, *Annual Report, 1889* (Washington, 1890), 38-39.

38. *The Maritime Reporter and Seaboard* (New York), 4 Jul. 1889.

39. Cited in White, *The Republican Era*, 173-174.

40. *New York Evening Post*, 19 Mar. 1889, and *Brooklyn Daily Times*, 18 Mar. 1889. Tracy's intentions also appeared in a much publicized letter to an employee at the Washington Navy Yard, discharged for inefficiency despite his status as a Union veteran; see *New York Times*, 23 Mar. 1889.

41. Favorable response to Tracy's intentions may be found in Corresp. to Tracy including W. G. Low, 2 Apr. 1889, Box 1; criticism in T. C. Platt, undated, Box 15, H. C. Lodge, 8 May 1889, and M. P. Wentworth-Thomas Reed, 23 Apr., 2 May 1889, all Box 1; and Tracy's retrenchment in his letters to S. F. Fischer, 2 Nov. 1889 and D. L. Braine, 30 Dec. 1889, Box 24, all BTLC.

42. *Washington Evening Star,* 3 Apr. 1889; *Philadelphia Item,* 7 Apr. 1889; *New York World,* 29 Jul. 1890.

43. Quoted in Herrick, *American Naval Revolution,* 48; also Luce–Porter, 9 Mar. 1889, quoted in Albert Gleaves, *Life and Letters of Rear Admiral Stephen B. Luce, U. S. Navy* (New York, 1925), 185-186.

44. Luce–Tracy, 19 Mar. 1889, Box 7, BTLC; Tracy–Luce, 30 Mar. 1889, Box 9, SLLC.

45. Luce, "Our Future Navy," 541-559 with all quotes therefrom.

46. Tracy–McCann, 16 Jul. 1889 printed as Appendix A to U.S. Congress, Senate, Letter from Secretary of the Navy, 51st Cong., 1 sess., Senate Ex. Doc. 43, 29 Jan. 1890. Other board members included Captain R. L. Phythian, Captain W. T. Sampson, Commander W. M. Folger, Lieutenant Commander W. H. Brownson, Naval Constructor B. Gatewood, and Ensign Philip R. Alger as Recorder.

47. *New York Times,* 31 July 1889.

48. For differences of opinion as to Mahan's influence on Tracy and others at this time see W. E. Livesey, *Mahan on Sea Power* (Norman, 1947), 272; Herrick, *American Naval Revolution,* 43, relying upon Richard S. West, *Admirals of American Empire* (Indianapolis, 1948), 149.

49. U.S. Navy Department, *Annual Report, 1889,* 35; *The Army and Navy Journal* (Philadelphia), 5, 19 Oct. 1889; *New York World,* 19 Nov. 1889.

50. Compare the traditional interpretation of Mahan's influence on the document as found in Herrick, Sprout, La Feber, and Walter R. Millis, ed. *American Military Thought* (Indianapolis, 1966), Document 26, 226-239 with that of Grenville and Young who offer a more plausible attribution to Luce's influence since even Tracy's figure of capital ships coincided with that of Luce's in "Our Future Navy."

51. U.S. Navy Department, *Annual Report, 1889,* 5. That Tracy was thinking about battleships in the early fall emerges from his letter to Eugene Hale, 27 Sept. 1889, Letterbook, 17 Jul. 1889-5 May 1890, Box 24, BTLC.

52. U.S. Navy Department, *Annual Report, 1889,* 5.

53. Ibid., 49-50.

54. *New York Daily Tribune,* 6 Dec. 1889; *New York Times,* 2 Dec. 1889, *St. Louis Republic,* 3 Dec. 1889, and *The Army and Navy* Journal, 7 Dec. 1889.

55. Chadwick–Tracy, 26 Dec. 1889; Catlin–Tracy, 3 Dec. 1889, both Box 4 BTLC; Mahan–Luce, 3 Dec. 1889, Box 9, SLLC.

56. Millis, *American Military Thought,* 226-227 and *Arms and Men: A Study in American Military History* (New York, 1956), 156-157; Herrick, *American Naval Revolution,* 43, 68; Sprout, *Rise of Naval Power,* 207; La Feber, *New Empire,* 122-124; West, *Admirals of American Empire,* 146; John K. Mahon, "Benjamin F. Tracy," *New York Historical Society Quarterly,* XLIV (April 1960), 185: and Vincent Davis, *The Admiral's Lobby* (Chapel Hill, 1967), 103-106.

Notes to Chapter 5

1. *New York Tribune,* 31 Dec. 1890.

2. Hale–Tracy, 10 Oct. 1889, Box 3 BTLC. Hale also requested any "advanced sheets" of Tracy's annual report due at the end of November.

3. U.S. *Congressional Record,* 51st Cong. 1st sess., 3163-3170; *New York Mail and Express,* 6 Dec. 1889.

4. Luce–Tracy, 18 Mar. 1892, Box 9, SLLC.

5. Chandler–Tracy, 9, 10 Jan. 1890, Box 24, BTLC; *Brooklyn Times,* 13 Jan. 1890.

6. "Report of the Policy Board," *Proceedings of the United States Naval Institute,* XVI (1890), 207-273.

7. Peter Karsten, "The Naval Aristocracy: United States Naval Officers from the 1840's to the 1920's; Mahan's Messmates," (Unpublished Ph.D Dissertation, University of Wisconsin, 1968), 373, also 372, 475.

8. "Report of the Policy Board," especially 206-209, 211; U.S. *Congressional Record,* 51st Cong., 1st sess., 6398. See also U.S. Navy Department, *Annual Report, 1887* (Washington, 1888), 3. La Feber, *The New Empire,* 123 states the report made "Tracy's paper seem almost anti-expansionist."

9. 51st Cong., 1st sess., Senate Executive Document 43, 1-2. Donald W. Mitchell, *History of the Modern American Navy* (New York, 1943), 21-22 suggests that the report was so out of touch with Congressional sentiment as to be quite devoid of effect as the earlier Rodgers Board report in 1882.

10. Chester–Luce, undated but 1890, Box 9, SLLC.

11. Expansionist press reception is reflected in *New York Herald,* 31 Jan. 1890, *New York Globe,* 8 Feb. 1890; Quaker opposition in U.S. *Congressional Record,* 51st Cong., 1st sess., XXI, No. 4, 3166-3167.

12. Tracy–William C. Sanger, 21 Jan. 1890, Box 24; Hale–Tracy, 24 Jan. 1890, Box 15, BTLC; L. F. Watson–Tracy, 14 Feb. 1890, Case 6807, Letters Received, 1890, Office, Secretary of the Navy (OSN), RG 80, GRN.

13. Miller–Howard Cole, 3 Feb. 1890, cited in Harry Sievers, *Hoosier President,* 143, n. 7. *Harper's Weekly,* 15 Feb. 1890 gives a full account of the fire. The *New York Tribune,* 4 Feb. 1890 carried a front page diagram of Tracy's house calling it the best known in Washington. Harrison wrote to Ambassador Whitelaw Reid in Paris; "Tracy . . . is entirely well in body and shows a brave spirit. He said yesterday that he wanted to resume his work and will probably do so in a few days." Harrison–Reid, 7 Feb. 1890, WRLC.

14. *New York Herald,* 17 Mar. 1890; *New York Daily Tribune,* 5 Mar. 1890.

15. *Brooklyn Daily Eagle,* 26 Mar. 1890; *Washington Post,* 19 Mar. 1890; 51st Cong., 1st sess., Senate Executive Document 89; and *Boston Evening Transcript,* 24 Mar. 1890.

16. Boutelle–Tracy, 7 Mar. 1890, Herbert–Tracy, 10 Mar. 1890, Box 5 BTLC. See also Hugh B. Hammett, "Hilary Abner Herbert, A Southerner Returns to the Union," (Unpublished Ph.D Dissertation, University of Virginia, 1969), 187-199.

17. Porter–Boutelle, 3 Jan. 1890, Box 8, General Correspondence, 1890-1899, DPLC; Luce–Boutelle, 29, 30, 1889, 1 Mar. 1890, all Box 9, SLLC.

18. Boutelle–Luce, 6 Mar. 1890, Box 9, SLLC, 51st Cong., 1st sess., House Report 1178, 26. Thus Boutelle's committee tacitly endorsed the arguments of both Tracy and the Policy Board.

19. U.S. *Congressional Record,* XXI, 3161-3171, 3221-3223, 3256-3261 for House; 5173-5182, 5236-5238, 5276-5297 for Senate. See also minority report of Senate Naval Affairs Committee in 51st Cong., 1st sess., Senate Report, 174, 1-7; *New York Tribune,* 10 Apr. 1890; *Washington Post,* 10 Apr. 1890.

20. See Lodge's remarks in *Congressional Record, Ibid.,* 3169-3170. Voting totals included in the House 131-105 and Senate 33-18 with sectional and partisan spirit blurring in the upper chamber. 26 House Democrats voted for the new style vessels and 24 of them represented coastal constituencies; of the 23 Republicans in opposition, 22 represented the hinterland, Ibid., 3395-5297.

21. U.S. Department of the Navy, *Navy Yearbook 1917* (Washington, 1917), 739, 758, 766.

22. U.S. Navy Department, *Annual Report, 1890* (Washington, 1891), 13, 14, 37. Tracy's statement indicates the possibility that even the original figure was negotiable. Herrick, *American Naval Revolution,* 83, discusses these other provisions.

23. Testimony of Tracy, 6 Feb. 1896, 54th Cong., 2d sess., Senate Report 1457, *Prices of Armor for Vessels of the Navy,* 11 Feb. 1897, 122.

24. Herrick, *American Naval Revolution,* 64; Dean Allard, "The Influence of the U.S. Navy upon the American Steel Industry, 1880-1900," (Unpublished M.A. thesis, Georgetown University, 1959), especially chapter II; American Iron and Steel Association, *History of the Manufacture of Armor Plate for the United States Navy,* (Philadelphia, 1890), 17-21. On steel inspection, see President Steel Inspection Board-Assistant Secretary of the Navy, 21 Oct. 1890, Case 10019, Letters Received, 1890, OSN, RG 80, GRN, NARS. Also U.S. Navy Department *Annual Report, 1886* and *1887,* 10-12 and iii-v respectively. Congress decreed in 1886 that builders of American warships should use only materials of "domestic manufacture."

25. American Iron and Steel Association, *History of Armor Plate,* 1; 59th Cong., 2d sess., House Document 193, *Cost of Armor Plate and Armor Plant,* 6 Dec. 1906, 6-7; W. H. Jasques, "Description of the Works of the Bethlehem Iron Company," *USNIP,* XV, (1889), 531-540.

26. Senate Report, *Prices of Armor,* 122; Bisphan–Tracy, 15 May, 1889, Box 2, BTLC. The all-steel plate was a homogeneous plate while the compound plate was a steel hard-surface plate welded upon a softer back, the object being to present a hard surface which would break up the projectile upon the initial point of contact before it entered the plate.

27. Senate Report, *Prices of Armor,* 122-124; Tracy–Ritchie, 7 Mar. 1892, Letterbook 3, Box 26; George A. Evans–Tracy, 15 Oct. 1889, Box 3, both BTLC. Tracy stated incorrectly in his annual report for 1890 that the department became aware of Riley's talk in July 1890.

28. Senate Report, *Prices of Armor,* 24; F. M. Barber–Tracy, 16 Nov. 1889, Box 4, BTLC, portray's Creusot's opposition.

29. U.S. Navy Department, *Annual Report, 1892* (Washington, 1893), 14; Vice President of Bethlehem Iron Company—Tracy, J. W. Philip—Tracy, both 23 Dec. 1889, Barber—Tracy, 19 Jan. 1890, all Box 4, BTLC.

30. Robert Lindemann–Tracy, 25 Jan. 1890 in U.S. Navy Department, *Annual Report, 1890,* (Washington, 1891), and *1891* (Washington, 1892), 17-18 and 19 respectively.

31. Senate Report, *Prices of Armor,* 143, also 131-132.

32. Various undated correspondence Carnegie–W. L. Abbott, October 1889-April 1890, traces these developments, Volume 240, A-L, ACLC.

33. J. S. Morgan–Carnegie, 7 June 1890; F. Rey–Abbott, 6 and 30 May, 1890, all Volume 11 ACLC. These documents reflect the extent of negotiations between Carnegie, Phipps and Company and Le Ferro Nickel with Rey representing the latter's London office.

34. Abel Rey–Carnegie, 16, 23, 26, June 1890; Morgan–Carnegie, 20 Jun. 1890; W. H. Emory–Carnegie, n.d. and 26 June 1890; Abbott–Carnegie, 23 June 1890, all Volume 11, ACLC; also Naval Attache–London–Chief, Bureau of Navigation, 16, 18, 21, June 1890, London Attache Letterbook, 1890, RG 38, ONI, NARS. Both Abbott and the London attache briefed Carnegie on these developments.

35. Carnegie–Tracy 5 July 1890; Abbott–Tracy, 17 July 1890, Box 6, BTLC; Senate Report, *Prices of Armor,* 143-145.

36. Carnegie–Tracy, 19 July 1890; Emory–Carnegie, 30 June 2, 3 Jul. 1890; Rey–Carnegie, 3 July 1890; J. F. Hull–Carnegie, 4, 6 July 1890; J. Scott–Carnegie, 6 July 1890; Carnegie–Carnegie, Phipps, and Company, 7 July 1890, all Volume 11, ACLC.

37. Carnegie–Tracy, 23 July 1890; various telegrams, Carnegie–home office, Volume 11 ACLC.

38. R. H. Sayre–Tracy, 24 July 1890, Box 6, BTLC; Carnegie–Tracy, 27 Aug. 1890, Volume 11, ACLC; also U.S. Navy Department, *Annual Report, 1890,* 18.

39. U.S. Navy Department, *Annual Report, 1890,* 20-21; L. A. Kimberly, "Report of the Board on the Competitive Trial of Armor Plate," *USNIP,* XVI, (1890), 620-645.

40. Barber–Tracy, 19 June 1890; S. J. Ritchie–Tracy, 28 June, 28 Aug., 8 Sept., 1890, all Box 6, BTLC.

41. Carnegie–Tracy, 10 Sept. 1890; Ritchie–Carnegie, Phipps and Company, 28 Aug., 1890, copy, both Box 6, BTLC; Abbott–Carnegie, 23 June 1890, Volume 11, ACLC.

42. Tracy–McKinley, 15 Mar. 1890, Box 25; Ritchie–Tracy, 30 Mar. 1891, Box 8, BTLC.

43. Folger–Luce, 24 Feb. 1890, Box 9 SLLC; U. S. *Congressional Record,* 51st Cong., 1st sess., 1890, XXI, part 2, 10452, 10460-10463. Allard, "Influence upon Steel Industry," 100-101. Gorman opposed flaunting naval stimulation of domestic refining and manufacturing industries. Also U.S. Navy Department, *Annual Report, 1890, 1892,* 21-22 and 21 respectively.

44. *New York Tribune,* 29 Oct. 1890; Corresp. Folger–Tracy, 18 Oct. 1890; Abbott–Tracy, 12 Sept. 1890; Carnegie–Tracy, 10 Sept. 1890; Joseph Wharton–Tracy, 25 Sept. 1890, all Box 6, BTLC; also U.S. Navy Department, *Annual Report, 1890,* 21.

45. *New York Times,* 6 Oct. 1890; Abbott–Tracy, 14 Oct. 1890; David Reeves–Tracy, 15 Oct. 1890, Cases 9984 and 9985 and Case 9499 with respect to conference scheduled for 7 Oct. 1890, all in Letters Received, 1890, OSN, RG 80, GRN, NARS.

46. U.S. Navy Department, *Annual Report, 1892*, 19; Copy of contract in Folder, Contract for Steel Armor, 1890, BR Armor and Armament, Subject Files, RG 45, NRC, NARS. See also Carnegie–Tracy, 27 Nov. 1890, Box 7, BTLC; Carnegie–Tracy, 1 Dec. 1890, Case 10388, Letters Sent; 1890, OSN, RG 80, GRN, NARS.

47. President, Steel Inspection Board–Tracy, 28 Nov. 1890, Case 10882, Letters Received, 1890, RG 80, GRN, NARS; *The Pittsburg* (Pa) *Dispatch*, 7 Dec. 1890.

48. Tracy–Cameron, 4 Nov. 1890, Box 24, BTLC; *New York World*, 23 Aug. 1890; Commandant, New York Navy Yard–Chief, Bureau of Construction and Repairs, 5 Dec. 1890, Case 11705; Report of the U.S. Torpedo Boat *Cushing*, 18 Oct. 1890, Case 10104, both in Letters Received, 1890, OSN, RG 80, GRN, NARS.

49. *Brooklyn Daily Eagle*, 12 June 1890; F. F. Bowles–Tracy, 10 Feb. 1890, Box 4, BTLC; Commandant New York Navy Yard–Chief, Bureau of Yards and Docks, 1 Apr. 1890, Case 7174, D. L. Braine–Tracy, 19 Nov. 1890, Case 10660, both Letters Received 1890, OSN, RG 80, GRN, NARS; 51st Cong., 1st sess., House Executive Document 315, 35; *New York Press*, 19 Nov. 1890.

50. Herrick, *American Naval Revolution*, 78.

51. Richard K. Morris, *John P. Holland, 1814-1914: Inventor of the Modern Submarine* (Annapolis, 1968), 62.

52. U.S. Navy Department, *Annual Report, 1890*, 38. Tracy may have taken this allusion from John R. Spears, "The American Navy," *The Chautauquan*, XI (May, 1890), 171-181, especially 178. Even Porter warned Boutelle on the defenselessness of the East Coast in a letter 3 Jan. 1890, Box 8, DPLC.

53. U.S. Navy Department, *Annual Report, 1890*, 40. Tracy later told a reporter: "Before I wrote my report I sent a naval officer to New York on a reconnoitering tour, and if I had repeated all that he said in his report I would have been called an alarmist. There is no question at all of the danger to which we are exposed should a foreign fleet come to attack us." See *Washington Post*, 2 Apr. 1891.

54. U.S. Navy Department, *Annual Report, 1890*, 41.

55. Compare *Memphis Commercial*, 7 Dec. 1890 with *New York Tribune*, 1 Dec. 1890, *New York Daily Press*, 5 Dec. 1890, and *New York Times*, 5 Dec. 1890.

Notes to Chapter 6

1. Wayne H. Morgan, *From Hayes to McKinley: National Party Politics, 1877-1895* (Syracuse, 1969), 354-356; Sievers, *Hoosier President*, 181.

2. *New Orleans Times Democrat*, 21 Apr. 1891; *St. Louis Republic*, 2 May 1891.

3. Hale–Tracy, 30 Dec. 1890; Copy, Boutelle–Luce, 19 Dec. 1890, both Box 7 BTLC. For Tracy's comments to reporter, see *New York Daily Tribune*, 6 Mar. 1891.

4. 51st Cong., 2d sess., House *Report on Naval Appropriations* Bill, No. 3339, 20 Dec. 1890, 12; U.S. *Congressional Record*, Senate, 51st Cong., 2d sess., XXII, 3, 2428.

5. Carnegie–Tracy, 9 May 1891, Box 9, BTLC; Carnegie–Blaine, 10 May 1891, Letterbook 17, ACLC; *Pittsburg* (Pa.) *Dispatch*, 19 Feb. 1891.

6. Cramp-Tracy, 27 Feb. 1891, Box 8, and 10 Nov. 1891, Box 10; also T. W. Hyde-Tracy, 23 Nov., 1891, Box 10, all BTLC.

7. Assistant Secretary of Navy-Commandant New York Navy Yard, 24 Dec. 1891, Letterbook, Assistant Secretary of Navy, 1892, RG 90, GRN, NARS. See also, Assistant Naval Constructor-Secretary of Navy, 12 Jul. 1891, Box 9, BTLC.

8. Henry Sanger-Tracy, 2 Mar. 1891; W. Potts-Tracy, 13 Mar. 1891, both Box 8; Tracy-R. Doliot, 10 Mar. 1891, Box 25, all BTLC. On Harrison and civil service reform see Sievers, *Hoosier President,* 73 n, 75-76, 134, 136.

9. Speech text in Speech Book, Box 27, BTLC. Newspapers apparently received the crux of Tracy's statement several days early, see, *New York Herald,* 5 Apr. 1891; *Boston Herald,* 8 Apr. 1891.

10. Tracy explained these procedures to the Chairman of the New York Republican Committee in September 1892, Tracy-Thomas H. Carter, 28 Sept. 1892, Box 26, BTLC.

11. *New York Sun,* 7 Apr. 1891; *New York Tribune,* 11 Apr. 1891; Correspondence to Tracy from John Leech, 6 Apr. 1891; F. C. Cocheu, 17 Apr. 1891; L. B. Swift, 22 Apr. 1891, all Box 8; and Scrapbook, 9 Apr.-27 Jul. 1891, Box 37, all BTLC.

12. *New York Herald,* 5 Apr. 1891; *The Army and Navy Register,* (Washington D.C.), 11 Apr. 1891.

13. U.S. Navy Department, Special Orders, "Reorganization of Civil Force Navy Yards, 1891-1892;" Board Minutes and Correspondence, OSN, 1891, RG 80, GRN, NARS; U.S. Navy Department, *Annual Report, 1891* (Washington, 1892), 49-51, and *1892* (Washington, 1893), 49-53.

14. Platt-Tracy, 18 Sep. 1891; Reed-Tracy, 1 Aug. 1891; C. W. Fish-Tracy, 20 Nov. 1891, all in BTLC and quoted in Herrick, *American Naval Revolution,* 137.

15. U.S. Navy Department, *Annual Report, 1889* (Washington, 1890), 32.

16. *New York World,* 28 Nov. 1891.

17. Sievers, *Hoosier President,* Chapter 10; Decker, Howell and Co.-Tracy, 12 Sept. 1890; Platt-Tracy, 12 Sept. 1890, both Box 6, BTLC; W. Windom-Harrison, 14 Sept. 1890; Tracy-Harrison, 13, 14, 16, Sept. 1890, Series I, Reel 29, BHLC.

18. On Barrundia affair see, John B. Moore, *A Digest of International Law* (2 vols., Washington, 1906), II, 871-876; A. F. Tyler, *The Foreign Policy of James G. Blaine* (Minneapolis, 1927), 103-106.

19. Accounts of the Haitian affair may be found in Ludwill Lee Montague, *Haiti and the United States, 1714-1938* (Durham, 1948), Chapter 9; Rayford Logan, *The Diplomatic Relations of the United States with Haiti, 1776-1891* (Chapel Hill, 1941).

20. Allan B. Spetter, "Harrison and Blaine: Foreign Policy 1889-1893," (Unpublished Ph.D dissertation, Rutgers University, 1967), especially Chapter VII. Herrick, *American Naval Revolution,* 96-97 suggests Tracy's indebtedness to Clyde evolved from the latter's service as stock broker for the general as well as retainership of Tracy's law firm by Clyde's steamship lines.

21. "Notes For Reports and Speeches, 1889-1892," Box 31, BTLC.

22. Douglass's assignment was apparently a reward for services to the Republican party in 1888 and much of the racism can be traced to local naval officer dislike of

the Negro diplomat. Gherardi–Tracy, 7 Jan. 1891, Box 31, BTLC; *New York Mail and Express,* 26 Mar. 1891; *New York World,* 21 Aug. 1891.

23. Gherardi–Tracy, 11 Jan. 1890, 11; Tracy–Blaine, 28 May 1890, 218, both in Letterbook 1, Letters to Cabinet Officials, RG 24, BNP, NARS; also Clyde–Tracy, 21 Apr. 1891, Box 8; Clyde–Tracy, 16 Aug. 1890 (telegram and letter), Box 6, BTLC.

24. *New York Herald,* 24 May 1891; Douglass–Blaine, 21 Apr. 1891 (copy), Letters Received, 1891, OSN, RG 80, GRN, NARS; Gherardi–Tracy, 21 Apr. 1891, Letter-book, Translations of Messages Received in Cipher, RG 45, NRC, NARS; Tracy–Gherardi, 24 Apr. 1891, Box 8; Clyde–Tracy, 14, 18, 27, May 1891, Box 9, both BTLC.

25. Blaine–Harrison, 10 Aug. 1891 in Albert T. Volwiler, (ed.), *The Correspondence Between Benjamin Harrison and James G. Blaine* (Philadelphia, 1940), 173; W. Wharton–Tracy, 3 Aug. 1891, enclosing Carry–Blaine, 17 Jul. 1891, Box 31, BTLC. Contrary to Herrick, *American Naval Revolution,* 91, n. 18, Tracy did nothing about the Danish islands later in his tenure.

26. On the Portugeese negotiations see Herrick, *American Naval Revolution,* 92-93; La Feber, *New Empire,* 110.

27. *New York Herald,* 23 May 1891; *New York Daily Tribune,* 9 Aug. 1891 rejoiced at Tracy's failure to get a naval base site which it contended would only involve the nation unduly in Latin American political affairs.

28. La Feber, *New Empire,* 130-131; Herrick, *American Naval Revolution,* 108-110.

29. McCann–Tracy, 30 Mar. 1891, Translations of Messages Received in Cipher, RG 45, NRC, NARS. See U.S. Navy Department, *Annual Report, 1891,* Appendix D, for ship movements.

30. Harrison–Miller, 6 May, 1891, Volume 122, BHLC. A useful chronology prepared later appears attached to D. W. Knox–Severino A. Russo, 21 Mar. 1946, Correspondence Relative Chile, 1892-1910, Folder VI, Subject File, VI, Class 2, International Relations and Politics, RG 45, NRC, NARS.

31. Osgood Hardy, "The Itata Incident," *Hispanic American Historical Review,* V, (May 1892), 195 ff; La Feber, *New Empire,* 132; Herrick, *American Naval Revolution,* 111.

32. Tracy–Brown, 26 Mar. 1891, quoted in U.S. Navy Department, *Annual Report, 1891,* 23-25; Tracy–McCann, 20 May 1891, Trans. Mess. Recd. and Sent in Cipher, 1891, RG 45, NRC, NARS.

33. U.S. Navy Department, *Annual Report, 1891,* 27; Osgood Hardy, "Was Patrick Egan a Blundering Minister?" *Hispanic American Historical Review,* VIII, (February 1928), 66-87.

34. Harrison–Blaine, 26 Sept. 1891 in Volwiler, *Correspondence of Harrison and Blaine,* 196; Reid–Blaine, 9 June 1891 (copy), Letters Received, 1891, OSN, RG 80, GRN, NARS.

35. *New York Herald,* 5 Sept. 1891, 19 Jan. 1892; Harrison–Wharton, 2 Sept. 1891; Miller–Harrison, 7 Sept. 1891, both Series I, Reel 32, BHLC.

36. A good synopsis of this affair appears in Herrick, *American Naval Revolution,* 118-121.

37. Carnegie–Harrison, 26 Oct. 1891, Volume 31, ACLC; Sievers, *Hoosier President,* 193; La Feber, *New Empire,* 134-136.

38. Tracy quoted in W. E. Curtis, *From the Andes to the Ocean* (Chicago, 1900), 411.

39. *New York Morning Advertiser,* 19 Jan. 1892; Robley D. Evans. *A Sailors Log: Recollections of Forty Years of Naval Life* (New York, 1903), 277. Harrison's private secretary noted in his diary that the whole cabinet was for war. While not strictly true, considering Blaine's ambivalence, Tracy's clandestine work of uniting the cabinet in support of Harrison's policy apparently produced results. See Sievers, *Hoosier President,* 195; La Feber, *New Empire,* 134.

40. Sievers, *Hoosier President,* 183-190; Herrick, "General Tracy's Navy, 229-230. The crisis resulted from a lynching of Italian Mafia members by a New Orleans mob in 1890. Tracy told Harrison that the American navy was incapable of fighting the stronger Italian fleet. The crisis passed with Tracy somewhat the beneficiary since he used the war scare to point up the need for more warships and coastal defenses. See *Brooklyn Daily Eagle,* 1, 2, Apr. 1891; *Chicago Inter-Ocean,* 2 Apr. 1891.

41. U.S. Navy Department, *Annual Report, 1892,* 37-38; Curtis, *From the Andes,* 412-413; A. T. Volwiler, "Harrison, Blaine, and American Foreign Policy," *American Philosophical Society Proceedings,* LXXXIX (1938), 643-647; Unidentified Memorandum, "List of Vessels of U.S. Navy ready in view of possible service against Chili" and Unidentified clipping from *Buenos Aires Herald,* showing Chilean naval strength, both in Box 31, BTLC.

42. Report, Lieutenant A. G. Winterhalter on Chilean War Vessels, 14 Nov. 1891, Ltrs. Recd. 1891, OSN, RG 80, GRN; Forsythe–Tracy, 6 Jan. 1892; Walker–Tracy, 20 Jan. 1892, both in Area File 4, RG 45; all NARS.

43. Tracy quoted in *New York Times,* 30 Jan. 1892.

44. Albert Gleaves, *The Life of an American Sailor: Rear Admiral William Hemsley Emory, United States Navy; From His Letters and Memoirs* (New York, 1923), 133, 148. Platt quoted in Albert Daggett–Tracy, n.d., Box 15, BTLC.

45. La Faber, *New Empire,* 136.

46. Stephen Gwynne, (ed.), *The Letters and Friendships of Sir Cecil Spring-Rice* (Boston, 1929), II, 118.

47. B. F. Tracy, "Our New Warships," *North American Review,* CLL, (June 1891), 655. See also J. H. Biles–Tracy, 13 Mar. 1891; Engineer in Chief-Secretary of Navy, 28 Apr. 1891, both in Ltrs. Recd. 1891, OSN, RG 80, GRN, NARS; Harrison Loring–Tracy, 31 Mar. 1891, Box 8, BTLC.

48. Gwynne, *Letters of Spring-Rice,* I, 64; John Garraty, *Henry Cabot Lodge* (New York, 1953), 646.

Notes to Chapter 7

1. U.S. Navy Department, *Annual Report, 1891* (Washington, 1892), 31-33.

2. Ibid., 38; also *New York Press, New York World,* both 13 Aug. 1891; *New York Herald,* 16 Sept. 1891.

3. List of Vessels, enclosed with Chief Intelligence Officer-Secretary of Navy, 30 Nov. 1891, Case 7303, Subject File (OD), Ships of Navy Distribution, Box 356, RG 45, NRC, NARS. Of the fifty-one, seven were regarded as unserviceable, twelve were sailing vessels including two ships of the line, and fourteen were tugs.

4. Richardson, *Messages and Papers of the Presidents.* IX, 200-201.

5. Morgan–Tracy, 25 Nov. 1891, Box 10; Whitney–Tracy, Box 11, both BTLC.

6. A. C. Buell–Charles H. Cramp, 17 Sept. 1891, Box 10 BTLC.

7. Luce–Tracy, 18 Mar. 1892, Box 9, SLLC.

8. Boutelle–W. B. Remey, 17 Apr. 1892, Box 12, BTLC.

9. Debate on this bill can be followed in U.S. *Congressional Record,* 52d Cong., 2d sess., House, XXIII, pt. 4, 3223-3331, 52d Cong., 1st sess., XXII, pt. 5, Senate 4215-4221, 4245-4267, 4309-4325, 4352-4368; pt. 7, 6137-6190. Chandler originally introduced legislation reflecting Tracy's desires—3 battleships, 2 coast defense vessels, 5 gunboats, and 8 torpedo boats.

10. Barber–Tracy, 30 July 1891, enclosing Schneider and Company-Secretary of Navy, 7 July 1891, Box 9; Barber–Tracy, 29 Aug. 1891, Box 10, all BTLC. Also "The Armor Tests, December 10, 1891," *Proceedings of the United States Naval Institute,* XVIII, 1892, 61, 147-148; Cramp–Tracy, 24 Sep. 1891, Case 5776, Letters Received and Sent, 1891, OSN, RG 80, GRN, NARS; Carnegie–Tracy, 10, 28 Dec. 1891, Box 11, BTLC; and *Philadelphia Evening Bulletin,* 14 Oct. 1891.

11. Joseph Frazier Wall, *Andrew Carnegie,* (New York, 1970), Chapter XVI, describes the crisis; see also President, Bethlehem Iron Company-Chief, Bureau of Ordnance, 1 Apr. 1892, Case 2615, Ltrs. Recd., 1892, OSN, RG 80, GRN; Folger–Herbert, 8 Jun. 1892, Papers Relating to HR 7093, No. 1, Drawer 3854, Committee on Naval Affairs, 1st sess., RG 233, HR, both NARS.

12. *Philadelphia North American,* 15 Oct. 1892. Buell–Tracy, 15 Oct. 1892, Box 13, BTLC shows that Tracy's division of work was not unique and that the expedient may even have been employed a year earlier. Also W. C. Cowles-Assistant Secretary of Navy, 27 Aug. 1892, Case 6189, filed with Case 5341, Ltrs. Recd. and Sent, 1892, OSN, RG 80, GRN, NARS.

13. Secretary of Navy-Bethlehem Iron Company, 10 Oct. 1892, Box 25, BTLC.

14. *Philadelphia North American,* 15 Oct. 1892; Tracy–National Advisory Board of the Amalgamated Association of Iron and Steelworkers, 5 Nov. 1892, Box 25, BTLC; *Pittsburg* (Pa) *Dispatch,* 12, 15 Oct. 1892; *Brooklyn Daily Eagle,* 14 Oct. 1892.

15. *New York Commercial Gazette,* 18 Oct. 1892.

16. Tracy's involvement receives attention in Herrick, *American Naval Revolution,* 145-147.

17. Elliott–Tracy, 15 Oct. 1891, Box 10; C. G. Gunthers and Sons-Elliott, 25 Feb. 1891, with Tracy Memo. n.d., Box 8, both BTLC.

18. Gwynn, *Letters of Spring-Rice,* I, 138.

19. On American war planning see Kenneth Bourne, *Britain and the Balance of Power in North America, 1815-1908* (Berkeley, 1967), 322-323, n. 1.

20. Gwynn, *Letters of Spring-Rice*, II, 118; Charles S. Campbell, Jr., "The Bering Sea Settlements of 1892," *Pacific Historical Review*, XXII (November 1963), 359 quotes another British legation secretary (besides Spring-Rice) as thinking Harrison wanted a convenient war by citing Michael Herbert–Eric Barrington, 22 Jan. 1892.

21. Blaine–Harrison, 6 Mar. 1892 in Volwiler, *Correspondence between Harrison and Blaine,* 242, Blaine adding: "Not a man in a million believes we should ultimately have war." *Philadelphia Public Ledger and Daily Transcript,* 10 Mar. 1892 hinted at the frequency of the Tracy–Foster conferences during the period that Blaine was away from his desk ill.

22. John W. Foster, *Diplomatic Memoirs* (Boston, 1909), II, 27-35. Tracy published his findings in "The Behring Sea Question," *North American Review*, CLVI, (May 1893), 438, 513-542.

23. William Williams, "Reminiscences of the Bering Sea Arbitration." *American Journal of International Law*, XXVII (October 1943), 562-584; James Bassett Moore, 53d Cong., 2d sess., HR, Misc. Doc. 212, *History and Digest of the International Arbitrations to Which the United States Has Been A Party* (Washington, 1898), I, 755-989 and II, 2123-2131.

24. Foster, *Diplomatic Memoirs,* II, 28.

25. Tracy–Harrison, 5 Aug. 1890, Series I, Reel 28, BHLC.

26. Roosevelt–Tracy, 12 Nov. 1895, quoted in Foster, *Diplomatic Memoirs,* II, 28.

27. Tracy, "The Behring Sea Question," 542.

28. Quoted in Foster Rhea Dulles, *America's Rise to World Power, 1898-1854* (New York, 1954), 24.

29. Herrick, *American Naval Revolution,* 102-103 places great emphasis upon the influence of Mahan's imperialist thought upon Tracy. Actually, the secretary understood the larger naval requirements and their link with expansionist interests of the nation even without Mahan's codification in various articles on Hawaii and the Isthmus. Kimberly told Tracy of the need for American naval forces to maintain order in the Hawaiian islands as early as the fall of 1889 and similar letters were received from Brown as well as copies of diplomatic correspondence from Stevens in 1890 and 1891. See, Kimberly–Tracy, 18 Oct. 1889, Area 9, Roll 296, Area Files, and Brown–Tracy, 29 July 1890, Subject File VI, International Relations–Hawaii, RG 45, NRC, NARS. Sylvester K. Stevens, *American Expansion in Hawaii, 1842-1898* (Harrisburg, 1945) 210, notes: "The reports from such a source as to conditions in Hawaii . . . must have had an important part in leading both Tracy and Blaine to sense that the issue of annexation was likely to be raised."

30. La Feber, *New Empire,* 144.

31. Stevens, *American Expansion,* 208; La Feber, *The New Empire,* 147, contends that Tracy's desire to round out control of the sea, for which possession of Hawaii was essential, led him to fill the vacuum left by Blaine's departure. This assertion may be true in light of the Chilean affair. Certainly during this time, Tracy had departmental officials conduct background investigations on the Hawaiian islands and public opinion on the question of annexation. See Memo. Lieutenant F. Singer–Secretary of Navy, Subject: Hawaiian Islands, 1 Feb. 1893; and "Opinion of Leading Newspapers on Hawaiian Question," n.d. both in Box 31, BTLC.

32. Harrison–C. C. Hines, 3 Feb. 1893, quoted in Sievers, *Hoosier President,* 253, n. 13.

33. *New York Herald,* 13 Sep. 1892. The charges appeared first in the issue of 22 Aug. and were expanded on 29, 31 Aug. The matter probably arose from a request in April 1892 by Bethlehem Iron for an additional $150 per ton on "inclined turret armor" which the company claimed was harder to fabricate. The technical problem reached no solution when the *Herald* broke the story; see Bethlehem Iron Company Request, Case 3691, Ltrs. Recd., 1892, OSN, RG 80, GRN, NARS.

34. Gordon–Tracy, 9 Feb. 1892, Box 11, BTLC.

35. Tracy–Gordon, 26 Feb. 1892, Box 11; I. S. Catlin–Tracy 3 Mar. 1892, Box 12; both BTLC.

36. *Boston Herald,* 5 Mar. and 11 Feb. 1892; *New York Evening Telegram,* 15 Feb.; *New York Recorder,* 26 Feb.; and *Portsmouth* (NH) *Daily Chronicle,* 23 Apr.; all 1892.

37. *Philadelphia Inquirer,* 2 Sept. 1892.

38. Tracy–William Smythe, 15 Jun. 1892, Letterbook 3, Box 26, BTLC. For Platt's comment, see Lang, *Platt Autobiography,* 246-247. Smythe, an Owego editor, was a life-long friend of both men and may have been cast in the role of middleman at this time.

39. *New York Mail and Express,* 3 Aug.; *Brooklyn Daily Eagle,* 6 Aug.; *Brooklyn Daily Times,* 1 Sept; all 1892; Gowdy—Tracy 9 Sept. 1892 and Tracy's endorsement, Box 13, BTLC. Tracy's decision to return to private life may also have been dictated by financial considerations.

40. *Brooklyn Daily Times* 28 Nov. 1892.

41. *Boston Daily Globe,* 27 Jan. 1892; *Brooklyn Daily Eagle,* 31 Jan. 1892.

42. American Iron and Steel Association, *History of Armor* Plate, 1-2.

43. U.S. Navy Department, *Annual Report,* 1892, 3-5; Richardson, *Messages and Papers,* 5758-5759; *New York Times,* 7 Dec. 1892. Tracy failed to mention that many of the naval vessels were of wooden construction and even many of the newer steel ships carried full sail equipment. See Silas Casey–Gherardi, 22 May, 1892, Case 3646, Ltrs. Recd. and Sent, 1892, OSN, RG 80, GRN, NARS.

44. U.S. Navy Department, *Annual Report, 1892,* 5; Cramp–Tracy, 22, 23 Nov. 1892, Box 14, BTLC; Estimation of Completion List, accompanying Tracy–Herbert, 24 Feb. 1892, 52d Cong., 1st sess., Comm. on Naval Affairs, Papers Relating to HR 7093, Drawer 3855, RG 233, HR, NARS; *Philadelphia Public Ledger,* 15 Nov. 1892.

45. U.S. Navy Department, *Annual Report, 1892,* 31. The *Brooklyn Daily Eagle,* 27 Sept. 1892 predicted Tracy would limit his requests to cruisers and battleships, not torpedo boats and Congress pared down his final request to only one $400,000 light-draught gunboat in February 1893; see *New York Daily Tribune,* 15 Feb. 1893.

46. U.S. Navy Department, *Annual Report, 1892,* 22. Also Statement of Guns–Hon. H. L. Davis, 9 Jan. 1891; Request for Information, Guns–Hon. A. J. Cummings, 8 Feb. 1892, Case 935, both in Ltrs. Recd., 1892, OSN, RG 80, GRN, NARS.

47. U.S. Navy Department, *Annual Report, 1892,* 25-29; also Lodge–Tracy, 12 Oct. 1892, Box 26; C. Y. Wheeler–Tracy, 22 Nov. 1892, Box 14, both BTLC.

48. U.S. Navy Department, *Annual Report, 1892,* 52-53; *Baltimore American,* 13 Dec. 1892.

49. U.S. Navy Department, *Annual Report, 1892,* 33 (also 37, 43) citing 52d Cong., 1st sess., HR 621, Appropriations for the Navy, 10 Mar. 1892, 15.

50. U.S. Navy Department, *Annual Report, 1892,* 37. On the review, see Folder, Fleet Review at Hampton Roads and New York, 1893, No. 1, Box 00 (5) Operations of Fleets, etc., Subject File, RG 45, NRC, NARS; *New York Times,* 1-4 May, 1893.

Notes to Chapter 8

1. *Brooklyn Standard Union,* 12 Nov. 1892; *St. Louis Republic,* 13 Nov. 1892 noted the possible partnership. Soley's relationship appears in Tracy–Boardman, 1 Mar. 1893, Box 26 BTLC.

2. Emma Wilmerding–Tracy, 19 Jun. 1892, Box 13, *ibid.*

3. A full description of the Greater New York movement appears in Allan Nevins and J. A. Krout (eds.), *The Greater City: New York, 1898-1948* (New York, 1948), 41, passim.

4. *New York Tribune,* 1 Jan. 1898. Material relating to Tracy's role appears in Box 39, BTLC.

5. D. Albert Shaw quoted in Lothrop Stoddard, *Master of Manhattan: The Life of Richard Croker* (New York, 1931), 180. The election may be followed in Cleveland Rogers and Rankin, Rebecca B., *New York: The World's Capital City: Its Development and Contributions to Progress* (New York, 1948), 82.

6. Undated Acceptance Speech, Box 27, BTLC.

7. Rogers and Rankin, *New York,* 82; Herrick, "General Tracy's Navy," 239 suggests Platt's intransigence.

8. *New York Times,* 15, 17 Mar. 1893.

9. Tracy renewed his request that Harrison permanently extend the civil service rules to the navy yards, Tracy–Harrison, 21 Feb. 1893, Reel 38, Ser. 1, BHLC. Interestingly, Herbert continued the system and improved it; see U.S. Navy Department, *Annual Report, 1893* (Washington, 1894), 51-52 and *1894* (Washington, 1895), 38-39.

10. Hammett, "Hilary Abner Herbert," especially chapter 8.

11. La Feber, *New Empire,* 229-231.

12. 59th Cong., 2d sess., HR Doc. 193, *Cost of Armor Plate and Armor Plant,* 6-9, 16, 22-23.

13. 53d Cong., 3d sess., Sen. Doc. 56, *Letter From the Secretary of the Navy in Reply to Senate Resolution of January 28, 1895,* 4 Feb., 1895, 1-3.

14. *Cost of Armor Plate and Armor Plant,* 130, xi-xii, 22.

15. Ibid., 154, also vii, 163-166. Tracy also admitted to being employed in 1896 by the Harvey Company to defend the patent for its process.

16. 54th Cong., 2d sess., Sen. Rep. 1457, *Prices of Armor for Vessels of the Navy,* 11 Feb. 1897, xiii-xiv. Both Bethlehem and Carnegie refused to forge armor at $300 a ton and a stalemate ensued until 8 May 1898, when war fever prompted Congress to raise the figure to $413 per ton.

17. Herbert–Tracy, 29 May 1895, Box 16, BTLC.

18. Catlin–Lamont, 15, 20, June 1895, both Box 16, BTLC.

19. Speech before Middlesex Club, Boston, 12 Feb. 1898, Box 27, ibid. *New York Sun,* 13 Feb. 1898.

20. See various letters of the Roosevelt–Tracy correspondence 1892-1907, Box 23, ibid. The Schley–Sampson controversy involved the actions of principal American naval commanders in the Santiago campaign of 1898, see West, *Admirals of American Empire,* chapter 19. Herrick, *American Naval Revolution,* chapter XI and epilogue summarizes succinctly the performance of Tracy's "Battle fleet" in 1898.

21. *New York World,* 14 Jan. 1897.

22. La Feber, *New Empire,* 283.

23. Sievers, *Hoosier President,* 268. Harrison termed the British legal brief of sixty-five pages "a great surprise and disappointment," Harrison–Tracy, 12 Jan. 1899, Reel 41, Ser. 1, BHLC.

24. Sievers, *Hoosier President,* 273-274; Harrison–Miller, 7 Oct. 1899, Ser. I, Reel 42, BHLC. Sievers uncovered confidential documents of Mallet-Prevost which provided a strong case for the counsel's assertion.

25. J. M. Sayre–Tracy, 5 Oct. 1908, Box 16; Financial Statements, 1908-1915, Box 29, both BTLC.

26. Tracy recommended several people to Taft and sent advice and praise concerning the president's position on neutrality in the Mexican crisis of 1911-1912; Taft–Tracy, 6 Mar. 1909, Box 17; Tracy–Taft, 1 May 1911, Box 18; 15 Mar. 1912, Box 20; all BTLC. On New York debt, see Bureau of Municipal Research, *New York City's Debt* (New York, February 1909); on Saratoga, see Secretary to Governor–Tracy, 28 Jan. 1910, Box 17, BTLC.

27. *New York Sun,* 26 Apr. 1912.

28. Tracy–Secretary of State, 11 Aug. 1914; State Department–Tracy, 17 Aug. 1914. Tracy wrote Emma on 14 July that he and granddaughter Alys had visited the Roosevelts at Oyster Bay for tea and that the ex-President "seemed glad to see me." On Tracy's concern about his son's business ventures, see for example, Tracy–Frank, 21 May 1914; all Box 22, BTLC.

29. On Evans reception, Printed invitation, Navy League–Tracy, 8 Jan. 1909, Box 6; on other naval matters, *New York Times,* 31 Mar. 1913; Acting Chief Bureau of Yards and Docks–Tracy, 11 Aug. 1914; Tracy–Chief Bureau of Yards and Docks, 13 Apr. 1914, all ibid.

30. *New York Sun,* 25 Apr. 1915.

31. *New York Herald,* 27 June 1915.

32. On the accident, *Brooklyn Daily Eagle,* 31 May 1915; on death announcements, *New York Sun,* 9 Aug. and *New York Times,* 10 Aug., both 1915; for typical obituaries, *New York Evening Post; New York American; New York Sun,* all 9 Aug. 1915.

33. *New York Times,* 8 Aug. 1915.

34. *New York Herald,* 27 June 1915 with successive quotes from this issue.

35. Statistics based upon B. R. Tillman, Jr., compiler, *Navy Yearbook, 1915,* (Washington, 1915), Table 23. From the redevelopment of an efficient battleship type around 1890 to the eve of World War II the size of the battle fleet was the generally accepted standard of relevant naval power. It was not a good standard since other types were also important in the naval calculation and other factors were omitted such as total national maritime strength, gunnery ability, total personnel in the naval establishment and their training and efficiency, and national logistical ability to support naval forces overseas. But the battleship remained the great symbol of naval strength for some forty to fifty years.

36. Daniels–Tracy, 27 May 1915, Box 23, BTLC.

Bibliographical Note

This bibliography provides a guide to the life and services of Benjamin F. Tracy. It is not intended to be inclusive, seeking merely to indicate channels for investigating his career. Tracy remains something of an elusive character if only because his personal papers portray a terse, business-like approach to life, and lack comment on private and family considerations.

John K. Mahon first cited the neglect of Tracy by modern historians in his brief article, "Benjamin Franklin Tracy, Secretary of the Navy 1889-1893," *The New York Historical Society Quarterly,* XLIV, (April 1960), pp. 179-201. Walter R. Herrick expanded upon this pioneering work in "General Tracy's Navy: A Study of the Development of American Sea Power, 1889-1893" (Unpublished Ph.D dissertation, University of Virginia, 1962) which formed the core of *The American Naval Revolution* (Baton Rouge, Louisiana State University Press, 1966). Herrick overstates the case for a "revolution" and for Mahan's influence upon Tracy, but he clearly delineates Tracy's major contributions: the battleship concept, his support of the Naval War College, and his role in Harrisonian expansionism. The book fails to show the work of congressional committees and the ideological framework of expansionism, nor does it capture the human dimensions of Tracy. The latter emerges better in shorter sketches such as E. G. Dunnell, "Secretary of the Navy, Benjamin F. Tracy," *The Epoch*, V (June 7, 1889), p. 285, and F. H. Platt, *Memorial to Benjamin Franklin Tracy* (New York, 1916); Charles E. Fitch, *Encyclopedia of Biography of New York*, 3 vols. (New York, The American Historical Society, 1916); Dumas Malone and Allan Johnson, *Dictionary of American Biography*, 20 vols. (New York, Charles Scribners, 1946); H. R. Stiles, *The Civil, Political, Professional and Ecclesiastical History and Commercial and Industrial Record of the County and the City of Brooklyn N.Y. from 1683 to 1884* (New York, 1884); S. W. Tracy (compiler), *The Tracy Genealogy, Being Some of the Descendants of Stephen Tracy of Plymouth Colony 1623* (Rutland, Vermont, Tuttle, 1936); J. W. White (editor), *National Cyclopedia of American Biography* 6 vols. (New York, James T. White, 1888-1893); and Benjamin Franklin Cooling III, "Benjamin Franklin Tracy: Lawyer, Soldier, Secretary of the Navy," (Unpublished Ph.D dissertation, University of Pennsylvania, 1969). Tracy's views on various subjects emerge best from his own writing such as: "The Behring Sea Question," *North American Review*, CLVI (May 1893), pp. 513-542; *New York City's Debt: Facts and Law Relating to the Constitutional Limitation of New York's Indebtedness. . . .* (New York, Bureau of Municipal Research, 1909); and "Our New Warships," *North American Review*, CL (June 1891), pp. 643-655.

The principal sources of the present study are in the Benjamin F. Tracy papers in the Library of Congress and in official Navy Department records in The National Archives and Records Service, both in Washington D.C. Tracy's papers cover the period 1870-1915 and include correspondence, memoranda, position papers, and scrapbooks of newspaper clippings together with miscellaneous material of social and personal nature and a few photographs. The absence of original material before 1870 poses problems, but gaps in the personal papers for 1889-1893 can be filled by recourse to Record Group 80, General Records of the Navy, and Record Group 45, Naval Records Collection of Office of Naval Records and Library; Record Group 38, Records of Office of Naval Intelligence; Record Group 24, Records of Bureau of Naval Personnel—all in National Archives. Several other collections in the Library of Congress are indispensable, including those of Nelson A. Aldrich, James G. Blaine, Charles Boutelle, Andrew Carnegie, George Dewey, Eugene Hale, Stephen B. Luce, Benjamin Harrison, Alfred

Thayer Mahan, David D. Porter, Mathew B. Quay, Thomas B. Reed, Whitelaw Reid, and William C. Whitney. The Edwin D. Morgan papers, New York State Library, Albany, and the records of the U.S. House of Representatives and the U.S. Senate, both in National Archives, have some use.

Published United States Public Documents include the pertinent volumes of the *Congressional Record* for the years 1889-1893, various House and Senate documents, *(House Reports, House Miscellaneous Documents, House Executive Documents, Senate Executive Documents, Senate Miscellaneous Documents, Senate Reports,* and *Senate Documents)* dealing with such subjects as appropriations, armor, the Chilean affair, naval stations, the Revenue Marine, Navy Department organization and personnel, the Policy Board, the Phythian Board and the Bering Sea sealing issue. Especially valuable are the annual reports of the Navy Department, and various general orders (numbered and unnumbered), regulation and special circulars, and special orders of the Navy Department 1889-1893, John B. Moore, *A Digest of International Law,* 2 vols. (Washington, Government Printing Office, 1906), and James D. Richardson (editor), *A Compilation of the Messages and Papers of the Presidents,* 20 vols. (Washington, Government Printing Office, 1907), provide much insight into the navy and the nation at this time.

Chapter notes of this book reflect the principal newspapers consulted and clipping scrapbooks in Tracy's private papers expedited the huge task of sifting through such material. No researcher on the U.S. Navy should neglect the *Proceedings of the United States Naval Institute* in order to gain insight into matters which concerned the profession during the Tracy period. Other useful periodicals include *The Army and Navy Journal, The Army and Navy Register, Frank Leslie's Illustrated Newspaper, Harpers Weekly,* and the *Nation.*

Material pertinent to Tracy's formative years is in D. S. Alexander, *A Political History of the State of New York,* 4 vols. (New York, Holt, 1906-1921); S. David Brummer, *Political History of New York State During the Period of the Civil War* (New York, Columbia University, 1911); William B. Gay, *Historical Gazateer of Tioga County New York, 1785-1888* (Syracuse, W. B. Gay Company, 1906); Edward Hungerford, Men of Erie: A Study of Human Effort, (New York, Random House, 1946); Henry B. Peirce and

Duane Hamilton Hurd, *History of Tioga, Chemung, Tompkins, and Schuyler Counties New York,* (Philadelphia, Evarts and Ensing, 1879); State of New York, *Journal of the Assembly of the State of New York, 85th Session, January 7, 1862,* (Albany, Van Benthuysen, 1862). General information on Tracy's part in the Civil War may be found in his Compiled Service Record in Record Group 15, Records of the Veterans Administration; Record Group 94, Adjutant Generals Office Records; Record Group 249, Records of Office of Commissary General of Prisoners; and Record Group 110, Records of Provost Marshal General's Office, all in National Archives. Also indispensable are U.S. War Department, *War of the Rebellion: A Compilation of the Official Records of the Union and Confederate Armies,* 128 vols. (Washington, Government Printing Office, 1880-1901); Frederick Phisterer (compiler), *New York in the War of the Rebellion, 1861-1865,* 5 vols. (Albany, F. B. Lyon and Company, 1912); and State of New York, *Annual Report of the Adjutant General of the State of New York, January 27, 1863* (Albany, Comstock and Cassady, 1863). James A. Rawley, *Edwin D. Morgan, 1811-1883: Merchant in Politics* (New York, Columbia University Press, 1955), provides insight into the situation in New York in 1861-1862. Edward Steere, *The Wilderness Campaign* (Harrisburg, Stackpole, 1960), clearly describes the tactical action in which Tracy participated and Eugene C. Murdock's *Patriotism Limited, 1862-1865; The Civil War Draft and Bounty System* (Kent, Kent State University Press, 1967), and *One Million Men* (Madison, State Historical Society of Wisconsin, 1972), as well as Leonard L. Lerwill, *The Personnel Replacement System in the United States Army* (Washington, Government Printing Office, 1954), show the problems of Civil War recruitment and processing of personnel.

Examination of Tracy's involvement with the Elmira prison camp should begin with William B. Hesseltine, *Civil War Prisons: A Study in War Psychology* (Columbus, Ohio State University Press, 1930); and proceed to Morgen Allen Powell, "Cotton For the Relief of Confederate Prisoners," *Civil War History,* 9 (March 1963), pp. 24-36. James I. Robertson, Jr., "The Scourge of Elmira," *Civil War History,* VIII (June 1962), pp. 184-201 presents a remarkably slanted view of the problems of the Elmira camp, while the older work, Clayton W. Holmes, *The Elmira Prison Camp: A History of the Military Prison at Elmira, New York, July 6, 1864 to July 10, 1865,*

(New York, G. P. Putnams, 1912), remains the fullest account. Personal reminiscences of Elmira prisoners include; Susan Williams Benson (editor), *Berry Benson's Civil War Book; Memoirs of a Confederate Scout and Sharpshooter,* (Athens, University of Georgia Press, 1962); A. M. Keily, *In Viniculus; or The Prisoner of War; Being the Experience of a Rebel in Two Federal Pens . . .,* (New York, Blelock, 1866); John R. King, *My Experiences in the Confederate Army and in Northern Prisons* (Clarksburg, West. Va., n.p., 1917); Southern Historical Society (compiler), "The Treatment of Prisoners During the War Between the States," *Southern Historical Society Papers,* I, (April 1876), pp. 224-230, and Marcus Toney, *The Privations of a Private,* (Nashville, By Author, 1905). Frank Wilkeson, *Recollections of a Private Soldier in the Army of the Potomac* (New York, G. P. Putnam's Sons, 1887), presents the observations of a Union guard at Elmira and Haywood J. Pearce, *Benjamin H. Hill: Secession and Reconstruction* (Chicago, University of Chicago Press, 1928), reflects the postwar controversy surrounding Elmira.

Tracy's postwar and post-cabinet life can be placed in a larger context by consulting works on Brooklyn and New York such as Edward Robb Ellis, *The Epic of New York City,* (New York, Coward-McCann, 1966); Allan Nevins and J. A. Krout, *The Greater City: New York 1898-1948* (New York, Columbia University Press, 1948); Cleveland Rodgers and Rebecca B. Rankin, *New York, The World's Capital City: Its Development and Contributions to Progress* (New York, Harper and Bros., 1948); as well as the Stiles volume on Brooklyn. Local politics can be analyzed in Harold C. Syrett, *The City of Brooklyn, 1865-1898: A Political History* (New York, Columbia University Press, 1944), and D. S. Alexander, *Four Famous New Yorkers* (New York, Holt, 1903). Original sources on the district attorneyship may be found in Record Group 60, General Records of the Department of Justice, Attorney Generals Office, in National Archives. Tracy's relationship to the Platt machine is reported in Harold T. Gosnell, *Boss Platt and His New York Machine: A Study of the Political Leadership of Thomas C. Platt, Theodore Roosevelt and Others,* (Chicago, University of Chicago Press, 1924), and Louis J. Lang (editor and compiler), *The Autobiography of Thomas Collier Platt* (New York, B. W. Dodge and Company, 1910). On the Beecher trial, see Chester L. Barrows, *William M. Evarts; Lawyer, Diplomat, Statesman,* (Chapel Hill, University of North Carolina

Press, 1941), and Paxton Hibben, *Henry Ward Beecher: An American Portrait* (New York, George H. Doran and Company, 1927). Also useful are Donald B. Chidsey, *The Gentleman from New York: A Life of Roscoe Conkling* (New Haven, Yale University Press, 1935), and Lothrop Stoddard, *Master of Manhattan: The Life of Richard Croker* (New York, Longmans, Green and Company, 1931).

One should begin the study of the resurgence of American naval power in the eighties and nineties by looking to British influence and the classic work of Arthur Marder, *The Anatomy of British Sea Power: A History of British Naval Policy in the Pre-Dreadnought Era, 1880-1905* (New York, Alfred A. Knopf, 1940). General histories of the U.S. Navy in the late nineteenth century are fairly familiar and include among the older works: Frank M. Bennett, *The Steam Navy of the United States* . . . . (Pittsburgh, Warren and Company, 1896); George T. Davis, *A Navy Second to None: The Development of Modern Naval Policy,* (New York, Harcourt Brace, 1940); Donald W. Mitchell, *History of the Modern American Navy: From 1883 Through Pearl Harbor* (New York, Knopf, 1946); James R. Spears, *The History of Our Navy From Its Origin to the End of the War With Spain 1775-1898* (New York, Charles Scribners, 1899); Harold and Margaret Sprout, *The Rise of American Naval Power, 1776-1918* (Princeton, Princeton University Press, 1939), and Richard S. West, Jr., *Admirals of American Empire* (Indianapolis, 1948). All present a somewhat conventional interpretation of the decline of American naval power after the Civil War and the resurgence under the aegis of Mahanite doctrine. Revisionist studies have begun to alter this view in part. They include Herrick's volume; Robert Seager II, "Ten Years Before Mahan: The Unofficial Case for the New Navy, 1880-1890," *Mississippi Valley Historical Review,* XL (December 1953), pp. 491-512; Stanley Sandler, "A Navy in Decay: Some Strategic Technological Results of Disarmament, 1865-1869 in the U.S. Navy," *Military Affairs,* XXXV (December 1971), 138-142; and several fine doctoral dissertations, Lance C. Buhl, "The Smooth Water Navy; American Naval Policy and Politics 1865-1876," (Unpublished Ph.D dissertation, Harvard University, 1969), portrays the navy of the Reconstruction period as caught in the same conflict of legislative and executive powers as the army yet fully capable of fulfilling the modest demands imposed upon it by both branches of government. Kenneth J. Hagan, "Protecting American Commerce and Neutrality: The Global Gunboat Diplomacy of the Old Navy 1877-1889," (Unpublished Ph.D dissertation, Claremont Graduate School, 1970, published as *American Gunboat Diplomacy and The Old Navy, 1877-1889*, Westport, Ct., Greenwood, 1973), notes that the cruiser-commerce protection theory of naval policy of the Gilded Age was a rational expression of national feeling and in keeping with accepted notions of U.S. strategic policy during peacetime periods. Also valuable for understanding naval development in the period is Robert Greehalgh Albion, "The Naval Affairs Committees, 1816-1947," *Proceedings of the United States Naval Institute*, 78, (November 1952), pp. 1227-1237 and Stephen H. Evans, *The United States Coast Guard 1790-1915: A Definitive History, With a Postscript 1915-1950* (Annapolis, United States Naval Institute, 1949).

The interaction of naval and diplomatic affairs leads naturally to an examination of the entire question of American expansionism during the Harrison administration. Older, standard works remain valuable: Foster Rhea Dulles, *America's Rise to World Power 1898-1954* (New York, Harper and Row, 1954), J. W. Pratt, *Expansionists of 1898* (Baltimore, Johns Hopkins University Press, 1936), and Alice Felt Tyler, *The Foreign Policy of James G. Blaine* (Minneapolis, University of Minnesota Press, 1927). These should be compared with much new material. Kenneth P. Bourne, *Britain and the Balance of Power in North America* (Berkeley, University of California Press, 1967), describes Anglo-American relations in the late nineteenth century. J. A. S. Grenville and George B. Young, *Politics, Strategy, and American Diplomacy* (New Haven, Yale University Press, 1966), integrates American strategic concerns with the more conventional elements of diplomatic affairs. Walter LaFeber, *The New Empire: An Interpretation of American Expansion, 1860-1898* (Ithaca, Cornell University Press, 1963), and William A. Williams, *The Roots of Modern American Empire: A Study of the Growth and Shaping of Social Consciousness in a Marketplace Society* (New York, Random House, 1970), both advance the cause of economic motivation for expansionism, a position towards which Ray Ginger leans in *Age of Excess: The United States from 1877 to 1914* (New York, Macmillan, 1965). Ernest R. May, "The Emergence of the United States as a World Power," in John A. Garraty, *Interpreting American History: Conversations with Historians* (New York, Macmillan, 1970), remains more conventional while commenting revealingly, "I really don't see much connection between foreign affairs and naval policy even in the 1890's." The opposite view emerges from Allan B. Spetter, "Harrison and Blaine: Foreign Policy 1889-1893," (Unpublished Ph.D dissertation, Rutgers, The State University, 1969), who advances Tracy as a prime mover in Harrisonian diplomacy. Other scholars see more diverse and complex strands in the expansionism of the period and provide important new interpretations. David F. Healy, *US Expansionism: The Imperialist Urge in the 1890s* (Madison, University of Wisconsin Press, 1970), sets the American experience in a wider context encompassing European nations as well. Paul S. Holbo, "Economics, Emotion, and Expansion; An Emerging Foreign Policy," in H. Wayne Morgan, *The Gilded Age, Revised and Enlarged Edition* (Syracuse, Syracuse University Press, 1970); Milton Plesur, *America's Outward Thrust: Approaches to Foreign Affairs 1865-1890* (DeKalb, Northern Illinois University Press, 1971), and Marilyn Blatt Young, "American Expansion, 1870-1900: The Far East," in Barton J. Bernstein, (editor), *Towards A New Past: Dissenting Essays in American History* (New York, Random House, 1968), all provide multicausative interpretations, and David Pletcher, *The Awkward Years, American Foreign Relations Under Garfield and Arthur* (Columbia, University of Missouri Press, 1962), simply exhausts the ramifications of expansionism in the early 1880s. An interesting reverse side of the imperialist coin appears in E. Berkeley Tompkins, *Anti-Imperialism in the United States: The Great Debate, 1890-1920,* (Philadelphia, University of Pennsylvania Press, 1971).

Specific cases of naval-diplomatic involvement during Tracy's tenure are recorded in the following works. On Chile see: W. E. Curtis, *Between the Andes and the Ocean* (Chicago, Stone, 1900); Osgood Hardy, "The Itata Incident," *Hispanic American Historical Review,* V (May 1922), pp. 195-226 and "Was Patrick Egan a Blundering Minister?" *Hispanic American Historical Review,* VIII (February 1928), pp. 66-87; J. B. Moore, "The Late Chilean Controversy," *Political Science Quarterly,* VIII (September 1892), pp. 467-494 and Frederick B. Pike, *Chile and the United States 1880-1962: The Emergence of Chile's Social Crisis and the Challenge to United States Diplomacy* (South Bend, University of Notre Dame Press, 1963). For the Haitian imbroglio see: Frederick Douglass, "Haiti and the United States; Inside History of the Negotiations for the Molé St. Nicholas," *North American Review*, Part I, 153 (September 1891), pp. 337-345 and Part II, (October 1891), pp. 450-460; Myra Himelhoch, "Frederick Douglass and Haiti's Mole St. Nicholas," *The Journal of Negro History*, LVI, (July 1971), pp. 161-180; Rayford W. Logan, *The Diplomatic Relations of the United States with Haiti, 1776-1891* (Chapel Hill, University of North Carolina Press, 1941); and Ludwell L. Montague, *Haiti and the United States 1714-1938* (Durham, Duke University Press, 1940). Richard Wellington Turk, "Strategy and Foreign Policy: The United States Navy in the Caribbean, 1865-1913," (Unpublished Ph.D dissertation, Fletcher School of Law and Diplomacy, 1968), provides a useful analysis of naval policy and operations in that area. Hawaii may be investigated through William A. Russ, *The Hawaiian Revolution, 1893-1894* (Selinsgrove, Susquehanna University Press 1959); Sylvester K. Stevens, *American Expansion in Hawaii 1852-1898* (Harrisburg, Archives Publishing Company, 1945); and Merze Tate, *The United States and the Hawaiian Kingdom, A Political History* (New Haven, Yale University Press, 1965). On the Bering Sea, see: Charles S. Campbell Jr., "The Anglo-American Crisis in the Bering Sea, 1890-1891," *Mississippi Valley Historical Review*, XLVIII, (December 1961), pp. 393-414, and "The Behring Sea Settlements of 1892," *Pacific Historical Review*, XXXII, (November, 1963), pp. 347-367; as well as William Williams, "Reminiscences of the Bering Sea Arbitration," *American Journal of International Law*, XXVII, (October 1943), pp. 562-584. On Samoa see: J. A. C. Gray, *Amerika Samoa: A History of American Samoa and Its United States Naval Administration* (Annapolis, United States Naval Institute, 1960), and George H. Ryden, *The Foreign Policy of the United States Relative to Samoa* (New Haven, Yale University Press, 1933).

The political aspects of the period are well covered in various syntheses and biographies. Most useful is H. Wayne Morgan, *From Hayes to McKinley, National Party Politics, 1877-1896* (Syracuse, Syracuse University Press, 1969), although he makes the puzzling observation that Tracy was not well known to Platt! Robert D. Marcus, *Grand Old Party, Political Structure in the Gilded Age 1880-1896* (New York, Oxford University Press, 1971) effectively examines the political parties while Donald Marquand Dozer, "Benjamin Harrison and the Presidential Campaign of 1892," *The American Historical Review*, LIV (October 1948), pp. 49-77, examines factors surrounding Harrison's defeat although neglecting Tracy's role. David J. Rothman, *Politics and Power: The United States Senate 1869-1901* (Cambridge, Harvard University Press, 1966), carefully portrays maneuvers on one side of Capitol Hill in the period. Leonard D. White, *The Republican Era: A Study in Administrative History, 1869-1901* (New York, Macmillan, 1958) remains the best approach to its subject. On Benjamin Harrison and James G. Blaine, see Harriet S. Blaine Beale, *Letters of Mrs. James G. Blaine,* 2 vols. (New York, Duffield and Company, 1908); David S. Muzzey, *James G. Blaine; A Political Idol of Other Days* (New York, Dodd, Mead, and Company, 1939), as well as Albert T. Volwiler, "Harrison, Blaine, and American Foreign Policy," *American Philosophical Society Proceedings,* LXXIX (November 1938), pp. 637-648 and *The Correspondence Between Benjamin Harrison and James G. Blaine, 1882-1893* (Philadelphia, American Philosophical Society, 1940). Harry J. Sievers, *Benjamin Harrison: Hoosier President, The White House and After* (Indianapolis, Bobbs-Merrill, 1968), forms the weakest of Siever's trilogy on the twenty-third president but provides good anecdotal material and covers the Tracy-Harrison preparation of the Venezuelan boundary case. Other biographies and memoirs of the cast of the period recapture the atmosphere and events and include: John W. Foster, *Diplomatic Memoirs,* 2 vols. (Boston, Houghton, 1909); John Garraty, *Henry Cabot Lodge* (New York, Knopf, 1953); Stephen Gwynn (editor), *The Letters and Friendships of Sir Cecil Spring-Rice: A Record,* 2 vols. (Boston and New York, Houghton-Mifflin, 1929); Oscar Doane Lambert, *Stephen Benton Elkins* (Pittsburgh, University of Pittsburgh Press, 1955); and Martin Meyers, "Eugene Hale and the American Navy," *American Neptune,* XXII (July 1962), pp. 187-193.

A picture of the naval service and personalities seems to appear best in biographical accounts such as: George Dewey, *Autobiography of George Dewey, Admiral of the Navy* (New York, Charles Scribners, 1913); Robley D. Evans, *A Sailors Log; Recollections of Forty Years of Naval Life* (New York, D. Appleton-Century, 1903); Edwin A. Falk, *Fighting Bob Evans* (New York, Jonathan Cape and Harrison Smith, 1931); Bradley Fiske, *From Midshipman to Rear Admiral* (New York, Century, 1919); Albert Gleaves, *The Life of An American Sailor: Rear Admiral William Hemsley Emory, United States Navy; From His Letters and Memoirs* (New

York, George H. Doran and Company, 1923); C. M. Remey, *The Life and Letters of George C. Remey* (Washington, n.p. 1937); and Winfield S. Schley, *Forty-Five Years Under the Flag* (New York, D. Appleton and Company, 1904). Peter Karsten, "The Naval Aristocracy: United States Naval Officers from the 1890's to the 1920's: Mahan's Messmates," (Unpublished Ph.D dissertation, University of Wisconsin, 1968) and *The Naval Aristocracy: The Golden Age of Annapolis and the Emergence of Modern American Navalism* (New York, Free Press, 1972) provide an excessively critical but lucid analysis of the naval officer corps and environment in the period.

The roles of Porter, Luce, and Mahan in the Tracy period are treated satisfactorily in the following: On *Porter* see; Kenneth J. Hagen, "Admiral David Dixon Porter: Strategist for a Navy in Transition," *Proceedings of the United States Naval Institute,* 94 (July 1968), pp. 140-143 and James R. Soley *Admiral Porter* (New York, Appleton, 1913); on *Luce,* see Albert T. Gleaves, *Life and Letters of Rear Admiral Stephen B. Luce, U.S. Navy; Founder of the Naval War College* (New York, Putnam, 1925), and John D. Hayes, "The Writings of Stephen B. Luce," *Military Affairs,* XIX (Winter 1955), pp. 187-196, as well as Luce's own writings such as "Our Future Navy," *North American Review,* CXLIX (July 1889), pp. 54-65 and "How Shall We Man Our Ships," *North American Review,* 152, (January 1891), pp. 64-70; On *Mahan* see, Kenneth P. Bourne and Carl Boyd, "Captain Mahan's 'War' with Great Britain," *Proceedings of the United States Naval Institute,* 94 (July 1968), pp. 72-78; W. E. Livezey, *Mahan on Sea Power* (Norman, University of Oklahoma Press, 1947), and W. D. Puleston, *Mahan, The Life and Work of Captain Alfred Thayer Mahan, USN* (New Haven, Yale University Press, 1939), as well as Mahan's own memoirs, *From Sail to Steam: Recollections on Naval Life,* 2 vols. (New York, Harper Brothers, 1908), and writings like, "Hawaii and Our Future Sea Power," *Forum,* XV (March 1893), pp. 1-11; "The Isthmus and Sea Power," *Atlantic Monthly,* LXXII, (October 1893), pp. 459-472; and "U.S. Looking Outward," *Atlantic Monthly,* LXVI (December 1890), pp. 816-824.

Administration of the U.S. Navy can be followed first in existant works on the secretaries: Gardner W. Allen, (editor), *Papers of John D. Long, 1897-1904* (Boston, Massachusetts Historical Society, 1939); Mark D. Hirsch, *William C. Whitney: Modern War-*

wick (New York, Dodd Mead and Company, 1948); Thomas H. Hunt, *The Life of William H. Hunt* (Brattleboro, E. L. Hildrith and Company, 1922); Leon Burr Richardson, *William E. Chandler, Republican* (New York, Dodd Mead and Company, 1940); and Hugh Bernard Hammett, "Hilary Abner Herbert: A Southerner Returns to the Union," (Unpublished Ph.D dissertation, University of Virginia, 1969). More conceptual studies of naval administration appear in Paul Y. Hammond, *Organizing For Defense: The American Military Establishment in the Twentieth Century* (Princeton, Princeton University Press, 1961), and Alfred Thayer Mahan, *Naval Administration and Warfare, Some General Principles With Other Essays* (Boston, Little, Brown, 1948), while the classic work remains the series of articles by Charles Oscar Paullin gathered together recently as *Paullin's History of Naval Administration: A Collection of Articles from the U.S. Naval Institute Proceedings* (Annapolis, United States Naval Institute, 1970). Other important but lesser known accounts are Julius A. Furer, *Administration of the Navy Department in World War II,* (Washington, Government Printing Office, 1954); A. W. Johnson, *A Brief History of the Organization of the Navy Department,* (Washington, U.S. Army Industrial College, 1933); Elting Morison, "Naval Administration; Selected Documents on Navy Department Organization, 1915-1940," unpublished typescript in Navy Department Library; Robert W. Neiser, "The Department of the Navy," *American Political Science Review,* XI (February 1917), pp. 59-75; and D. W. Taylor, "Navy Department Organization, Past, Present, Future," unpublished typescript in Navy Department Library. Intracacies of the bureau conflict are covered nicely by James E. Hewes, Jr., "Management vs. Bureaus," *Marine Corps Gazette,* 51 (February 1967), pp. 39-41 and Thomas W. Ray, "The Bureaus Go On Forever . . ." *Proceedings of the United States Naval Institute,* 94 (January 1968), pp. 50-63. More specific studies include Robert G. Albion, "A Brief History of Civilian Personnel in the U.S. Navy Department," typescript in National Archives Library; Bill Appler, "History of the Navy Supply Corps," *The Review* [Defense Supply Administration] XLVII (May-June 1968), pp. 46-48, 123, 125, 127, 129, 130; Henry P. Beers, "Historical Sketch of the Bureau of Equipment, dated April 10, 1941, Navy Department," unpublished typescript, National Archives Library, and Harold Thomas Wieand, "The History of the Development of the United States Naval Reserve,

1889-1941," (Unpublished Ph.D dissertation, University of Pittsburgh, 1952). Different aspects of the shore establishment are noted
in: Organization Planning Staff, Navy Management Office, "Evolution of the Naval Shore Establishment," unpublished typescript
dated October 5, 1962, Navy Department Library; W. J. Coggeshall
and J. E. McCarthy, *The United States Naval Torpedo Station,
Newport Rhode Island 1658-1920* (Newport, Training Station
Press, 1920); "History of Puget Sound Naval Shipyard," unpub-
lished typescript, Navy Department Library; Arnold S. Lott, *A
Long Line of Ships: Mare Island's Century of Naval Activity in
California* (Annapolis, United States Naval Institute, 1949);
Taylor Peck, *Round Shot to Rockets: A History of the Washington
Navy Yard and U.S. Naval Gun Factory* (Annapolis, United
States Naval Institute, 1949); Ronald H. Spector, "Professors of
War: The Naval War College and the Modern American Navy,"
(Unpublished Ph.D dissertation, Yale University, 1967); Thaddeus
V. Tuleja, "A Short History of the New York Navy Yard," unpub-
lished typescript and James H. West, "A Short History of New
York Navy Yard," February 23, 1941, unpublished typescript,
both in Navy Department Library as well as Lucien Young, *A Brief
History of the United States Navy Yard and Station, Pensacola,
Florida and Its Possibilities* (Pensacola, Naval Station Press, 1964
reprint).

The extremely important but relatively unexplored armor question has been best covered by Dean C. Allard, "The Influence of
the United States Navy Upon The American Steel Industry, 1880-
1900," (Unpublished M.A. thesis, Georgetown University, 1959)
and Walter I. Brandt, "Steel and the New Navy, 1882-1895," (Unpublished Ph.D dissertation, University of Wisconsin, 1920). On
Carnegie's contribution, the best portrait of the steelmaker as a
shrewd manipulator emerges from Joseph F. Wall, *Andrew Carnegie* (New York, Oxford University Press, 1970) although older
works should be consulted including Andrew Carnegie, *Autobiography of Andrew Carnegie* (Boston, Houghton-Mifflin, 1920), and
Burton J. Hendrick, *Life of Andrew Carnegie*, 2 vols. (New York,
Doran and Company, 1932). Other useful sources include: American Iron and Steel Association (compilers), *History of the Manufacture of Armor Plate for the United States Navy* (Philadelphia,
American Iron and Steel Association, 1899), and the contemporary accounts in the *Proceedings of the United States Naval Insti-*

tute: "The Armor Tests, December 10, 1891," XVIII (1892), pp. 147-148; J. G. Eaton, "Domestic Steels For Naval Purposes," XV (1889), pp. 317-337; Albert Gleaves, "The Naval Ordnance Proving Ground," XV (1889), 457-461; W. H. Jacques, "Description of the Works of the Bethlehem Iron Company," XV (1889), pp. 531-539; and W. Richards and J. A. Potter, "The Homestead Steel Works," XV (1889), pp. 431-441.

Index